T0302600

CASTLES
PALACES & STATELY HOMES

CASTLES
PALACES & STATELY HOMES

THE ILLUSTRATED GUIDE TO THE ARCHITECTURAL, CULTURAL AND HISTORICAL HERITAGE OF GREAT BRITAIN AND NORTHERN IRELAND

CHARLES PHILLIPS
CONSULTANT: PROFESSOR RICHARD G. WILSON FRHISTS

LORENZ BOOKS

CONTENTS

INTRODUCTION

Castles summon a stirring vision of the past, including mounted knights and their ladies, jousting in the lists, fearless swordfighting and the heroic deprivations of siege warfare. When we visit castle sites in England and Wales, we find evocative ruins or romantic Victorian reconstructions to encourage these reveries of the 'age of chivalry'.

No English or Welsh castles survive in their original form from the Middle Ages because they were brought to ruin by natural decay, damaged in the fighting of the English Civil War or deliberately slighted (made indefensible) by the victorious Parliamentary army. In Scotland, however, castles survived for longer. Some played a part in the Jacobite conflicts of the 18th century, when an alliance of highlanders, English rebels and foreign supporters failed to restore the House of Stuart to the throne.

One cause of the enduring appeal of castles (and the key reason why some 19th-century landowners wanted to rebuild their great country houses with turrets and gatehouses) is that these fortresses are centuries-old symbols of social status and authority.

Below: The oldest-surviving part of the Tower of London, the White Tower of c.1078, was once painted with whitewash.

Above: Harlech Castle in North Wales, built by Edward I c.1283, has the double defensive walls of the 'concentric castle'.

THE FEUDAL SYSTEM

Castle-building was introduced to England by William the Conqueror and his Norman army in 1066. (A few English castles in Herefordshire and Essex did predate the Conquest, but they were built by Norman friends and associates of Edward the Confessor.) The invaders swept aside the Anglo-Saxon aristocracy, imposing a new Norman ruling class bound to King William I and his descendants by the ties of the feudal system. The castles they built were symbols of feudal authority. They were the fortified homes of knights and great lords, who held them as vassals of the king or a superior lord in return for military support and loyal service.

Castles were, of course, regal as well as lordly residences. Most medieval English kings were great castle-builders, from William I to Edward I and beyond. At the Tower of London and Windsor, William I founded great royal strongholds that have endured to this day as embodiments of royal tradition.

FROM TIMBER TO STONE

In the early years, most Norman castles were timber and earthwork fortifications. The typical early Norman castle was the 'motte and bailey'. The motte, or mound, stood within its own defensive barrier, and often supported at its summit a tower containing the lord's living apartments. The bailey was the larger area around the motte, enclosed by a ditch and a bank topped with a palisade. The motte might be a natural hill or outcrop, or it might be a man-made mound; it was usually linked by a wooden bridge to the bailey, which contained essential buildings such as stables, kitchens, chapel and hall.

Gradually, timber and earthwork were replaced with stone – although in a few cases, for instance at Richmond in Yorkshire and Ludlow in Shropshire, castles were built partly or mostly in stone from the start. Castles were usually enlarged and improved in a piecemeal fashion, and often details of history or topography dictated the kind of solution found in a particular place to a particular need.

When the summit of the motte was encased in stone, the result was what historians call the 'shell keep', which often, as at Windsor and Restormel, enclosed timber or stone buildings for the lord's use in an inner courtyard. Elsewhere, the lord's stronghold was often in a great stone tower – the *magna turris* ('great tower') of contemporaries and the 'tower keep' of historians. Some tower keeps were built in the late 11th century, such as the Tower of London and Colchester. Throughout the following century, tower keeps, whether rectangular, cylindrical or polygonal, were regularly added to castles.

The tower or shell keep, like the palisaded motte in the early castles, formed an inner stronghold to which the lord and his bodyguard, could retreat. This stronghold within the castle was called the 'dungeon' (from the Latin *dominium* via French *donjon*, meaning lordship). The word acquired its modern meaning, of a dank and dark prison for the lord's enemies, only in later times.

TOWERS AND GATEHOUSES

Stout towers were an important feature of the defensive walls around the bailey. If they were projecting from the wall, they provided a strong position from which defenders could shoot at anyone trying to scale or undermine the wall. They also provided a raised shooting point from which defenders could attack people who had gained access to the top of the wall.

The entrance was a particularly vulnerable point, and towers built above it or to either side of it resulted in the development of the gatehouse. This became a major feature (and the most secure part of the castle at Caerphilly and Beaumaris in Wales), containing some of its most prestigious apartments.

Above: At Dover, the vast stone square keep built by Maurice the Engineer for Henry II after 1168 still dominates the castle.

THE CONCENTRIC CASTLE

In the late 13th century, the concentric castle – regarded by historians as the climax and perfection of British castle design – was developed in Wales, most notably at Caerphilly, built *c.*1271–80 by Gilbert de Clare, Lord of Glamorgan, and at Beaumaris, begun in 1295 by Edward I. This design consisted of two rings of fortifications – an outer wall overlooked and protected by a taller and more heavily fortified inner wall. This idea was as old as ancient Egypt, but was new to Britain. Edward and others had seen its effectiveness on Crusade.

THE FORTIFIED MANOR HOUSE

In early medieval warfare, the possession of castles provided the key to victory. King Stephen's long struggle against the Empress Matilda – through the '19 long winters' (1135-54) remembered by chroniclers – was conducted as a series of castle sieges. King John's battle against rebel lords in 1215 climaxed in a two-month siege of Rochester Castle. However, by the time of the Wars of the Roses in the 15th century, conflicts were decided on the battlefield.

Lords still wanted battlements and gatehouses on their property – partly because a fortified house was prestigious, and partly because lawlessness had by no means been entirely eliminated – and so applied for a royal 'licence to crenellate'. But, increasingly, they looked more for comfort than security. At Penshurst Place in Kent and Stokesay Castle in Shropshire, the level of fortification was sufficient only to deter passing marauders.

Left: The imposing gatehouse tower of Pembroke Castle, built in the 13th century by William Marshall, Earl of Pembroke.

USING THIS BOOK

Many of the houses described in this book changed over time as architects added new buildings to the original design or modernized old structures. Therefore, some great historic houses appear in several sections of the book.

The Tudor age brought about social changes in England and Wales as profound as those that followed the Norman Conquest of 1066. The accession of Henry Tudor as Henry VII in 1485 ended the long Wars of the Roses: as the heroic age of warrior lords and knights drew to a close, a new elite class of merchants and statesmen arose to take their place. Then, *c.*1536-41, as Supreme Head of the Church of England, Henry seized the lands and assets of the country's religious houses, including around a quarter of England's agricultural land, in the Dissolution of the Monasteries. To raise money, he sold much of it to the merchants and political operators of the new Tudor gentry, resulting in an unprecedentedly extensive and swift change of land ownership in England.

A NEW LEVEL OF COMFORT

Great new country houses were built by these men, houses constructed and decorated by the masons and craftsmen who had previously worked for the Church. Initially, many lords continued to raise battlements and gatehouses, but increasingly, also, they fitted their houses with large glass windows – a sign that they did not fear attack.

By 1540, Henry VII and Henry VIII had between them reigned for more than 50 years. Although there were continuing fears of foreign invasion, particularly since the establishment of the Church of England had inspired a Franco-Spanish Roman Catholic alliance, the Tudors had resoundingly succeeded in delivering the domestic peace they promised the people following the Wars of the Roses.

The new Tudor country houses offered far greater comfort: the windows let in more light and the fitting of flues led to the introduction of coal-burning fireplaces and chimneys. The houses also began to provide more private living space for their owners. The Great Hall began to be neglected in favour of the warm 'solar' room and other private chambers on the first floor of the house.

TUDOR PALACES

The early Tudor decades were also a time of lavish palace building. Henry VII replaced his fire-ravaged palace at Sheen in Surrey with the vast and ornate Richmond Palace, laid out over 10 acres (4ha) around wide courtyards and with a magnificent timber-roofed Great Hall 100ft (30m) in length. He also built a new palace at Greenwich, where Henry VIII was born in 1491, and developed Baynard's Castle from a Norman fortification in London.

Above: The west front at Hampton Court was the entrance in Tudor times. Henry VIII's arms are carved above the gateway.

Henry VIII created magnificent royal residences at Whitehall and Hampton Court out of houses seized from Cardinal Wolsey; he took possession of great episcopal palaces such as Hatfield House in Hertfordshire and Knole in Kent; he built many new houses, for example at Bridewell in London and Beaulieu in Essex; and he established the extravagantly splendid new palaces of St James's in London, Oatlands at Weybridge and Nonesuch near Ewell (both in Surrey). By his death in 1547, Henry possessed more than 40 palaces and houses – more than any other English monarch.

PRODIGY HOUSES

Edward VI, Mary and Elizabeth I added nothing to the collection of royal palaces, beyond minor additions and

Left: Fit for Queen Elizabeth I. Sir William Cecil's 'prodigy house' at Burghley, Lincolnshire, was 32 years in construction (1555–87).

Above: Holyroodhouse Palace, in Edinburgh, was founded as a priory in 1128. It is the Queen's official residence in Scotland.

necessary maintenance under Elizabeth. But although no new royal buildings were erected, the 45-year reign of Elizabeth saw the construction of a series of astonishingly grand country houses built in her honour. Burghley House in Linconshire, Longleat in Wiltshire, Holdenby in Northamptonshire, Wollaton Hall in Nottinghamshire and Loseley House in Surrey were all 'prodigy houses', built by leading courtiers competing to create a country estate worthy of the monarch revered as England's greatest treasure, and fit to receive her on one of her annual 'summer progresses' around England.

The desire to create a country house grand enough to receive a monarch also inspired lords in the reign of James I, when Robert Cecil, 1st Earl of Salisbury, built the majestic Hatfield House in Hertfordshire and Thomas Howard, 1st Earl of Suffolk, built Audley End, Essex. Like Knole in Kent, Hatfield was originally an ecclesiastical palace and then one of Henry VIII's many grand residences, before it was transformed into the country seat of England's leading political family. Mary I and Elizabeth I spent much of their childhood at Hatfield, and Elizabeth received the news there that she was queen.

CLASSICAL ARCHITECTURE

The era of James I and Charles I saw the rise of Inigo Jones, one of the greatest English architects. With the creation of the Queen's House in Greenwich, the Banqueting House in Whitehall and Wilton House in Wiltshire, Jones became the pioneer in England of 'classical' building inspired by both ancient Roman and Italian Renaissance architecture, and particularly by the writing and designs of Andrea Palladio. Jones's elegant buildings were a major influence on future generations of patrons and architects – especially on the members of the 18th-century Palladian movement, who drew their inspiration from the works of Palladio.

Below: The honey-coloured Montacute in Somerset, built in the 1590s, is one of the loveliest of Elizabethan country houses.

ROYAL BUILDERS

The first decades that followed the accession of the Hanoverian dynasty in 1714 represent the nadir of royal building in England. When in London, George I and George II made do with the modest Kensington Palace, created by William III, and the increasingly shabby redbrick St James's Palace, built by Henry VIII; they did not attempt to rebuild the previous royal residence in London, Whitehall Palace, which had been destroyed by fire in 1698. Neither king liked England much and their affections really lay with their preferred palace of Herrenhausen in Hanover.

For much of the 18th century, indeed, many Englishmen were rather uncomfortably aware that the monarchy lacked a grand palace in the capital. St James's was considered inadequate: the novelist and journalist Daniel Defoe dismissed it as 'really mean' in comparison to the glories of the royal court it housed. He also added that, while the English court was more magnificent than any other in Europe. 'this palace comes beneath those of the most petty princes'.

Below: The Prince Regent and John Nash used an Islamic-influenced 'Hindoo' style for the Brighton Pavilion, begun in 1815.

LATE GEORGIAN CHANGES

In his 60-year reign (1760-1820), George III did undertake improvements at Windsor Castle, previously left empty. He also bought Kew Palace and – as a family retreat from court life at St James's – Buckingham House, which in the 19th and 20th centuries was to become the kind of grand metropolitan palace that might have pleased Defoe. But it was only with George III's son, first as Prince of Wales, then as Prince Regent (1811-20) and finally as George IV (1820-30) – that royal building really began once more. With Jeffry Wyatville, George was largely responsible for transforming Windsor Castle into the picturesque 'Gothic' residence that wins the admiration of visitors from all over the world; with John Nash, Henry Holland, Thomas Hopper and James Wyatt, he created the extravagant Carlton House in central London (demolished in 1827); and, again with Nash, he built the exotic Royal Pavilion in Brighton and began the transformation of Buckingham House into a great palace.

VICTORIA'S CONTRIBUTION

In Queen Victoria's reign, Buckingham Palace was named the monarch's official London residence and given the east front that is now its celebrated 'public face', facing the courtyard and the Victoria Memorial and, beyond, the Mall. However, Victoria's principal contribution to royal building was the result of her carrying to new lengths the separation between the monarch's public and private lives that George III had begun when he bought Buckingham House as a family home. With her husband, Prince Albert, she built two substantial family retreats far removed from London: Osborne House on the Isle of Wight and Balmoral Castle in the Grampian region of Scotland. Balmoral Castle has remained popular with the royal family and together with Sandringham House in Norfolk – acquired by Edward VII in 1862 while still Prince of Wales – is Elizabeth II's principal retreat from royal life at Buckingham Palace, Windsor Castle and Holyroodhouse in Edinburgh.

Above: Robert Adam transformed the 16th-century Osterley House, Middlesex, by adding a 'neoclassical' facade in c.1763.

BRITISH COUNTRY HOUSES

In the 18th century, when Britain's kings occupied the rundown St James's Palace and the uninspiring Kensington Palace, the country's powerful Whig aristocrats lived and entertained in extravagant style in country houses such as Castle Howard in Yorkshire, Stowe House in Buckinghamshire and Chatsworth in Derbyshire. With buildings designed by architects of genius, such as John Vanbrugh, William Kent, Nicholas Hawksmoor and Colen Campbell, standing in gardens and parklands designed by Charles Bridgeman, Kent and 'Capability' Brown, 18th-century aristocrats may well have enjoyed the period of highest achievement in the history of the British country house.

In the 19th century, the wealth generated by Victorian Britain's empire and industry funded another great age of country house building. Architects such as Anthony Salvin and William Burges romantically renovated some great castles such as Alnwick, Muncaster, Cardiff and Castell Coch.

Above: Belvoir Castle, Leicestershire, is one of many castles rebuilt in the 'Gothic Revival' style in the 19th century.

DECLINE AND FALL

In the 20th century, however, although fine new houses such as Castle Drogo and Manderston were built, the general picture for country houses was bleak. Following agricultural depression and swiftly moving social changes, partly resulting from wider democratization, and in the face of heavy taxation and punitive death duties of potentially 80 per cent of the estate, many owners of great houses struggled to survive. Houses fell into ruin, and were demolished or sold for institutional use, while treasured collections of paintings, sculpture and books were sold to overseas buyers.

Below: Robert Adam evoked the grandeur of ancient Rome in his lavish decoration of the Ante-room at Syon House, Middlesex.

SAVED FOR THE NATION

Some estate owners showed great ingenuity in making their houses pay: in the 1960s, Henry Thynne, 6th Marquess of Bath, introduced lions to his estate at Longleat in Wiltshire to help attract paying visitors in order to fund the house; at Loseley Park in Surrey, James More-Molyneux established a thriving dairy business. Many other houses were saved by the Country House scheme of 1937, under which owners unable to meet death duties could pass the property to the National Trust, an independent charity founded in 1895, and later government schemes under which restoration and maintenance grants were made and tax concessions granted in return for house owners opening their doors to the public for an agreed number of days each year.

House after house passed from private hands into those of the National Trust and English Heritage (a government organization charged with caring for England's historic environment) or to their equivalents in Scotland, Wales and Ireland. As they did so, they found a new status as cherished repositories of British achievements in art and architecture.

The country house was for many centuries a central point in local life: its owner was supported by and supportive of the locality, and had many responsibilities as a result. In the 19th and early 20th centuries, these houses briefly became little more than a locus of privilege, a treasured private possession. Since the end of World War II, however, they have become part of a shared and treasured national heritage – an embodiment, like the ruined castles that also dot the countryside, and the palaces and other royal residences, of the glories and storied achievements of Britain's past.

PART ONE

ANCIENT CASTLES

TO 1485

In the years after 1066, the great Norman lords built castles wherever they settled. Castles were immensely effective as instruments of war, yet they were also the proud homes of the new Norman aristocracy. Fortifications became symbols of lordly authority, and so were added to country houses; later, fortified manor houses were built that combined comfort with security.

Left: The original Pembroke Castle was built by Roger, Norman Lord of Dyfed. William Marshall, Earl of Pembroke, added the cylindrical tower keep (centre) c.1200.

ENGLAND TIMELINE, TO 1485

Above: The Round Tower at Windsor Castle, Berkshire, was built in the 12th century.

Above: Middleham Castle, North Yorkhire, was the childhood home of Richard III.

Above: Bodiam Castle, East Sussex, is one of the finest examples of medieval building.

TO 1086

*c.*300BC At Maiden Castle in Dorset, Iron Age Britons begin building a vast hillfort. In AD43 the Roman army takes it from the Durotriges tribe.

*c.*AD75 Fishbourne Villa near Chichester, West Sussex, is a palace for King Cogidubnus of the Regnenses tribe.

*c.*AD250 At Porchester in Hampshire, the Romans build one of a series of 'Saxon shore forts'. Remains of other forts are at Richborough, Lympne and Pevensey.

*c.*AD850 Leede builds the original Leeds Castle in Kent.

1066 Duke William's army builds castles at Pevensey, Hastings, Dover, Canterbury, Wallingford, Berkhamsted and London.

1068 William the Conqueror founds castles at Warwick, Nottingham, York, Lincoln, Huntingdon and Cambridge.

*c.*1070 Alan Rufus, Earl of Yorkshire, builds Richmond Castle.

1072 William founds castles in Durham and at Bambrugh in Northumberland.

1075 William founds Windsor Castle.

*c.*1076 William orders the rebuilding in stone of the original earthwork castle in London. The White Tower at the Tower of London is complete by 1100.

*c.*1076 Norman monk Gundulf begins building Colchester Castle on the site of the Roman Temple of Claudius.

1085 Roger de Lacy builds Ludlow Castle in Shropshire.

1087–1299

1087-9 Rochester Castle, originally built of earth and stone, is rebuilt in stone by Bishop Gundulf of Rochester.

1097 King William Rufus begins building Westminster Hall on the site of King Edward the Confessor's palace.

*c.*1100 Roger de Bigod builds Framlingham Castle in Suffolk.

*c.*1140 Aubrey de Vere III, Earl of Oxford, builds Castle Hedingham in Essex.

1145 Reginald, an illegitimate son of Henry I, builds a castle on the site of an Iron Age Celtic fortress and Saxon fort at Tintagel in north Cornwall.

*c.*1150 Robert Fitz-Ranulph builds Middleham Castle in North Yorkshire.

1153 Robert Fitz-Harding, 1st Lord Berkeley, builds Berkeley Castle in Gloucestershire.

1165 Henry II builds the polygonal keep at Orford Castle in Suffolk.

1180 Hamelin de Plantagenet builds a cylindrical keep at Conisbrough Castle in South Yorkshire.

*c.*1250 Henry III makes lavish improvements to Westminster Palace, creating the superb King's Great Chamber.

1280 William de Valence, uncle of King Edward I, begins rebuilding Goodrich Castle in Hereford and Worcestershire.

1290 Wool merchant Lawrence of Ludlow fortifies his fine manor house of Stokesay Castle in Shropshire.

1300–1485

1300 Sir John de Broughton builds Broughton Castle near Banbury, Oxfordshire.

1302 A fire destroys much of the royal palace at Winchester, but the Great Hall survives.

*c.*1340 Sir John de Poulteney begins major rebuilding at Penshurst Place in Kent; Thomas, 3rd Lord Berkeley, builds the superb Great Hall at Berkeley Castle in Gloucestershire; Sir Thomas Cawne builds the Great Hall in the moated manor house of Ightham Mote, near Sevenoaks, Kent.

1370 The magnificent Banqueting Hall is built at Haddon Hall, Derbyshire.

*c.*1375 The Neville family builds Raby Castle in County Durham.

1385 Sir Edward Dakygrigge begins building Bodiam Castle in East Sussex.

1432 Sir John Falstaff begins building Caister Castle in Norfolk and Ralph, Lord Cromwell, builds his Great Tower at Tattershall Castle in Lincolnshire.

1441 Sir Roger de Fiennes begins building the fine fortified manor house of Herstmonceux Castle in East Sussex.

1477 King Edward IV begins building St George's Chapel at Windsor Castle.

*c.*1480 Edward IV builds a splendid Great Hall at Eltham Palace in Kent.

1482 Sir Edward Bedingfeld begins building the fortified manor house of Oxburgh Hall, near King's Lynn, Norfolk.

N
W
E
S
SCOTLAND
Chesters Roman Fort
Housesteads Roman Fort
Raby Castle
Richmond Castle
North Sea
Middleham Castle
Norton Conyers
Irish Sea
ENGLAND
Peveril Castle
Haddon Hall
Tattershall Castle
The Wash
Belvoir Castle
Stokesay Castle
Oxburgh Hall
Caister Castle
Ludlow Castle
Warwick Castle
Framlingham Castle
WALES
Goodrich Castle
Sudeley Castle
Broughton Castle
Orford Castle
Castle Hedingham
Berkhamsted Castle
Tower of London
Layer Marney Tower
Palace of Westminster & Jewel Tower
Lullingstone Roman Villa
Colchester Castle
Berkeley Castle
Windsor Castle
Rochester Castle
Bristol Channel
The Vyne
Hever Castle
Ightham Mote
Dover Castle
Winchester Castle Great Hall
Leeds Castle
Penshurst Place
Great Dixter House
Strait of Dover
Bignor Roman Villa
Maiden Castle
Porchester Castle
Lewes Castle
Camber Castle
Tintagel Castle
Launceston Castle
Fishbourne Roman Palace
Herstmonceux Castle
Pevensey Castle
Hastings Castle
English Channel

SCOTLAND, WALES

AND NORTHERN IRELAND TIMELINES, TO 1485

Above: Edinburgh Castle houses the Scottish Crown Jewels and the Stone of Destiny.

SCOTLAND, TO 1485

1093 Queen (later Saint) Margaret of Scots builds a chapel in Edinburgh Castle. St Margaret's Chapel is the oldest surviving part of the castle.

1204 Alan, 2nd High Steward, begins work on Rothesay Castle, Isle of Bute.

1279 Unknown builders begin the unusual triangular castle of Caerlaverock in Dumfriesshire.

1296 William Wallace captures Dunnottar Castle, Aberdeenshire.

1300 King Edward I repairs Hermitage Castle, Borders, during the Scottish Wars of Independence.

1368–72 The future Robert II of Scots builds the 60ft(18m)-high David's Tower at Edinburgh Castle, the first known example in Scotland of the tower house.

1375 1st Earl of Douglas begins building Tantallon Castle, East Lothian, on a rocky promontory opposite the Bass Rock.

1424 King James I of Scots begins rebuilding Linlithgow Palace in West Lothian.

*c.*1435 King James I of Scots builds a Great Chamber at Edinburgh Castle.

*c.*1440 The main tower is added to Glamis Castle, Angus.

1460 Robert, 2nd Lord Maxwell, completes the building of Caerlaverock Castle, Dumfries & Galloway.

Above: Beaumaris Castle, Wales, is the most technically perfect medieval castle in Britain.

WALES, TO 1485

1067 Chepstow Castle built.
1090 Abergavenny Castle built.
1106 Kidwelly Castle begun.
*c.*1200 Pembroke Castle begun.
1271 Caerphilly Castle begun.
1277 Edward I begins building Flint and Rhuddlan Castles, Denbighshire.
1283 Edward I begins building Conwy, Caernarfon and Harlech castles.
1295 Edward I begins Beaumaris Castle.
1430 Sir William ap Thomas builds the Yellow Tower at Raglan Castle.

Above: Carrickfergus Castle, Northern Ireland, is dominated by its great keep.

NORTHERN IRELAND, TO 1485

*c.*1177 John de Courcy builds Dundrum Castle on the site of a Celtic hillfort overlooking Dundrum Bay.
*c.*1180 De Courcy builds Carrickfergus Castle overlooking Belfast Lough.
*c.*1180 De Courcy builds Killyleagh Castle to protect the inhabitants from Viking invaders.
1200s Building of Dunluce Castle begins.
1300s Building of Ardglass Castle begins.

ENTRY TO THE TRAITORS GATE

CHAPTER ONE

FROM ROMAN VILLAS TO NORMAN CASTLES

TO 1154

Few buildings and fortifications remain of those that were constructed before the Norman followers of William the Conqueror invaded England in 1066. Wood and other biodegradable building materials have decayed, and what stone structures there were have generally been dismantled or incorporated into later buildings. With a few exceptions, we cannot visit pre-Norman buildings. However, there are extensive archaeological remains from which we can get an idea of the houses, palaces and fortresses built by native Britons, Romans and Anglo-Saxons.

Chronicle accounts of the dramatic events of 1066 repeatedly make plain the Normans' reliance upon the castle as both a military base and a means of overawing the people they came to conquer. Upon landing at Pevensey, Duke William of Normandy built a castle amid the remains of the Roman fort there, and at Hastings he raised another. At Dover, within days of the Battle of Hastings, he built a further castle, then at Canterbury yet another. Before the year was out, he had even erected a fortification at the south-east corner of the city wall of London itself.

By 1100, the Normans had built 400 castles in England. Each of the major Saxon towns had its Norman castle, and the borders were securely guarded by fortresses. Most comprised earthwork fortifications and timbers, and they were gradually rebuilt in stone in the late 11th and 12th centuries. Indeed, before the end of William I's reign in 1087, the first castles made entirely of stone were being built.

Left: The imposing Norman White Tower at the Tower of London was begun in 1078, using stone specially imported from William the Conqueror's homeland in France.

BEFORE THE NORMANS

ROMAN AND ANGLO-SAXON BUILDING

The ancient Romans' version of the country house or palace was the summer villa, an elegant building often lavishly decorated with murals and mosaics and equipped with the latest comforts, such as underfloor heating, and set in a well-tended estate. During the Roman occupation of Britain, villas were considered to be a status symbol both for the Romans and for the richest and most prominent of their subjects – as is still evident from the impressive remains of those buildings that have been excavated.

Above: The ancient British fort of Maiden Castle, Dorset, covers 45 acres (18ha). Vespasian's forces captured it in AD43.

ROMAN VILLAS

At Fishbourne, near Chichester in West Sussex, are the remnants of a magnificent villa built *c.*AD75 for King Cogidubnus (or Togidubnus) of the Regnenses tribe. Archaeologists have determined that the villa had four wings arranged around a central courtyard, with a large reception chamber in the west wing. As many as 100 rooms at Fishbourne had mosaic floors, of which 20 survive, including a beautiful one representing the Roman love god Cupid riding a dolphin.

Below: The broch of Gurness, a fort on Orkney, is around 65ft (20m) across and was probably in use until around AD100.

Fishbourne was probably the grandest villa in the whole of Britain, and it was so large that it bears comparison with imperial villas in Italy. Other less magnificent but still remarkable Roman villas in Britain include Bignor near Arundel in West Sussex, Chedworth in Gloucestershire and also Lullingstone in Kent.

ANGLO-SAXON PALACES

There are also a few tantalizing remains of the palaces and grand houses built by Anglo-Saxon kings in the years after the Roman withdrawal from Britain. The kings of Northumbria, for example, built a palace complex on raised ground at Yeavering in Northumberland in the 7th–9th centuries AD. The most important building of the complex, the Great Hall, was built entirely of wood and had a great central hearth and entrances in the long sides of the building. Roof posts were erected in pairs down the length of the building, which had the effect of dividing the space into three separate aisles.

Archaeologists have uncovered what may be the remains of palaces kept by the great King Offa of Mercia at Sutton in Herefordshire and on the banks of the River Thames at Chelsea in London. Another great Anglo-Saxon hall that may have been a palace was found at Northampton; while at Cheddar in Somerset, a building once thought to be a palace is more likely to have been a less grand building, perhaps a hunting lodge.

FORTS AND FORTRESSES

The remains of more than 2,500 hilltop fortresses built by ancient Britons have been identified. Most are small, and offered protection to just a few peasants and their cattle, but the remnants of very extensive hilltop fortresses from the 1st millennium BC can be seen at Maiden Castle in Dorset, Hengistbury Head in Hampshire and Old Sarum in Wiltshire.

In northern Scotland and on Orkney and the Shetland Isles, locals seeking protection against raiders built fortified round towers, or brochs, at about this time. The Broch of Gurness on Orkney is 65ft (20m) across and once stood 32ft (10m) tall; Mousa Broch, on the isle of Mousa off Shetland, still stands 42ft (13m) tall and is 50ft (15m) in diameter.

When the Romans conquered Britain, they very rarely used the existing British fortifications as strongholds, preferring to build their own fortresses. Some of these Roman forts have been excavated, giving an indication of their size and importance. Caerleon in Monmouthshire was a 50-acre (20-ha) fort. Its wall had defensive turrets every 150ft (46m) and the fortress had an amphitheatre for both military manoeuvres and entertainment.

At the northern limit of their empire, the Romans built Hadrian's Wall, which ran for 73 miles (117km) from Newcastle to Carlisle. After every mile (1.6km), soldiers built a small 'Mile Castle' fortification, and after every 4 miles (6.5km), they erected a garrison fort, such as the one at Housesteads in Northumberland, which was built c.AD124 and has been fully excavated. It had room to garrison up to 1,000 men.

Below: The Roman camp at Caerleon was one of three permanent legionary forts in Britain in the late 1st century AD.

Above: This mosaic from the Roman villa at Lullingstone, Kent, shows the god Jupiter (in the form of a bull) carrying off Europa.

In south-east England are the remnants of Roman coastal fortifications, the Saxon shore forts, built to repel a possible sea-borne invasion. The most complete remains are at Portchester Castle in Hampshire. The 9-acre (3.6-ha) fort had walls 20ft (6m) high and 10ft (3m) thick, with D-shaped towers every 100–200ft (30–60m), from which defenders would have fired catapults. Large parts are still standing.

Anglo-Saxon kings needed to fortify their palace settlements against Viking raiders. King Alfred (r.871–99), for instance, garrisoned a series of forts for this purpose throughout his kingdom of Wessex, remains of which can be seen.

Many Roman and Anglo-Saxon forts later formed the basis of Norman stone castles: including the Roman fortresses at Pevensey, Porchester, Caerleon and Caerphilly. Excavations at Goltho, Lincolnshire, reveal how an Anglo-Saxon hall-palace complex was given ditch and bank defences in AD850–1000 and then was the site of a Norman motte-and-bailey castle in 1080–1150.

Below: King Alfred the Great – for whom this fine jewelled bookmark head was made – established around 30 fortified burghs (boroughs) to keep the Vikings at bay.

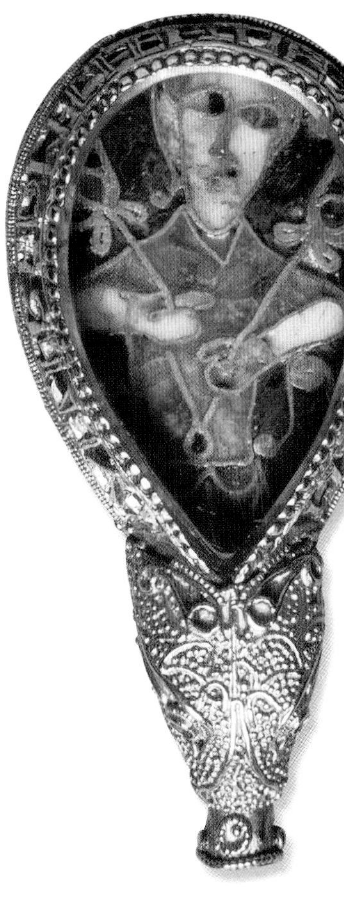

PEVENSEY AND HASTINGS

THE FIRST CASTLES

Along with Hastings, Dover and Canterbury, Pevensey Castle was among the first four Norman castles built in England. Duke William of Normandy began to build a castle at Pevensey within the west gate of the Roman fort there, on the very first day of the Conquest campaign, 28 September 1066. According to one chronicler, William's invasion force carried with it, packed in boxes, the materials needed for quickly raising a wooden tower and other defensive structures.

OCCUPATION OF ANDERIDA

The Roman fort of Anderida at Pevensey – later one of the Saxon shore line of fortresses – was sited on a peninsula overlooking the sea, for at the time of the Roman occupation, and indeed of the Norman Conquest, the waves came in as far as the castle walls, although the sea has now fallen back to leave marshland. In 1066, the fort was the site of an Anglo-Saxon burgh, or fortified town, and the remains of a chapel excavated within the castle walls are probably those of this burgh. William and his Norman forces encountered no resistance when they took control and hastily erected their castle.

ROBERT, COUNT OF MORTAIN

In the autumn of 1066, Duke William did not linger at Pevensey, but moved his army swiftly on to Hastings. After the Conquest, he gave Pevensey Castle and its lordship to his half-brother Robert, Count of Mortain. Robert was also made Lord of Berkhamsted, Lambeth and Bermondsey, and in 1072 of Cornwall. He was England's second-largest lay landowner, although he spent little time in the country, preferring to live in Normandy.

Above: Pevensey Castle in Sussex survived sieges by the forces of King William Rufus (1088) and Simon de Montfort (1264).

PEVENSEY CASTLE

Robert strengthened the existing walls of the Roman fort at Pevensey to form the outer bailey wall of the castle. He repaired the eastern gateway and built a new entrance to replace the ancient one at the south-west. He then erected a second walled enclosure within and at the eastern end of the ancient fort.

The castle's stone tower-keep was probably built after Robert's death (1095), in the early 1100s, when many of the wooden Conquest castles were rebuilt in stone. It made use of part of the Roman wall and a Roman tower. On the other three sides of the inner bailey (or enclosure), the walls and D-shaped towers were probably erected in the mid-1200s by Peter of Savoy, Earl of Richmond and uncle of Henry III's wife, Queen Eleanor. Henry made Peter Lord of Pevensey in 1246. Peter built residential apartments set against the inside of the castle walls in a very grand style befitting his status.

As the sea retreated, uncovering Pevensey Marshes, the castle declined in importance. By the Tudor period, it had begun to fall into ruins. Nevertheless, it was partially refortified as a gun emplacement in the 1580s to defend

MOTTE-AND-BAILEY CASTLES

The early Norman castles combined a motte (a mound) surrounded by a ditch and a bailey (an enclosed, defended area). The bailey was enclosed by a wooden fence, and outside that by another ditch or a moat. Sometimes the motte was a hill; at other times it was an artificial mound built up using the earth that had been dug out when the ditch was made.

On the motte stood a keep (a look-out tower), in the early years also made of wood. It often contained accommodation for the castellan (keeper of the castle). Within the bailey were the buildings necessary to house and maintain the garrison – perhaps a Great Hall, kitchens, chapel, stables and other farm buildings.

In the late 11th–12th century, the wooden keep was often rebuilt in stone. The outer wall around the bailey was also remade in stone, with the addition of a strong 'gatehouse' and a drawbridge across the moat.

Right: At Launceston, Cornwall, a timber keep was built on a steep motte c.1067. The stone castle is late 12th century.

Above: The original timber motte-and-bailey castle of 1066 at Hastings, Sussex, was rebuilt in stone as early as 1070.

against a Spanish invasion. Almost 400 years later, it housed military billets and machine-gun posts during World War II.

HASTINGS CASTLE

An image in the Bayeux Tapestry shows William's men digging to create a ditch and raise a motte at Hastings. As he would later do at Dover, he built the motte of his castle within the outline of an Iron Age hill fortress and an Anglo-Saxon burgh, and close to a pre-existing church, which is now known as St-Mary-in-the-Castle. The castle occupied a commanding position on a coastal hill-top overlooking the beach and harbour. A tower was added in the 12th century; an eastern curtain wall (with a twin-towered gatehouse) and the South Tower were built in the 13th century. Later the cliff was so severely eroded by the sea that parts of the castle fell into it.

After victory at Hastings, and building a castle at Dover, William marched in a circuitous route on London and erected castles *en route* at Canterbury in Kent, Wallingford in Oxfordshire (where Archbishop Stigand of Canterbury submitted to him) and Berkhamsted in Hertfordshire. Earthworks and other castle remains can still be seen in all these towns.

Right: At Hastings, William, then Duke of Normandy, supervises his men digging out a ditch and using the earth to build a motte, in this scene from the Bayeux Tapestry.

DOVER CASTLE

THE STONE KEEP

In October 1066, within days of victory at the Battle of Hastings, and after building Pevensey and Hastings Castles, William the Conqueror began to build his castle at Dover. He set to work inside the boundaries of an Iron Age hillfort that had been adapted by the Romans and then become a fortified town. The pre-Norman church of St Mary-in-Castro, dating from the late 10th or early 11th century, survives within the castle precincts – alongside a Roman *pharos*, or lighthouse. The earth bank and ditch outside the castle's later 12th-century walls are probably the remains of the fortifications that were established on the site by its Iron Age colonizers.

According to the account of William of Poitiers, the first Norman castle at Dover was built in just eight days. Presumably, it was an earthwork and wooden motte-and-bailey fortification. This would have been quite a feat, as motte construction was very labour intensive, and the soldiers needed to be on constant guard. All that remains today is a stretch of the ditch and bank alongside the south transept of the church. King William made his half-brother Bishop Odo of Bayeux the first constable of the castle at Dover.

Left: Henry II, who built the great keep at Dover, brought stability to England after the civil war of King Stephen's reign.

THE STONE KEEP

William's castle at Dover was greatly strengthened by Henry II (r.1154–89) and his architect Maurice the Engineer in 1168–88. Maurice built the vast square stone keep, or tower, which is the dominant building in the castle complex to this day. Measuring 96 x 96 x 98ft (29 x 29 x 30m), with walls 16–21ft (5–6.5m) thick, this massive rectangular stone keep was the largest in Europe. It contained four great rooms measuring 20 x 50ft (6 x 15m), and two chapels, in addition to a further 12 rooms, each roughly 10 x 15ft (3 x 4.5m), within the extremely thick walls.

THE CASTLE WALLS

Maurice also raised the inner bailey wall at Dover, complete with ten rectangular towers, and two twin-tower gateways with barbicans (outer fortifications defending a drawbridge or gateway) – one to the north (the King's Gate) and one to the south (the Palace Gate). Furthermore, Henry and Maurice began work on an outer curtain wall, in this way anticipating the principles of the concentric castle design, with its twin defensive walls, around 100 years ahead of the design's more general application in the reign of Edward I.

Below: English stronghold. Constables of Dover Castle have included Henry V and Henry VIII (while princes), the Duke of Wellington and Sir Winston Churchill.

Above: The castle at Dover with (beyond, left) the Church of St Mary-in-Castro and the Roman lighthouse.

NORMAN RINGWORKS

In addition to motte-and-bailey castles, the Normans built fortifications known as 'ringworks' – defensive strongholds enclosed by earthworks but without a motte. These were sometimes quite small, less than 30m (100ft) across within the earthworks, but in other places they were of considerable size: a ringwork excavated at Huttons Ambo in Yorkshire measured 120 x 180ft (35 x 55m) within its bank and ditch defences.

Historians emphasize that the castle was a symbol of high status within the rigidly hierarchical feudal system, adding that ringworks may have been built for landowners who did not have sufficient feudal standing to justify a motte and a castle. Another explanation is that ringworks were preferred in places where a large garrison force was needed, since the castle and motte fortification could leave little room to house defenders.

The outer wall of the castle was completed by King John (r.1199–1216). At the close of John's reign, when the King was in open conflict with many of his barons, the castle was besieged by Prince Louis of France, who had been invited by the barons to invade. Despite the great expenditure on its walls by King Henry II, and a determined defence by constable Hubert de Burgh, the castle came close to being captured when Louis of France and his engineers succeeded in undermining the King's Gate, part of which collapsed. However, King John's death brought the conflict to an end before matters could get worse.

Henry III (r.1216–72) carried out extensive improvements at Dover Castle. Most notable was the erection of the Norfolk Towers in place of the former King's Gate and the addition of the Constable's Gate, containing residential quarters for the castellan or keeper of the castle, *c.*1227.

LATER YEARS

Dover Castle's position ensured that it remained an important element of England's maritime defences across the centuries. Many later alterations were made that, sadly, damaged the remains of the medieval castle. These included knocking down towers in the outer wall to establish gun emplacements during the Napoleonic War, when an extensive network of tunnels was first dug into the cliff beneath the castle. In World War II, Operation Dynamo (the May 1940 evacuation of 338,000 British soldiers from Dunkirk, northern France) was masterminded by 700 top-secret staff from the tunnels. Within the tunnels there was a hospital as well as a command centre that Churchill visited to see the plans that led to eventual victory.

Below: An early concentric castle in England? This reconstruction of Dover Castle in the mid-1300s shows inner and outer defences.

THE TOWER OF LONDON
AND WILLIAM I

Six weeks after their triumph at Hastings, the Normans marched into London from the north-west, following a route from the battlefield via Dover, Canterbury, Winchester, Wallingford and Berkhamsted. The main aim of this long march was to make an impressive show of military force and to cow the population into submission. William sent an advance party into London to build a castle there, and, after his coronation on 25 December 1066, he retreated to Barking until it was finished.

The first London fortification was built in the south-east corner of the city's Roman walls. With the River Thames to the south and the city walls also to the south and to the east, the castle-builders built trenches and an earthwork wall with a wooden palisade to the north and west. The trenches were 25ft (8m) wide and 11ft (3.5m) deep.

Above: The Tower of London was already being used as a prison by 1100, when Bishop Flambard of Durham escaped through a high window using a rope.

THE SQUARE KEEP

The rectangular tower of Colchester Castle and the White Tower of London are the earliest examples of the square keep in England. The former, at 107 x 151ft (32.5 x 46m), was larger even than the White Tower. These towers may have been based on the design of the ducal palace at Rouen of *c.*950. They were intended more as an expression of the might of the Norman invaders than as military strongholds.

Below: The vast Norman keep at Colchester was built over the vaults of the ruined Roman Temple of Claudius.

THE WHITE TOWER

Around a decade later, in 1078, William ordered the building of a great square stone keep, the White Tower, which was intended to strike fear into the hearts of any subversive Londoners. This vast and forbidding building, which survives to this day (see also page 102), was largely complete by *c.*1100. The tower, 90ft (27m) high with walls 11–15ft (3.5–4.5m) thick, measured 105 x 118ft (32 x 36m). It contained a basement beneath two floors of residential apartments, both containing a hall, chamber and chapel. The top floor was set aside for the King himself. The tower's sole entrance was on the south side, some 15ft (4.5m) above ground and accessed by steps that could be removed. The White Tower was probably designed by Gundulf, a Norman monk who became Bishop of Rochester.

WESTMINSTER HALL

HEART OF THE PALACE

When William the Conqueror was satisfied with the fortifications he had built in the city of London, he moved his court into King Edward the Confessor's palace at Westminster. Edward had built this in 1060 on ground between the River Thames and the abbey church of Westminster (subsequently Westminster Abbey).

Above: This engraving by Wenceslaus Holler shows Westminster Hall (centre) as it appeared in the English Civil War.

KING WILLIAM RUFUS

William the Conqueror's son, William Rufus, had grand plans to build a new palace on the site, and in 1097 he built the first stage: Westminster Hall. His structure is the only part of the 11th-century palace still standing today, since it survived the fire that devastated the ancient buildings in 1834.

William Rufus's hall was used for banquets. It measured a massive 240ft (73m) in length and was almost 40ft (12m) high, with walls 6ft 8in (2m) thick.

A raised gallery ran around the hall 20ft (6m) above the ground. The walls were plastered and painted, and contained round-headed windows. The roof was supported by great timber posts, which divided the vast room into a central nave and two side aisles. Although William was reputedly not very impressed with the new building – declaring it a 'mere bedchamber' – he held a great banquet in 1099 to celebrate its completion. The Royal Council of bishops, nobles and ministers, which later assembled there, was the forerunner of the present House of Lords.

Below: King George IV's lavish Coronation Banquet was held in Westminster Hall, in 1821. The Earl of Denbigh wrote of the event that 'it exceeded all imagination'.

AFFAIRS OF STATE

The hall's appearance has significantly changed since King William Rufus's day. After it was damaged by fire in 1291, Edward II carried out restoration; in addition, Richard II made several major improvements in 1397–9, including installing a vast hammer-beam roof (see page 70). Later, the hall was the setting for the coronation feast of each new monarch, when, following tradition, the king or queen's champion would ride to the centre of the hall and challenge to single combat anyone who opposed the sovereign's right to rule. The last coronation feast held in the hall was for George IV in 1821, which was, like all his entertainments, incredibly lavish.

The hall has also been the setting for a number of important trials, including those of Sir Thomas More in 1535, the Gunpowder Plot conspirators in 1606 and King Charles I in 1649. Its main everyday function is as the vestibule of the House of Commons. Since the death of Queen Victoria, it has also been used for the lying-in-state of deceased royals, such as Edward VII (1910), George VI (1952) and Queen Elizabeth, the Queen Mother (2002).

CHEPSTOW CASTLE
NORMAN BUILDING IN WALES

William FitzOsbern was the childhood friend of William the Conqueror and veteran of the Battle of Hastings. He began work on a stone castle at Chepstow in south-east Wales in 1067. Created Earl of Hereford, FitzOsbern established Chepstow as a base for Norman penetration into Wales. It was built in stone from the beginning.

The castle was built in a strategic position – a long, high cliff overlooking the River Wye and the place where the Roman road from western England into South Wales forded the river. Its principal building was a stone Great Hall, initially of two storeys; this was altered and raised in the 13th century, but its original walls are still standing, making it Britain's oldest surviving stone castle building. FitzOsbern and his masons used bands of red tiles thought to be from the nearby Roman fort of Caerwent; they also inserted Norman round-headed windows on the ground floor, which can still be seen today. There are also surviving sections of the 11th-century stone defensive walls to the east (now in the middle bailey) and west (now in the upper bailey).

FitzOsbern's castle was largely complete by 1071, when the Earl was killed in battle in Flanders. By then he had made good use of his base to stamp his authority on much of the Welsh kingdom of Gwent. However, his son, Roger Fitzwilliam, lost possession of Chepstow when he joined the doomed uprising against the Conqueror in 1075. Roger was imprisoned, his castle and lands reverting to the Crown.

Left: Chepstow Castle's walls are 18ft (5.5m) thick in parts. They are notable for an early use of round and square towers.

WILLIAM MARSHALL

In 1115, Henry I gave the castle to the powerful de Clare family, who seem to have made no notable alterations. Then, in 1189, the de Clare heiress, Isabel, daughter of Richard 'Strongbow' de Clare, Earl of Pembroke, married the great knight William Marshall, and the castle passed into his hands along with all her other estates. Marshall upgraded the defences at Chepstow significantly, rebuilding the eastern defensive wall and adding two projecting round towers with arrow slits through which archers could defend the land immediately outside the wall. (The curtain wall he raised was, in his day, the eastern boundary of the castle, but because of subsequent developments, it is now the dividing wall between the middle and lower baileys.)

In the years to 1245, William Marshall's sons continued to redevelop the castle, adding a further enclosure to

THE NORMANS IN WALES

Chepstow was the earliest of several castles erected on the borders of Wales (the Marches) by the Norman 'Marcher lords', who took an iron grip on the English-Welsh border. (The term 'Marcher' derives from the Frankish *marka*, meaning 'boundary'.) Just as William FitzOsbern was given the earldom of Hereford and built a castle at Chepstow, so Roger of Montgomery was created Earl of Shrewsbury and raised a castle at Pembroke, South Wales, and Hugh de Avranches was made Earl of Chester and built a castle in that city. Many other Norman castles followed in Wales, including notable examples at Cardiff (built *c.*1091 by Robert Fitzhamon, Norman lord of Gloucester), Abergavenny (built *c.*1090 by Hamelin de Ballon), Kidwelly (built in the 12th century by Roger, Bishop of Salisbury) and Caerphilly (built from 1271 onward by Gilbert de Clare).

Below: Kidwelly Castle was rebuilt after c.1275 by Payn de Chaworth.

the east (now the lower bailey) with a twin-towered gatehouse, and at the other, western, end of the castle building a barbican with a cylindrical tower. They also improved the Great Keep, adding large windows on the safer northern side overlooking the Wye.

ROGER BIGOD III

In 1270–1300 the castle was in the hands of another great landholder, Roger Bigod III, Earl of Norfolk. He built a new hall along the northern (cliff) side of the lower bailey, including a cellar, kitchen, service rooms and accommodation, as well as the public space of the hall. In addition, he erected what is now known as Marten's Tower, containing elegant accommodation for the lord of the castle and a richly decorated chapel, at the south-east angle of the lower bailey. Earl Roger also built a new three-storey gatehouse for the barbican, added an extra storey to William FitzOsbern's Great Keep and erected the town walls for the developing

Below: Interior of Marten's Tower, Chepstow. Henry Marten, who was jailed there, was a leader of the Levellers in the Civil War.

Above: River fortress. The Wye runs along the north edge of the escarpment on which the elongated castle stands at Chepstow.

settlement alongside the castle. The town of Chepstow grew in the 13th and 14th centuries and received a charter in 1524.

The castle was garrisoned for Charles I and came twice under siege during the Civil Wars of the 17th century. In forcing its surrender, parliamentary guns caused damage, but the castle was later repaired and garrisoned by both Cromwell and Charles II. Marten's Tower takes its name from Henry Marten, one of the judges who signed Charles I's death warrant and who, after the Restoration in 1660, was imprisoned with his wife (in some comfort) in the tower by Charles II. Marten died there in 1680.

ROCHESTER CASTLE

STRONGHOLD IN STONE

The original Rochester Castle was one of the earliest Norman fortifications, built shortly after the Conquest as a show of strength and to guard the point at which the Roman road from London to Dover crossed the River Medway in Kent. It was constructed of timber and earthworks in the south-west angle of the Roman city wall at the point where the medieval bridge spanned the river. In 1087–9, the first years of King William Rufus's reign, Bishop Gundulf – architect of the White Tower in London – rebuilt the castle walls in stone. Rochester was therefore one of the first Norman castles to be reworked in stone.

THE SQUARE KEEP

In 1127, King Henry I granted the castle to William de Corbeil, Archbishop of Canterbury, and his successors. The archbishop built a remarkable square keep, 70 x 70ft (21 x 21m), 113ft (34.5m) high to the parapet, with turrets at the corners soaring another 12ft (3.5m). The walls were 12ft (3.5m) thick at their base. The keep was forbidding without but luxurious within: the second floor housed a chapel, a Great Chamber and a Great Hall, with magnificent carving around the fireplaces, windows and doors, and a raised gallery to the hall. The keep also contained a defensive cross wall, behind which defenders could retreat if the tower was partially breached, and which came in

Above: The square keep at Rochester Castle, showing the rounded south-east tower, rebuilt after damage in the siege of 1215.

Below: A 19th-century painting of Rochester shows how close the cathedral stands to the castle, which guards the crossing of the River Medway.

Above: The interior of the great keep of Rochester Castle is now little more than a shell, but the sheer size of the ruins gives a sense of its original luxury and grandeur.

useful for the castle defenders in 1215 (see below). A smaller tower, built against the north face of the keep, guarded the entrance, which was at first-floor level.

THE FIRST SIEGE

Archbishop de Corbeil's square keep at Rochester faced two major sieges in its history. The first came in 1215, when, with many of England's leading barons openly opposing King John, the Archbishop of Canterbury, Stephen Langton, refused to open the castle to the pro-Royalist Bishop of Winchester. King John and his army arrived, and laid siege for around two months, held at bay by a garrison of little more than 100 men. The King's men used five stone-throwing engines, which did great damage to the curtain wall but could make no significant impact on the tremendous fortifications of the keep itself, so instead they set out to undermine the south-east angle of the tower. They dug beneath the corner of the building and shored up the brickwork with wooden props, then set fire to the props, causing part of the tower to collapse. The defenders retreated behind the defensive cross wall and continued the fight, but the garrison was reduced to surrender by starvation.

After the siege of 1215, the damaged south-east corner of the keep was restored in the contemporary style as a cylindrical (circular) turret, in contrast to the square turrets at the other corners of the tower. Other repairs and improvements included reconstruction of the castle's outer gate and the building of a drawbridge in the southern curtain wall.

In 1264, Rochester Castle was besieged by Simon de Montfort and other rebels during the baronial uprising against King Henry III. The castle was badly damaged, but withstood the assault for a week, until de Montfort and his men withdrew at the news that the King's army was on its way to relieve the castle.

LATER YEARS

In later years, the castle fell into disrepair, but it was restored and rebuilt in the 14th century by Kings Edward III and Richard II. Then it suffered many more years of neglect before being passed from the Crown to private owners in the reign of James I.

MARCHER FORTRESS: LUDLOW CASTLE

Ludlow Castle in Shropshire was built in 1085 as a Norman stronghold to subdue the 'Marches' (the English-Welsh border). Its first lord, Roger de Lacy, was granted land in south Shropshire by William FitzOsbern, Earl of Hereford and builder of Chepstow Castle. At Ludlow, using locally quarried stone, de Lacy built one of the great stone keeps of the 12th century, on high land overlooking the River Terne. The de Lacy family lost the castle for some years, during which, *c.*1130, Sir Joyce de Dinan built a remarkable circular chapel in the Middle Ward, but the castle subsequently returned to its original owners. The town of Ludlow was laid out in the 12th century to the east of the fortress.

In later years, Ludlow Castle belonged to Roger Mortimer, the ruthless Earl of March; his descendants probably built the fortifications on the castle's northern front. The castle then passed to Edward IV. Many improvements were made to the castle in the Tudor period, when it was briefly the home of Prince Arthur (elder brother of the eventual King Henry VIII) and his bride, Catherine of Aragon. In the tower named after Prince Arthur, the sickly heir to the throne died in 1502 – an event with momentous consequences for England's royal family.

Below: In Ludlow's inner bailey stands the Chapel of St Mary Magdalene – the only round 'church' in an English castle.

CASTLE HEDINGHAM

THE GREAT TOWER

Castle Hedingham in Essex is celebrated as one of the most splendid 12th-century rectangular keeps in England. The vast stone tower, 110ft (33.5m) high, was built *c.*1140 by Aubrey de Vere III, probably to celebrate his elevation to the earldom of Oxford.

TOWER CASTLE

The keep has four floors above a basement: the first contains the entrance chamber and the second and third floors combine to make the great Banqueting Hall. Around the hall, built into the 12ft (3.5m) thick walls, runs an elevated minstrels' gallery. The hall and gallery make Hedingham comparable to the Great Keep at Rochester, built perhaps a decade earlier.

Above: The 28ft (8.5m) transverse arch in the Banqueting Hall at Hedingham is one of the largest Norman arches in England.

Castle Hedingham once had four corner turrets and a forebuilding on the west face containing the first-floor entrance to the tower, again as at Rochester. But two of Hedingham's turrets and most of the forebuilding have now been demolished. In other respects, however, it survives in remarkably good condition, with floors and roof intact.

The keep stood in the inner bailey, separated from the outer bailey to the east by a ditch (now crossed by a Tudor bridge). Remains of a Great Hall and a chapel have been found in the inner bailey. The inner and outer bailey were enclosed by earthwork and ditch defences.

The castle remarkably remained in the de Vere family until 1703, on the death of the 20th Earl of Oxford.

Left: Only two of the original four corner turrets survive on the four-floor rectangular tower at Castle Hedingham.

BERKELEY CASTLE

THE ROUND KEEP

The first documented castle at Berkeley in Gloucestershire was built by Roger de Berkeley, as recorded in the Domesday Survey of 1086. Earlier, the land had belonged to Earl Godwin of Wessex, father of Harold II, and after Harold's defeat at Hastings was granted by the Conqueror to the immensely powerful William FitzOsbern, Earl of Hereford, builder of Chepstow Castle and holder of large swathes of land in western and south-western England. There were fortifications on the site before Roger de Berkeley's castle.

Above: Edward II was murdered at Berkeley in 1327. The Berkeley descendants of Robert Fitz-Harding still live at the castle.

THE KEEP

The oldest surviving building at Berkeley is the magnificent round keep, completed in 1153 by Robert Fitz-Harding, 1st Lord Berkeley. Lord Robert received the estate from King Henry II, who had taken the castle from its previous lord, another Roger de Berkeley, following the lawlessness of King Stephen's reign. The keep stands 62ft (19m) high and is 90ft (27m) in diameter. Its walls enclose the mound of the earlier motte-and-bailey Norman fortification, although rather than being placed on top of the motte, the tower here surrounds it. The entrance was by a staircase on the eastern side, enclosed in a forebuilding in the 14th century. The ascent was by 'trip steps', made deliberately in varying sizes so that attackers mounting in a hurry would be likely to lose their footing.

Below: Berkeley Castle's inner bailey, 1822. In one of the apartments are the ebony bed and chairs used by Sir Francis Drake on his round-the-world voyage of 1577–80.

The keep originally had four semicircular turrets, all now gone. Two were incorporated into 14th-century buildings within the enclosure, one was replaced by a new gatehouse and the fourth by Thorpe Tower. The remodelling was carried out largely byThomas, 3rd Lord Berkeley, in 1340–50, when he added the magnificent Great Hall in the castle's inner bailey (see page 68). This hall, 32ft tall and 62ft in length (10 x 19m), was raised on the site of the original hall. It is hung with fine tapestries and has beautiful stained glass windows.

LATER HISTORY

Berkeley Castle was besieged by a parliamentary army during the Civil War in 1645, when their guns made a breach measuring 35ft (11m) in the walls of the keep. This breach has never been repaired, remaining to this day as a reminder of the castle's past as a working fortress.

RICHMOND CASTLE

NORTHERN STRONGHOLDS

The Norman castle of Richmond in North Yorkshire dates to within a decade of the Conquest and occupies a commanding position on a spur overlooking the River Swale. It was built by Alan Rufus of Brittany, Earl of Yorkshire, who was given the vast lands of Edwin, the Saxon Earl of Mercia, as a reward for loyal service to William the Conqueror at Hastings. Richmond Castle was probably built after the Normans had decisively stamped their authority on northern England in the ruthless 'Harrying of the North' during the winter of 1069–70.

Above: The two-storey building that survives in the corner of the triangular Great Court at Richmond is Scolland's Hall of c.1075.

SCOLLAND'S HALL

The oldest surviving part of the castle is Scolland's Hall, a sizeable, very early stone two-storey keep built *c.*1071–5. The now-ruined building once contained a Great Hall on the first floor, as well as private apartments for the lord and a tower containing a garderobe, or area for dressing. Alan Rufus also built a long curtain wall enclosing a large, roughly triangular bailey called the Great Court of around 2.5 acres (1ha), which takes its curious shape from that of the hilltop land it occupies. He fortified the south-west corner of the enclosure with a rectangular defensive tower and added three more towers along the eastern stretch of the curtain wall. In the most northerly of these, Robin Hood's Tower, was a fine chapel dedicated to St Nicholas. This tower is also believed to have been the prison of King William 'the Lion' of Scots in 1174 after he was captured at Alnwick. Another chapel (now gone) appears from archaeological evidence to have stood in the western part of the Great Court. Beyond Scolland's Hall to the south was an outer defensive ward called the Cockpit.

A gatehouse originally stood at the north end of the Great Court, but this was incorporated into a new keep, begun *c.*1170 by Conan, 5th Lord of Richmond, and completed by King Henry II, who took possession of the castle after Conan's death in 1171. In the 14th century, John, Duke of Brittany, carried out some improvements, adding

THE CONQUEROR'S NORTHERN EXCURSIONS

King William travelled north in 1068 to deal with a threatened revolt. In the Anglo-Scandinavian city of York, he founded two motte-and-bailey castles, now known as Clifford's Tower and Baille Hill. On his way, he established castles at Warwick and Nottingham, and on the way back south built castles at Lincoln, Huntingdon and Cambridge. He returned to York in early 1069 to relieve the castles and again later the same year to unleash the celebrated 'Harrying of the North' in the face of Danish raids and English insurrection. He refortified both York castles and celebrated Christmas 1069, the third anniversary of his coronation day, in Clifford's Tower.

Above: Clifford's Tower, York. It takes its name from Roger de Clifford, hanged there in 1322 for disloyalty to Edward II.

Above: Richmond's 12th-century keep has walls 11ft (3.4m) thick. The arch at its foot may be part of the original gatehouse.

a first-floor Great Chamber and chapel on the northern side of Scolland's Hall and raising the height of the curtain walls and some of the towers.

The castle is of great interest to archaeological historians because it was built with a keep-hall and a curtain wall but without any motte at a time when the Normans were building motte-and-bailey castles. At Richmond, the design was adapted to the location, which, due to its hilltop and riverside location, enjoyed excellent natural defences. Scolland's Hall is the second oldest surviving stone keep in England, after that at Chepstow Castle.

ROYAL RICHMOND

The earldom of Richmond has a famous history and many royal associations. Edward IV's brother, Richard of Gloucester, was Earl of Richmond and held on to the title after he became King Richard III. Henry VII took the title and then bestowed it upon his favourite palace of Sheen by the River Thames in Surrey, the palace he rebuilt following a calamitous fire of Christmas 1498. But the original Richmond Castle had a largely uneventful history. It was not attacked or besieged during either the Wars of the Roses or the English Civil War. Indeed, it was in a ruinous state as early as the mid-16th century.

NORMAN POWER

Other major Norman castles in northern England included the one at Bamburgh, ancient capital of the kings of Northumberland. Little today remains of the Norman fortifications, which may have been built by William the Conqueror in the 1070s; the castle underwent major restoration and rebuilding in the 18th and 19th centuries. The Conqueror also founded another once-significant castle at Lincoln. Begun in 1068, it was built in the south-west part of the walled city established by the Romans. The castle had stone walls from at least 1115, with gateways to east and west and two keep towers on the southern edge.

At Durham, the Normans built a magnificent motte-and-bailey castle to protect the Bishop of Durham, of which only the crypt chapel and part of the gatehouse survive. By the 1140s, Durham Castle consisted of a timber tower on the motte, with a stone curtain wall around the mound; in the bailey stood a chapel, a hall and a chamber block. The proud Norman Romanesque Cathedral, begun in 1093, already stood alongside the castle.

Below: Richmond Castle's isolated position meant that it did not play a significant part in any national conflicts.

CHAPTER TWO

PLANTAGENET MIGHT

1154–1307

The formidable warrior-king Edward I (1239–1307) was the greatest royal castle-builder in English history. He was memorialized on his tombstone as *Scotorum Malleus* ('the Hammer of the Scots') for his battle exploits beyond England's northern border, but he is also remembered for the brutally efficient campaigns he fought in Wales and the network of great castles he erected to impose English rule there. Of the ten castles Edward built during his campaigns against the Welsh, those of Beaumaris, Caernarfon and Harlech are lauded as elegant and innovative examples of the art of castle-building.

Before his accession to the throne, Edward travelled to the Holy Land on Crusade in 1271–2. There, he saw and admired Crusader castles, learning much from their 'concentric' design. The castles had two concentric sets of walls: troops on the higher inner walls could defend the outer walls that they overlooked, but, if necessary, could withdraw within the inner stronghold. On his way back from the East, Edward stopped in Savoy (France), where he met an ambitious castle-builder who had established his reputation by building the widely admired stronghold of St Georges d'Espéranche for Edward I's uncle, Count Philip I of Savoy. Called Master James of St Georges in honour of Count Philip's castle, he became Edward's chief military architect. As Master of the King's Works in Wales, he was largely responsible for the magnificent ring of 'Edwardian' castles erected there.

Left: Symbol of an English king's power in Wales. The eight drum towers and high curtain wall of Conwy Castle dominate the shore of the estuary.

ORFORD CASTLE
AND CYLINDRICAL KEEPS

Orford in Suffolk was once on the coast, but now the Orford Ness shingle bank intervenes between the village and the sea. The castle was built by King Henry II, both as a coastal defence against possible invasion and to strengthen the King's hand against the troublesome Earl of Norfolk, Hugh Bigod. Happily for the King, Orford Castle was finished in 1173, just in time to provide a royal stronghold in the face of a rebellion in Suffolk, supported by Bigod, in 1173–4. Following Henry's victory over the rebels, he destroyed Bigod's castles at Framlingham, Bungay, Thetford and Walton.

EXPERIMENTAL KEEPS

The keep, or tower, at Orford was polygonal (many-sided). Three rectangular turrets adjoined the keep, one of which had a forebuilding attached.

Above: The turrets of the polygonal keep at Orford are 90ft (27m) tall. The keep is all that survives of a once substantial castle.

In the later 12th and early 13th centuries, castle-builders experimented with new forms for the keep, the main stronghold of the castle. As the techniques and weapons of siege warfare developed during the 12th century, the traditional rectangular keep proved unsatisfactory in two ways: it was vulnerable to attack (its corners could be undermined or destroyed, as at Rochester, making it unstable), while its rectangular shape restricted the defenders' field of fire.

At Orford, the keep's inner design was also experimental. Above the basement, with its own well, were two self-contained residential quarters on the first and second floors, each with kitchen, chambers, garderobe and spacious circular hall. The upper 'apartment' was very grand and evidently intended for the King himself. The forebuilding, on the southern side, contained the entrance way on the ground floor, and the chapel on an upper level between the first and second floors of the main tower. Today, only the keep survives at Orford, but originally it stood within a large bailey, or enclosure, surrounded by a defensive wall set with rectangular defensive towers.

The design of the keep at Orford is unusual among English castles. As builders moved on from the 'square' (rectangular) keep, they more often built 'cylindrical' (circular) rather than polygonal towers.

Below: The thick wall, round mural towers and outer gatehouse complement the vast circular keep at Pembroke Castle.

Above: Dundrum Castle is one of John de Courcy's finest castles, set high on a hill overlooking Dundrum Bay.

CONISBROUGH CASTLE

Henry II's illegitimate half-brother, Hamelin Plantagenet, built a splendid keep at Conisbrough, in Yorkshire, in the 1180s. The castle at Conisbrough had been established a little over a century earlier by William de Warenne, a close friend of William the Conqueror. It came into Hamelin's hands on his marriage to Isabel, Warenne's descendant and heiress, in 1164. Hamelin built a circular tower-keep surrounded by six turrets that rise above the main tower to provide elevated defensive positions. These buttress towers are therefore similar to the ones built around ten years earlier at Orford. Archaeological historians also see a forerunner to the Conisbrough keep in Earl Hamelin's fortified cylindrical keep at Mortemer in Normandy.

At Conisbrough, the keep stood in the north-eastern part of an extensive bailey, surrounded by a thick curtain wall set with semicircular turrets. Within the tower was a basement with a well, a first-floor storage area and residential quarters on the second and third floors – a hall (second floor) beneath a chamber (third floor), both luxuriously fitted with fireplace, garderobe and washbasin. Adjoining the chamber, in the easterly turret, was a splendid chapel.

PEMBROKE AND DUNDRUM

Other fine cylindrical keeps were built in the late 12th century at Pembroke in South Wales and at Dundrum (then Rath) in Co Down, on the east coast of Northern Ireland. Built in the years either side of 1200 by William Marshall, Earl of Pembroke, the castle at Pembroke was on the site of an 11th-century stronghold raised by Roger, Earl of Montgomery and Norman Lord of Dyfed. The keep is 75ft (23m) high, with a basement beneath three floors of residential apartments and a domed stone roof. It has a large gatehouse and barbican tower – part of an extensive curtain wall that encloses a sizeable bailey. Pembroke was South Wales's strongest castle. It also has a significant place in history as the birthplace of Henry Richmond, the future King Henry VII.

Dundrum Castle was built by John de Courcy, a Somerset knight who travelled to Ireland in 1171 as part of the Norman incursion and, pushing north on his own, conquered parts of Ulster.

Above: The impressive courtyard at Pembroke Castle is so big that the whole of Harlech Castle could fit within it.

De Courcy established the castle in a formidable position, on the site of a former Celtic fort atop a 200ft (60m) hill overlooking Dundrum Bay. His cylindrical keep was 52ft (16m) high and contained two storeys above a basement. The walls were 8ft (2.5m) thick and in places contained passageways and chambers. The castle's boundary was defined by an imposing curtain wall that ran around the edge of the flattened hilltop.

Right: At Conisbrough Castle in Yorkshire, the cylindrical keep, with its six wedge-shaped buttresses, is 100ft (30m) in height.

FRAMLINGHAM CASTLE

THE THIRTEEN TOWERS

The construction of the first castle at Framlingham is traditionally credited to the Norman knight Roger de Bigod, who fought in William the Conqueror's army at Hastings and was rewarded with extensive landholdings. Later, he received the Framlingham estate from Henry I in 1101. Following his death six years later, the castle and land passed first to his eldest son, William, and then, after William died in the '*White Ship* disaster' in 1120, to Roger's second son, Hugh.

Hugh, the powerful and fiercely independent 1st Earl of Norfolk, provoked the wrath of King Henry II, as a result of which the castle of Framlingham was first confiscated by the Crown in 1157–65 and then partially destroyed in 1175, following the failure of a revolt (in which Hugh took part) in 1173–4.

THE CURRENT CASTLE

Hugh's son Roger, 2nd Earl of Norfolk, built Framlingham in its current form in 1190–1210. Earl Roger's design for Framlingham did away with the fortified keep altogether. Instead, probably in tribute to the Byzantine fortresses seen and admired by English knights on Crusade, the castle's main fortification was a curtain wall containing 13 towers. This enclosed an extensive inner bailey and was complemented by earthwork defences surrounding an even larger outer bailey to the south, west and east. It appears that these were never rebuilt in stone. Additional defence was provided by an artificial lake, on the castle's western side, created by damming the nearby river. In the inner bailey, Earl Roger built a Great Hall, which in later years was partially demolished and used as a poorhouse.

Above: Framlingham is a castle without a keep. Its strength lay in the 13 mural towers in the 44ft (13m) high wall.

Below: The rather inappropriate ornamental chimneys in the courtyard at Framlingham were added in the early 16th century by the castle's then owners, the dukes of Norfolk.

ROYAL VISITS

King John was entertained at Framlingham Castle in 1213. Three years later, he besieged and captured the Bigod stronghold in the course of the civil war that ended his reign. The castle was returned to the ownership of the Bigods, who later served as Marshals of England, but after once more falling foul of the Crown, they were finally removed from office and relieved of all their landholdings by King Edward I (r.1272–1307).

In 1553, at a time when the castle had been forfeited by the dukes of Norfolk to the Crown, Mary Tudor was staying at Framlingham when she received the news that she had become Queen of England.

CARRICKFERGUS CASTLE

THE NORMANS IN IRELAND

Above: Carrickfergus Castle commanded the waters of Belfast Lough and protected the walled town that grew up alongside it.

Situated on a rocky outcrop overlooking Belfast Lough is Carrickfergus Castle, which is celebrated as the most complete surviving early medieval castle in the whole of Ireland. John de Courcy, Norman knight and builder of Dundrum Castle in Co Down, built the earliest part of the castle (later its inner ward) in the 1180s.

CASTLE CONSTRUCTION

De Courcy was defeated by Hugh de Lacy, Earl of Ulster, at Carrickfergus. He took possession of the castle, and began work on a massive four-storey rectangular keep some 90ft (27m) high, with a principal chamber measuring 40 x 38ft (12 x 11.5m). De Lacy doubled the size of the castle by enclosing the remainder of the peninsula and raised a substantial curtain wall with projecting towers, arranged to allow for covering arrow fire. Architectural historians compare the layout of the curtain wall and its towers to that at Framlingham. Like Framlingham, Carrickfergus was besieged and captured by King John and passed to the Crown.

Below: The entrance to the four-storey keep at Carrickfergus is on the second floor.

The distinctive gatehouse at Carrickfergus had flanking towers and a high arch that supported a wooden platform used by the defenders. It was added *c.*1250, when the curtain wall enclosing the outer ward was raised.

SCOTTISH BESIEGERS

In 1315, Carrickfergus was besieged by the army of Edward Bruce, brother of King Robert I of Scots. Edward led a Scots force into Ireland that year and was proclaimed High King in 1316; but despite the arrival of reinforcements commanded by his royal brother, he was defeated and killed by Ireland's English rulers in 1318. At Carrickfergus, the English garrison withstood the siege for a full year, apparently forced to eat the flesh of eight dead Scottish prisoners to fend off starvation. However, the castle finally fell to Robert Bruce himself.

Almost 400 years later, the castle played a role in the 'Williamite War', fought to decide the future of the English monarchy after the deposition of King James II and his replacement by Prince William of Orange as William III.

In 1690, the 'Williamite' army under General Schomberg besieged and captured the castle. The following year, William himself landed at Carrickfergus to lead the campaign that ended in his victory at the Battle of the Boyne.

Below: The massive walls of Carrickfergus Castle are over 3ft (1m) thick.

MIDDLEHAM CASTLE

HOME OF RICHARD III

In some places the square keep remained in favour. At Middleham in North Yorkshire, *c.*1150–70, Robert FitzRanulph built one of the largest square keeps in western Europe, measuring 110 x 80ft (33.5 x 24m), with walls 12ft (3.5m) thick. Even in its ruinous condition today, it rises to a height of 66ft (20m). Architectural historians use the term 'hall-keep castles' for fortified buildings such as Middleham, which are dominated by substantial keeps containing large halls.

At Middleham, the keep was built close to an earlier castle, an earthwork motte-and-bailey fortification constructed in the last decade or so of the 11th century by Alan Rufus, first Norman Lord of Richmond, or his brother Ribald. The remains of this fortification, now known as 'William's Hill', can be examined today around 500 yards (460m) to the south-west of the main castle.

Below: The remains of Robert FitzRanulph's great square keep (centre back) still dominate the ruined castle at Middleham.

A KING AT HOME IN MIDDLEHAM CASTLE

Richard III loved Middleham Castle. It was the home of his wife, Anne, daughter of Richard Neville ('Warwick the Kingmaker'), and they lived there with her mother, the Countess of Warwick, and Richard and Anne's son, Prince Edward, who was born in the castle's south-west tower (henceforth known as the Prince's Tower) in 1473. It was at Middleham, on 9 April 1484, that Edward died aged just ten, the year before his father was killed at Bosworth Field.

Right: Richard III (1452–85) is often assumed to have been responsible for the murder of the Princes in the Tower.

FAVOURED ROYAL CASTLE

Middleham Castle was a residence fit for a king. Indeed, it later became a favoured royal residence in the 15th century as the home of Richard III and his wife, Anne. Although its builder, Robert FitzRanulph, Ribald's grandson, had close family ties to the lordship of Richmond, he came from only a minor branch of the family, which makes the grandeur of Middleham Castle therefore somewhat surprising.

The keep's two storeys were constructed above a vaulted basement with two wells. The ground floor was occupied by a large kitchen and an extensive cellar-pantry; two circular stone pits are thought to have been used for keeping live fish prior to their preparation for the table. A circular stair in the south-east corner led up to the first floor, which contained a buttery, pantry, small chapel and the Great Hall in its eastern half; beyond a central wall in the western half was a Great Chamber and a privy or private chamber for the Lord of Middleham's personal use. The Great Hall was used both for feasting and as a law court.

DEFENDED STAIRWAY

The keep's main entrance was on the first floor, approached by a heavily fortified stone staircase (now destroyed) on the building's east face. Anyone approaching the keep had to gain access via a manned gateway at the foot of the

Above: The compact castle at Middleham is square. Although once luxuriously fitted as a palace, it was also a sturdy fortress.

stairs, then pass through another guarded gatehouse halfway up the stairs, and a third at the top of the stairs. All the way up, people climbing the stairs could be watched or, if need be, attacked from a defensive wall with a wall-walk along the top and also from the battlements on top of the keep.

LATER ALTERATIONS

From 1270 onward, the castle was in the hands of a branch of the Neville family, whose descendants later rose to great prominence in the north and, indeed, nationally. Under the Nevilles, a curtain wall was added around the keep in the late 13th century. A three-storey gatehouse with battlements and a projecting 'gallery' from which defenders could throw missiles or pour boiling oil on attacking forces was built in the 15th century. The castle's four towers were built and gradually developed in stages from the 13th to the 15th centuries.

In the 13th century, a substantial three-storey building was raised on the eastern side of the keep, linking it to the castle's eastern wall. It contained two floors of living quarters and a large chapel on the third floor to replace the rather small chapel originally provided within the main keep.

LUXURIOUS ACCOMMODATION

In the late 14th century, Ralph Neville, created Earl of Westmoreland by Richard II, constructed a series of residential chambers within the castle's thick curtain wall to supplement the accommodation provided in the keep. Ralph had a total of 23 children, including 14 by his second wife, Joan Beaufort, the illegitimate daughter of John of Gaunt. In his time, King Henry IV stayed at Middleham Castle and was reportedly impressed by the luxurious accommodation provided.

Ralph's descendant Richard Neville, Earl of Warwick, was the celebrated 'Warwick the Kingmaker', a power-broker during the Wars of the Roses. On his death at the Battle of Barnet on Easter Sunday, 1471, Middleham Castle passed to Edward IV, who gave it to his brother Richard, Duke of Gloucester, subsequently King Richard III.

Below: Middleham's keep's original staircase has collapsed, but modern steps allow visitors to climb up for views of the town and surrounding Yorkshire countryside.

TINTAGEL CASTLE

KING ARTHUR'S BIRTHPLACE

The ruins of Tintagel Castle in north Cornwall, on a headland and adjacent outcrop, are among the most romantic military remains in Britain. Most of what is visible dates from the 13th century, but the castle's name is forever associated with the story of King Arthur of Camelot, the legendary king of Britain usually associated with a historical Celtic prince of the 5th–6th centuries AD.

Above: Gateway to a romantic past? Tintagel's dramatic setting encourages visions of Merlin, Arthur and Ygerna.

THE ARTHURIAN LEGEND

It was in Tintagel Castle, according to the 12th-century Welsh chronicler Geoffrey of Monmouth, that Arthur was conceived. The magician Merlin transformed Uther Pendragon, King of Britain, into the likeness of Gorlois, Duke of Cornwall, so that he could lie with Gorlois's ravishing wife, Ygerna. The result was Arthur, who may also have been born at Tintagel. Later, he became – according to the legend – Britain's greatest king, Celtic defeater of the Saxons, embodiment of chivalric virtue, lord of Camelot and leader of the knights of the Round Table. Some versions of his legend suggest that he himself held court at Tintagel.

FROM MONASTERY TO RUIN

The headland at Tintagel may have been used as an Iron Age Celtic fortress or later as a Saxon fort, but no evidence remains of these fortifications. Tintagel was certainly the site of a monastic community established by the Celtic Christian missionary St Juliot in the early 6th century, and there are traces of a monastic cell (dwelling) and of an underfloor heating system thought to have been used by the monks.

In 1145, Reginald, an illegitimate son of Henry I, built a castle on the headland; the chapel and Great Hall are believed to survive from his time. His castle was extended by Richard, 1st Earl of Cornwall and Knight of the Holy Roman Empire. Most of the surviving castle buildings are from his stronghold.

The gate and upper ward of the castle were constructed on the headland, while a separate ward containing the Great Hall stood on the outcrop, which could be reached by a very narrow rock causeway. This has since been eroded by the sea, and access to the outcrop is now by steps cut into the rock.

Tintagel Castle fell into ruins after Earl Richard's time, and it was for many years a largely unregarded, if beautifully situated, ruin. However, the 19th-century revival of interest in Arthurian legend put the castle back on the map.

Below: This watercolour of the remains of Tintagel Castle is by 19th-century American artist, William Trost Richards.

WINCHESTER GREAT HALL

AND THE ROUND TABLE

Winchester, in Hampshire, southern England, was the capital of the Anglo-Saxon kingdom of Wessex and the burial place of kings, including Alfred and Canute II. It remained England's principal city until the 12th century.

A Norman castle was built there soon after the Conquest, in the reign of King William I the Conqueror. King Henry III was born in the castle, on 1 October 1207, and in his time the Norman castle was rebuilt after having fallen into disrepair during King John's reign. Henry was a man of culture and refinement, whose reign saw the major rebuilding of Westminster Palace and Abbey, Windsor Castle and the construction of magnificent English cathedrals at Lincoln, Wells, Salisbury and St Alban's. At Winchester, the Great Hall is all that survives of his work.

ARTHUR'S ROUND TABLE

A magnificent round table that hangs on the wall of the Winchester Great Hall was for many years identified as the Round Table of King Arthur of Camelot. The table, 18ft (5.5m) in diameter and 2,640lb (1,200kg) in weight, is decorated with the names of the 24 knights of Arthur's company and a portrait of the King himself. According to the *Roman de Brut* (1155), one of the early medieval romances that developed the Arthurian legend, Arthur introduced a round table so that none of the knights could claim precedence over any other. Historians have established that the table in question was not made until the 14th century and was decorated in the reign of Henry VIII, who had a keen interest in knightly exploits, the Arthurian story and the chivalric tradition.

Above: The legend of King Arthur's round table inspired this vast 14th-century tribute, now hung in the Great Hall at Winchester.

THE KING'S HALL

The Winchester Great Hall was an early example of a new development in such buildings, a movement away from the dark and shadowy halls of the 12th century to a lighter, more elegant design. Henry's hall contained columns of Purbeck stone, fashionable plate tracery windows and pointed arches. Its walls were plastered and decorated in brilliant colours. When he was in Winchester, Henry used the hall for dining, sitting in council with leading barons and clergy and as a courtroom. It is a fine example of the early English Gothic style of architecture.

In the reign of Henry's successor, Edward I, a major fire destroyed most of the royal apartments at Winchester in 1302. Edward and Queen Margaret, his second wife, were in residence at the time and were almost burned alive.

CAERPHILLY CASTLE
CONCENTRIC DEFENCES

The forbidding Caerphilly Castle in Glamorgan, South Wales, was built in 1271–*c.*1280 by Gilbert de Clare (1243–95), Lord of Glamorgan and one of the most powerful men in the realm. It covers 30 acres (12ha), and is the largest castle in Wales, as well as the second largest British castle, after Windsor. Both in size and in the splendour of its residential quarters, Caerphilly Castle rivalled the great Welsh strongholds, such as Beaumaris and Harlech, built shortly after by King Edward. It is rightly regarded by historians and architects as one of the most splendid castles in all Europe and as one of the finest medieval buildings erected in the British Isles.

As a 'Marcher Lord' (a descendant of the Norman lords created by William the Conqueror to subdue the natives in the Welsh Marches), de Clare had the right to build castles without royal licence and to wage war on his own behalf. He had become a man of great wealth when he inherited the earldom of Gloucester in 1262 and had driven Welsh prince Gruffudd ap Rhys out of upland Glamorgan in 1266.

LLYWELYN'S THREAT

De Clare's vast castle at Caerphilly, begun at the very end of Henry III's reign when the future Edward I was abroad on Crusade, must by its overwhelming size have provoked some misgivings at the royal court. However, de Clare's principal concern was to counter the threat of Welsh prince Llywelyn ap Gruffudd, who had control of much of northern and middle Wales and was aiming to move southwards and capture Glamorgan. With his powerful siege engines, Llywelyn had in 1270 overrun and destroyed an earlier castle that de Clare had begun to build at Caerphilly.

Above: Gilbert Clare, Lord of Glamorgan. This Victorian image is based on a near-contemporary stained glass window (c.1340) at Tewkesbury Abbey Church.

THE CONCENTRIC CASTLE

A stronghold with two defensive boundaries (an outer wall overlooked and protected by a taller and stronger inner round of fortifications) is known as a concentric castle. The design was used by the Romans and put to very effective use in Crusader castles, such as Krak des Chevaliers in Syria. Shortly after the construction of Caerphilly, Edward I and his chief architect, Master James of St Georges, used the concentric design in the castle of Beaumaris, Anglesey, in 1295.

Below: This aerial view of Caerphilly shows impressive double walls – with higher inner fortifications – and extensive water defences.

WALLS OF DEFENCE

The surviving stronghold at Caerphilly is notable as Britain's first truly concentric castle, one with twin defensive walls. The low outer wall has two gatehouses, each with two towers, as well as a water gate in the south front. The inner wall is rectangular, fortified with one gatehouse facing east and one facing west, a great kitchen tower and a tower at each of the corners of the rectangle.

Above: As part of a programme of modern repairs to Caerphilly Castle begun c.1870 by John Crichton Stuart, the 3rd Marquess of Bute, the water defences were restored by reflooding the lake.

Along the south side of the inner rectangle were the Great Hall and luxuriously appointed state apartments. The Great Hall was remodelled in 1322–6, when the castle was in the possession of Hugh le Despenser the Younger, favourite of Edward II.

The castle's main stronghold was the eastern gatehouse of the inner wall, intended as the residence of the castle constable. Its entrance passage could be closed with door and portcullis towards both the outer ward (the area within the outer wall, but outside the inner wall) and the inner ward (the area enclosed by the inner wall), and so could be defended from both directions. If the castle were overrun, its remaining defenders could retreat to this gatehouse.

The castle's forbidding stone defences were supplemented by a vast encircling moat that was probably inspired by the siege of Kenilworth Castle in 1266, in which its water defences greatly prolonged the encounter, which de Clare witnessed.

CAERPHILLY'S LEANING TOWER

Caerphilly's south-eastern tower leans dramatically 9ft (2.75m) from the perpendicular. The most likely explanation for this is that it was partially demolished during the English Civil War by parliamentarian forces determined to spoil the castle defences.

A more romantic tale maintains that when Edward II, at the close of his reign, took refuge in Caerphilly Castle, then held by his favourite Hugh le Despenser, his estranged wife, Queen Isabella, pursued him with armed force. Edward moved on, but Isabella besieged the castle and captured the tower, later setting off a vast explosion that almost brought it down.

RESTORATION

In the early part of the 15th century, Owain Glyndwr held Caerphilly Castle in the course of his failed revolt against Henry IV. By 1536, the castle had become derelict, except for one part, which remained in use as a prison. The stronghold was restored *c.*1870 by the 3rd Marquess of Bute, the builder-restorer of Cardiff Castle and Castell Coch, and then by his son, the 4th Marquess, in the early 20th century. The 5th Marquess placed Caerphilly Castle in state care in 1950.

Below: Beyond the Lower Eastern Gatehouse at Caerphilly is the Inner East Gate, with the celebrated leaning tower to the left.

CAERNARFON CASTLE

CONSTANTINOPLE'S INFLUENCE

In 1283, Edward I began building an impressive castle and walled town at Caernarfon in North Wales, as a symbol of his conquest of the Welsh. The King was fresh from triumph in the Second Welsh War (1282–3), in which he had slain Welsh prince Llywelyn ap Gruffudd and captured his brother Dafydd, Prince of Gwynedd.

STRATEGIC POSITION

As he prepared to establish English government in Wales, Edward wanted to make a triumphalist expression of his imperial ambitions at Caernarfon. He chose the town because it was an ancient stronghold for the princes of Gwynedd and because of its strategic position overlooking the Menai Straits, where the River Seoint reaches the sea, and controlling access to Snowdonia – but principally because it was the site of Roman Segontium, which had defended the north-west frontier of the empire.

Below: With his magnificent fortress at Caernarfon, Edward wanted to impress his regal power on his new Welsh subjects.

AN EMPEROR'S DREAM CASTLE

In appearance and design, Caernarfon is quite different to the other great castles Edward raised in Wales, at Harlech, Conwy and Beaumaris. Caernarfon has polygonal rather than circular drum towers, and cross-banded masonry (alternate strips of light and dark stone) in the defensive walls.

Edward built Caernarfon as the fulfilment of a dream traditionally said to have come to Roman Emperor Magnus Maximus, son of Constantine I, in which he travelled to a land of mountains and found there a marvellous fortress with walls of varied hues, containing an ivory throne capped with golden eagles. The polygonal towers and cross-banded walls were apparently a homage to the Theodosian Wall at Constantinople, which Edward and his chief architect, Master James of St Georges, had seen while on Crusade.

King Edward and Master James incorporated into the castle an 11th-century Norman motte-and-bailey fortification built at Caernarfon by Hugh, Earl of Chester. In this way, Edward made the symbolic statement

Above: The towers of Caernarfon have stood proud for centuries. This watercolour shows the Eagle Tower c.1850.

HISTORY TIMELINE

1294 The castle is besieged by land forces in the Welsh uprising led by Madog ap Llewelyn; the benefit of its maritime location is proven as the garrison takes in supplies by sea and survives until a relieving army arrives in the spring of 1295.

1323 The castle assumes roughly its modern form, after 40 years' building.

1399 Richard II visits. Furnishings and decorations must be unfinished, for he has to sleep on straw.

1401-3 Owen Glendower tries unsuccessfully three times to take the castle. The third time, he uses heavy siege machinery, but is still repulsed by a garrison of only 28 men.

1646 During the English Civil War, the castle, garrisoned by Royalists, is captured by Major-General Mytton for the Parliamentarians.

***c*.1890** After centuries of neglect, the castle is repaired.

that his claim to Wales was merely the renewal of an ancient right established by the Normans. A walled borough, or town, was built alongside the castle, the two making a heavily fortified seat for English royal government in Wales. Defences were strengthened further by the tidal waters that the castle overlooks: originally the castle and town stood on a peninsula that was almost completely surrounded by water. The castle has an irregular oblong design because it was built in the shape of the rock it occupies.

At the western end of the castle stands the majestic Eagle Tower, at 124ft (38m) high one of the tallest single towers erected in the Middle Ages. When first built, it had a stone eagle on each of its three turrets. The tower contained the splendid residence of the castle's keeper, the Justiciar (or regent) of North Wales.

ENGLISH PRINCE OF WALES

On 25 April 1284, Edward I's wife, Queen Eleanor, gave birth to their first-born son at Caernarfon. According to tradition, he then presented the infant to his Welsh subjects as their next ruler, pointing out that the baby was currently without blame, had been born in Wales and spoke not a single word of English. Seven years later, again at Caernarfon, the boy was invested as Prince of Wales. In 1911, in a romanticized 'medieval' ceremony, Edward, eldest son of George V, was invested as Prince of Wales in the castle. The ceremony was devised for Prince Edward and his father by David Lloyd George, MP for Caernarfon. Some 58 years later, Queen Elizabeth II's eldest son, Charles, was invested as Prince of Wales at Caernarvon on 1 July 1969.

Right: Famous for his castle-building and battlefield exploits, Edward I also recodified English common law.

BUILT FOR DEFENCE

At Caernarfon, Master James designed a forbidding fortress. Defenders in the 13 polygonal towers could cover the entire circumference of the castle. In the south front, soldiers and archers could rain weapons on attackers from two 'firing galleries' that ran, one above the other, right along the wall. There were two main gateways: at the east end, the Queen's Gate gave into the inner bailey by way of a drawbridge; on the north front, the King's Gate gave access to the castle from the walled town. The latter had impressive defences, for it contained six portcullises and five doors.

Master James' plan was for the enclosure within the castle walls to be divided across the middle by the gatehouse, but the interior of the castle was never completed, as was a tower on the mound of the Norman castle within the walls. Building work on the castle went on until 1330, yet much of it was left unfinished. In its surviving form, it is the shell of a magnificent fortress.

Below: Coastal stronghold of Caernarfon. Edward built his major Welsh fortresses on the coast because the Welsh intercepted land supplies and he needed access to the sea.

CONWY CASTLE
DRUM TOWERS

The castle and walled town of Conwy in North Wales were built by King Edward I in just five years (1283–8). Again designed by Edward's great architect, Master James of St Georges, the castle comprises eight massive drum towers linked by a high curtain wall that is 15ft (4.5m) thick in parts. The sturdy walls of the adjacent town contain three gates and 21 strong towers; on average 24ft (7.5m) in thickness, they run for over ¾ mile (0.5km). They survive in good condition over seven centuries later.

Above: Stephenson's rail and Telford's road bridge run past Edward I's castle at Conwy.

RING OF STONE

Conwy was part of the ring of Welsh castles planned by King Edward I to impose English rule, enforced by English-garrisoned strongholds, on the Welsh. At Conwy, however, in contrast to Beaumaris, Caernarvon and Harlech, Master James elected not to raise strongly fortified gatehouses with twin towers. The drum towers in the castle walls defended both western and eastern entrances to the castle and made extra fortifications on the gate unnecessary.

INNER AND OUTER WARDS

Like Caernarvon, the castle at Conwy has a narrow, elongated shape because it was designed to fit the rock on which it stands: a high promontory in a commanding position alongside the tidal waters of the river estuary. Within the high defensive walls, the castle was divided by a gateway into the outer and inner wards on an east–west axis. Access from the town was via a drawbridge across the moat at the north-western end of the rock. A steep flight of steps led into the west barbican (outer defence), which was defended by the westernmost two of the castle's eight great towers. From there a gateway led into the outer ward, which contained the kitchen, stables and Great Hall. The constable had his quarters in the great towers overlooking the west barbican.

Right: Conwy Castle's intimidating towers and vast curtain wall appear to grow naturally from the rocky outcrop on which they stand.

The smaller inner ward was the heart of the castle, containing the royal quarters: the King's Hall, Privy Chamber and Presence Chamber. The castle's south-east tower housed the king's sleeping rooms, while the north-east tower contained a well-appointed chapel. Beyond was the east barbican and stairs leading down to a water gate.

'BASTIDE' FORTIFIED TOWN

Conwy Castle and town were, like Caernarvon and Flint, planned as a single defensive and trading unit.

MASTER JAMES OF ST GEORGES

Edward's chief architect, the builder of the 'Edwardian' castles of North Wales, was Master James of St Georges (*c.*1230–c.1308). A native of Savoy, Master James took his full title from the magnificent castle of St Georges d'Espéranche, which he built for Edward I's friend and relative, Count Philip of Savoy. Like the castle at Caernarvon, St Georges d'Espéranche had polygonal towers. Master James built eight Welsh castles for Edward I: Aberystwyth, Beaumaris, Builth, Caernarvon, Conwy, Flint, Harlech and Rhuddlan. Master James won a position of great eminence, was styled Master of the King's Works in Wales, and earned the then vast amount of three shillings a day.

Edward I had seen the success of building planned towns beside garrisoned castles in English-held Gascony (south-west France), and applied the idea in North Wales. The Welsh towns were planned as centres for the English administration of an occupied country. They were settled with English people, and the Welsh locals were often forbidden to enter the town or to trade with its people, and could risk hanging if found within the walls after sunset.

In 1401, according to tradition, a local carpenter won control of Conwy Castle from Henry IV's garrison. Gaining access to the stronghold on Good Friday, when the majority of the defending garrison were at church, he then opened the gates to Welsh rebels, who declared for Owen Glendower, self-styled native Prince of Wales. The occupation itself did not last long, however; Glendower's revolt against Henry IV failed, although subsequently, it is said, most of the rebels were granted pardons.

Above: Four of Conwy's eight towers guard the castle's outer ward, while the other four protect the inner ward.

Below: Looking down to the west from the King's Tower on Conwy's outer ward, the remains of the Great Hall lie on the left.

DECLINE AND RUIN

Over the next two centuries, the castle fell into disrepair. According to a state paper of 1609, it was already 'utterlie decayed', and in this condition was sold for £100 to Viscount Conway. The castle was repaired for use in the Civil War by John Williams, a Conwy man who had risen to be Archbishop of York. In the war, Conwy was besieged and captured by Parliamentarians commanded by Major-General Mytton and afterwards was slighted. In 1665, the 3rd Earl of Conway reduced the castle to little more than a ruin by removing all the ironwork, lead and timbers. It was restored in the 19th and 20th centuries.

RHUDDLAN, FLINT AND GOODRICH

CASTLES BY THE WATER

Rhuddlan Castle in Denbighshire, North Wales, was begun by King Edward I at the same time as its near-neighbour at Flint, in 1277. Rhuddlan and Flint, the first of the ten castles built by Edward I in Wales, were both raised alongside new towns set within earthwork fortifications. At Rhuddlan, the River Clwyd was diverted and canalized for 2–3 miles (3–5km) to allow seagoing vessels to approach the newly constructed landing stages, which were built separately for castle and town.

Rhuddlan was a long-established military and royal base. It was originally the setting for a fort built in AD971 by Edward the Elder, son of Alfred the Great, and was afterwards the kingly seat of Welsh ruler, Gruffydd ap Llywelyn. Gruffydd's stronghold was destroyed by Harold Godwinson in 1063. After the Norman Conquest, a motte-and-bailey castle was built there in 1073 by leading nobleman, Robert of Rhuddlan. In 1276–7, Edward I marched into the region to stamp out the threat posed by Welsh ruler, Llywelyn ap Gruffydd, self-styled 'Prince of Wales'. In the course of this campaign, Edward began the castles at Flint and Rhuddlan, and received the submission of Llywelyn at Rhuddlan in November 1277.

Edward's castle at Rhuddlan, raised around 650–1,000ft (200–300m) north-west of the Norman fortifications, was begun by Master Bertram de Saltu, a Gascon engineer, but finished by Master James of St Georges, to whom the castle is usually attributed. Rhuddlan Castle was built swiftly, and was largely complete by 1280.

Above: The remains of the south tower overlook the inner ward at Rhuddlan.

INNER WARD AND MOAT

The design was for a concentric castle, with a relatively low outer wall that was overlooked by the much more formidable fortifications of the inner ward. Beyond the outer wall was an artificial moat, itself protected by a further outer wall on three sides of the castle.

Below: Loading bay. At Rhuddlan, the smooth waters of a canalized stretch of the Clwyd approach the castle's landing stage.

GOODRICH CASTLE: BUILT IN RED SANDSTONE

Goodrich Castle in Hereford and Worcester was largely rebuilt by Edward I's uncle, William de Valence, and William's son, Aymer, in the years after 1280. The Valences' castle, which overlooks the River Wye and defends an ancient river ford, incorporates an earlier tower-keep (of the mid-1100s). The Valences rebuilt the curtain wall and added impressive angle towers together with ditches on the east and south sides, and an outer defensive wall to the west and north, with a barbican to the north-east. The barbican, in a half-moon shape, seems to be derived from the similar Lions' Tower raised by Edward I at the Tower of London.

Right: The south-east tower largely hides the square keep (centre left). A modern rail lines the approach to the gatehouse (right).

To the south, however, giving on to the river, a short section was filled with water and used as a dock. In fact, the other three sections of the moat appear to have been kept dry to serve as a defensive ditch.

The symmetrical inner ward took the shape of a diamond. Matching towers rose at the north and south corners of the diamond, and double-towered gatehouses stood at the east and west corners. Within, a Great Hall, chapel, private rooms and kitchens once stood against the curtain wall. The inner fortifications were forbidding, with four-storey towers and walls 9ft (3m) thick, with a plentiful supply of arrow slits for the defenders.

BEYOND THE CASTLE

Four gates led out from the castle's outer ward: the main one leading northwards to the newly built town, another gate giving on to the river, a third gate on to the dock, defended by a rectangular defensive tower, and a fourth, the Friary Gate (later blocked), opening to the south-east.

THE DONJON TOWER AT FLINT

The main strength of Flint Castle, completed with its adjacent town in nine years (1277–86), is its circular great tower at the south-east corner of the rectangular inner ward, which is set apart, surrounded by a moat. Castle historians liken the tower to the celebrated Tour Constance at the French port of Aigues-Mortes, from which Edward set sail with his troops for North Africa, while on Crusade in 1270.

The tower is the donjon, the lord's residence within the castle and the heavily fortified position to which the defenders would fall back as a last resort. It is supplemented by three more towers, one at each angle of the rectangular inner wall. (The French word *donjon* later became the English 'dungeon'; but in its earliest use in England, it signified the lord's dwelling rather than a gloomy jail-room.)

Another notable feature at Flint was the internal arrangement of rooms within the great tower. Above a large circular storage basement, the residential rooms and chapel on the first storey are arranged around a large, central, octagonal shaft, designed to bring light and air to residents. (Originally the building contained a basement and two storeys, although only the first storey now remains.) This arrangement is supposedly unique.

Below: The ruined north-east tower at Flint. The great tower at the south-east corner was complemented by three smaller towers at the other angles of the rectangular inner ward.

HARLECH CASTLE

IMPREGNABLE FORTRESS

At Harlech, Edward I and Master James of St Georges raised a concentric castle with a great twin-towered gatehouse on top of an imposing, steep-sided 200ft (60m) rock. When Edward and Master James built the castle in the late 13th century, the rock directly overlooked the sea and the tidal estuary of the River Dwyryd. Indeed, there was a landing stage for receiving seaborne supplies, accessed from the castle by a heavily fortified stairway, the 'Way from the Sea'. Today, however, the tidal creek is dry and the sea has retreated more than ½ mile (0.8km). Yet, because an approach up the cliff-like sides of the castle rock would be almost impossible, Harlech Castle retains an almost impregnable aspect – with land attack feasible only from the east. The castle was, in fact, taken four times: in 1404, 1408, 1468 and 1647.

The castle, begun in the summer of 1283 during King Edward I's second military campaign in North Wales, was built at a cost of £9,500 over the seven years to December 1290. At one point, in 1286, Master James had an army of 950 labourers at his disposal.

Above: Harlech Castle's position on a hilltop meant that space was tight. The outer ward is narrow and the inner ward small.

Below: Safe within the castle walls, the inner face of the gatehouse at Harlech can risk windows and a gentle staircase.

THE INNER WARD

The castle's outer defences are largely ruined, and the outer ward is very narrow, due to lack of space. However, the inner ward boasts four drum towers and the massively fortified gatehouse facing east. The gatehouse consists of two projecting semi-cylindrical towers flanking a narrow entranceway defended by three portcullises and gates, and seven 'murder holes' from which defenders could launch missiles or scalding water at the attackers.

The gatehouse contained guardhouses on the ground level at either side of the entrance, and on the first floor were the well-appointed quarters of the castle constable. On the second floor were even more luxurious rooms for the use of important visitors, doubtless including King Edward I. Both sets of rooms included a hall, a chamber, a bedchamber and a private chapel. Although the outer face of the gatehouse presents a stern aspect, its inner walls contain large windows, and there is a fine external

KIDWELLY CASTLE

Where Harlech Castle failed to repulse Owain Glyndwr, Kidwelly Castle in Dyfed succeeded, twice withstanding siege attacks by the 'Prince of Wales' in 1403–05. Kidwelly Castle was originally Norman, built by Roger, Bishop of Salisbury and Justiciar of England under Henry I, overlooking and commanding the upper tidal reaches of the River Gwendraeth. After being captured more than once by the Welsh and partially rebuilt by Lord Rhys in 1190, it passed to Edward I's nephew, Henry, Earl of Lancaster, in 1298. Around the inner castle with four drum towers, Henry built a heavily fortified outer defensive wall in imitation of the concentric castles of his uncle and Master James of St Georges. The impressive outer wall had four towers (one of which contained a chapel) and two gatehouses.

Left: The Great Gatehouse at Kidwelly Castle. On the first floor, directly above the gate, was a large and well-appointed hall.

staircase giving access to the constable's apartments, in which Master James, who was made the castle constable in July 1290, lived for the next three years.

There were further, less grand, residential rooms in the towers at the angles of the rectangular inner ward. Functional rooms, such as the Great Hall, buttery, granary, bake house and kitchens, were situated within the walls of the inner ward quadrangle.

HARLECH SIEGES

The castle may have been almost impregnable in the face of violent attack, but it could be vulnerable to being cut off from reinforcements and supplies. If the garrison maintained access to the sea, then all was well: when besieged by the troops of Madog ap Llywelyn in the 1294–5 uprising, the castle defenders received supplies by sea from Ireland. However, when the Welsh rebel and self-styled 'Prince of Wales', Owain Glyndwr, took the castle in 1401, he was able to block all supplies, since a fleet of his French allies was active in the waters beneath the rock while his own troops blocked land access.

During the Wars of the Roses in the 15th century, the castle was garrisoned by men loyal to the Lancastrian cause under Dafydd ap Iuean, and was besieged by a Yorkist army commanded by Lord Herbert, Earl of Pembroke. The garrison withstood immense hardship before surrendering in 1468 – a feat that inspired the marching song *Men of Harlech*. A royalist garrison defended Harlech Castle during the Civil War in the 17th century. Surrendered as late as March 1647, it was the last castle to fall to the Parliamentarian army.

Below: Harlech's rocky heights. The land falls steeply away on all sides save the east, and the position commands superb views.

BEAUMARIS CASTLE

MASTER JAMES' MASTERPIECE

Beaumaris Castle on Anglesey was the last of the great castles built in Wales for Edward I by his chief builder, Master James of St Georges. Although it remained unfinished, it is celebrated today as a triumphant culmination of Edward's two decades of Welsh castle-building. Its plan, an octagon enclosing a rectangle, is lauded as the perfection of the concentric castle design. Set amid meadows rich in bulrushes, with distant views across into Snowdonia, it is also known for the great beauty of its location.

Above: Beaumaris dwarfed by Snowdonia. In this view from the north, the waters of the Menai Strait are visible beyond the castle.

WELSH UPRISING

Beaumaris was begun in the spring of 1295. The previous year, during an uprising led by Llywelyn ap Gruffud's kinsman, Madog ap Llywelyn, Welsh rebels had overrun Anglesey and killed the royal sheriff, Roger de Pulesdon. Edward launched fierce reprisals over the winter of 1294–5 and was still in the area when the building of Beaumaris Castle began.

THREE LAYERS OF DEFENCE

Built on flat marshy land, the castle had no natural defences, save the sea to the south, and needed to be heavily fortified. The design called for three concentric layers of defence: a moat, 18ft (5.5m) wide and filled with tidal water, and two sets of defensive walls. The octagonal outer wall contained 12 towers and two gatehouses. The rectangular inner wall, in places 15ft (4.5m) thick, contained four round towers (one at each corner), two gatehouses and two D-shaped towers.

The main entrance in the outer wall to the south gave on to the sea at high tide. Known as the Gate-next-the-Sea, it overlooked a small dock area where ships could land supplies at high tide. The second gateway, called the Llanfaes Gate from the name of the Welsh town nearby, opened landwards to the north. The outer wall was lower and less thick than the forbidding inner fortification. The gates in the outer wall were set at an angle to those in the inner one, so that any attacker who succeeded in breaching the outer defences would have to make an awkward turn to the right under fire from the defenders of the inner stronghold. The outer ward, the area between the outer and inner walls, was just a narrow strip of land.

The two imposing inner gatehouses stood in the north and south stretches of the rectangular inner wall. The west and east walls, without gatehouses, contained formidable D-shaped towers, planned as three-storey buildings but never completed beyond the second floor. In addition, a circular tower rose

Below: The northern gate, or Llanfaes Gate, Beaumaris, viewed from the inner ward. A further storey was planned but never built.

Above: Stones piled high – the bulk of the castle at Beaumaris and its superb design made up for its lack of natural defences.

in each corner of the rectangle. The plans called for lavishly appointed chambers and halls, mainly in the first and second floors of the gatehouses. These were never fully built, but the castle's main room, the Great Hall on the first floor of the north gatehouse, gives an idea of the splendour awaiting the Prince of Wales or the king. The Chapel Tower, also part of the inner walls, contains a magnificently appointed chapel with vaulted ceiling and point windows. Within these formidable walls, the inner ward is surprisingly large, covering ¾ acre (0.3ha).

A WHITE ELEPHANT

Edward I poured lavish resources into the work: Master James employed no fewer than 200 quarrymen, 30 smiths and carpenters, 400 masons and 2,000 general labourers. He had spent £6,000 by the autumn of 1295. The bulk of the building was carried out in the three years after 1295; by 1298, royal funds for building were running low, and the King was increasingly focused on events and building works in Scotland and Gascony.

Further building was carried out at Beaumaris beginning in 1306 and continuing intermittently after Edward's death in 1307 until 1330, without ever reaching completion. The castle remains an example of 'what might have been': a magnificent plan that was never brought to fulfilment.

Above: Never finished, but formidable nonetheless - Beaumaris Castle in the 14th century has a moat and double walls.

Moreover, its formidable defences were never needed. Beaumaris, for all its might, saw little military action – for even by the time the castle was begun, Welsh resistance had been almost entirely crushed. Some 200 years later, it was garrisoned by Royalists in the Civil War, but was taken without a struggle by the Parliamentarian scourge of Edward's Welsh castles, Major-General Mytton, on 14 June 1646.

CAERLAVEROCK CASTLE, DUMFRIES

The builders of Caerlaverock were clearly influenced by Beaumaris and Master James's other great concentric castles. Caerlaverock combines a twin-towered gatehouse with two drum towers, the whole laid out to a triangular design within a defensive moat and an earthen rampart. The main defence and final refuge is the gatehouse, which – as at Beaumaris – contained the residential quarters of the castle constable.

Right: Within the castle lie the remains of 18th-century courtyard residences.

CHAPTER THREE

THE RISE OF THE FORTIFIED HOUSE

1307–1400

In 1290, wealthy wool merchant Lawrence of Ludlow obtained a royal licence to crenellate his manor at Stokesay in Shropshire. He declared that he needed to fortify the house because of the potential threat of the unruly Welsh just 20 miles (32km) away across the border. In fact, Edward I's forceful campaigns of the 1280s in Wales had effectively stamped out resistance there.

Lawrence's home, Stokesay Castle, was not a castle proper but an early example of a type of building that would become popular with wealthy householders in the 14th and 15th centuries: the fortified manor house. Other splendid examples include Penshurst Place, Hever Castle and Ightham Mote, all in Kent; Broughton Castle in Oxfordshire; and Raby Castle in Co Durham. Many of these buildings were fortified towards the end of the 14th century, when England had seemingly lost control of the English Channel and there were fears that France might invade. At this time (under Richard II) and again in the 15th century (under Henry VI), central authority was weak, so landowners needed to project at least an appearance of strength.

Yet, while fortified manor houses had a degree of defensive strength, none of them was a fortress. The houses may have been well enough defended to deter passing marauders, but they generally could not have withstood an attack by an organized army; they certainly could not have repelled a siege in the way that Rochester Castle almost did, and Kidwelly Castle in Dyfed twice succeeded in doing. The men who built the fortified manor houses put comfort before the needs of defence.

Left: The charming manor house of Ightham Mote, in Kent, combines a crenellated gatehouse and defensive moat with windows and a half-timbered upper storey.

STOKESAY CASTLE
AN ENGLISH STONE HOUSE

Stokesay Castle's name comes from that of a family – Say – who had their dairy farm ('stoke') here from around 1115. Wool merchant Lawrence of Ludlow fortified the house in the early 1290s.

Lawrence's father, John, had purchased the manor in 1281. Earlier, in 1240, the Says had built a tower at the north end of the house's west front. Lawrence added a new upper storey with projecting timberwork, which remarkably survives to this day. He also built a new Great Hall, 34ft (10.3m) high and measuring 52 x 31ft (16 x 9.5m), with partly shuttered, partly glazed windows – proof of his substantial wealth, for at this time glass cost so much that wealthy families with more than one house carried their window panes with them as they moved about. Much of the timberwork survives from the 13th century. The rafters are blackened by the smoke that rose from the chimney-less central hearth to find its way out via the louvres in the roof.

Above: The magnificent beams of the Great Hall's roof were made from whole trees.

A ROOM FOR RETIRING TO

Attached to the hall on the south side, Lawrence erected the 'solar block', containing a chamber to which the family withdrew from the more public space of the Great Hall. The private chamber, known as a 'solar' because the room was designed with large windows to allow in as much sunlight as possible, was on the upper floor, and reached by an external staircase, while the ground-level space beneath was used for storage.

DEFENSIVE ADDITIONS

At the Great Hall's south end, Lawrence built the impressive, three-storey South Tower, complete with battlements. The only access to this stout construction – whose walls are 5ft (1.5m) thick – was via a drawbridge from outside the entrance to the 'solar' room. He also added a defensive curtain wall, topped with battlements, a stone gatehouse,

Below: Stokesay Castle's spacious hall is flanked by the north tower (left) and the solar with the turreted south tower (right).

THE SOLAR ROOM

Solar rooms, so-called because they were designed to maximize the warming power of the sun, were places to which the lord of the manor and his family could retreat from the communal medieval Great Hall. As early as the late 14th century, the solar was often also known as a 'retiring room'. There are fine examples of solars at Penshurst Place and Ightham Mote; at Penshurst the solar room was later used as a reception room to entertain Queen Elizabeth I. At Stokesay Castle, the solar contains a beautiful original carved wooden overmantle above the fireplace, on either side of which are 'squints' – openings through which the family could survey the comings and goings in the Great Hall below.

a drawbridge and an encircling rock-cut moat supplied with water from a large pond just to the south-west. The wall originally stood 34ft (10.3m) high from the bottom of the moat. Yet, although Stokesay Castle had some defensive capability, it was not designed to withstand a serious attack. The Great Hall, for example, was built with large windows facing Wales, the direction from which Lawrence said he feared attack. As in other fortified manor houses, comfort was deemed more important than defence. However, although far from impregnable, Lawrence's fortified manor was certainly sufficiently grand for him to entertain the Bishop of Hereford and his retinue for ten days.

LATER DEVELOPMENTS

Lawrence did not live to enjoy his castle for long, as he drowned in a shipwreck in 1294. Nevertheless, his descendants remained in possession of Stokesay for more than three centuries, and in the 14th and 15th centuries often served as sheriffs of Shropshire. The castle and lands were sold to pay off debts in 1598. In the 1630s, Stokesay was let on a long lease to Charles Baldwyn, MP for Ludlow, who replaced the original stone gatehouse with a charming half-timbered building, which still survives. In the Civil War, Stokesay's then owner, Lord Craven, declared for the King, but surrendered to a parliamentary army in 1645 before any damage was done to the 'castle'. In line with their normal policy of slighting fortified defences, the Parliamentarians reduced the height of the curtain wall.

UNUSUAL ATTRIBUTES

Stokesay Castle is notable as one of the earliest English stone houses. It was built of local Silurian limestone, quarried just across the valley. Unless good-quality building stone was available locally, as here or in the Cotswolds, building in stone in this period was prohibitively expensive for all but the wealthiest landowners because it involved not only quarrying but also transporting the very heavy material over great distances. Generally, it was only the king, his leading barons and churchmen who could meet the necessary cost.

Stokesay Castle is also highly unusual in that its central buildings survive largely unaltered from the time of Lawrence of Ludlow in the 13th century. The buildings were unoccupied after 1706, and so were not altered in line with prevailing fashions. After 150 years, during which Stokesay fell gradually into picturesque ruins, and was used by a nearby farm, the 'castle' was bought and restored by Victorian philanthropist and glove-manufacturer J.D. Allcroft. It was further repaired in the 1980s and has been held by English Heritage since 1992.

Above: The gabled windows in the Great Hall were part-glazed: the upper part and the circular 'eye' above were glazed; the lower part was closed with shutters in the cold.

Below: The solar chamber in the South Tower was warmed by sunlight through the large windows and the fire of its chimneypiece.

PENSHURST PLACE

HOME OF SIR PHILIP SIDNEY

Penshurst Place in Kent is one of England's earliest and finest fortified manor houses. Celebrated above all for its later association with Renaissance poet and soldier, Sir Philip Sidney, and the Sidney family, Penshurst began life as a 13th-century house owned by Sir Stephen de Penchester (d.1299). In *c.*1340, Sir John de Poulteney, four times Lord Mayor of London, transformed the house into a country mansion where, within a day's ride of the capital, he could entertain and hunt.

HALL AND 'SOLAR'

The magnificent Barons' Hall, with a 60ft (18m) high roof made of chestnut wood and large octagonal central hearth, was completed in 1341. In this cavernous, smoky chamber, Sir John's servants ate and slept. Vast trestle-mounted wooden tables were used: the two wooden tables at Penshurst are 13th-century originals, the only surviving examples of their kind in England. As at Stokesay and in other medieval halls, the smoke rose to the ceiling to escape through smoke louvers or slatted openings.

Three Gothic screens disguise the passage to the kitchen and offices. A stone staircase leads up to the house's state apartments. The first was originally a 'solar room'. It subsequently became an ante-room (reception area) in the Elizabethan era and, later still, the State Dining Room. (In 1430, Henry V's brother, John, Duke of Bedford, built a second hall to the south-west of the solar block adjoining the original Barons' Hall. The new hall, now called the Buckingham Building, had mullioned windows added in the 16th century.)

A FORTIFIED MANOR

In *c.*1390, amid fears of a French invasion, the owner of Penshurst Place was granted a licence to crenellate, and fortified the

Above: Sir Philip Sidney served Elizabeth I and knew many other great figures of the age, including Sir Walter Raleigh.

Below: From the ornate fountain in the Italian Garden at Penshurst Place there is a splendid view of the south front of the house.

Left: The Long Gallery at Penshurst (1601) was typical of those added to country houses in Elizabeth I's reign.

mansion with a curtain wall containing eight defensive towers. As at Stokesay, the house was sufficiently well fortified to repel a minor assault, but a well-armed army would have had little difficulty in gaining entry. Today, the bulk of these fortifications have gone. Some were dismantled and others used as part of later extensions, but one tower remains, standing alongside a stretch of wall in the gardens to the south of the main house.

CROWN PROPERTY

In the late 15th and early 16th century, three dukes of Buckingham owned Penshurst, and all were beheaded. The third was Edward Stafford, who was executed on 17 May 1521, having been found guilty of high treason, supposedly for plotting the King's death and his own elevation to the throne.

As the property of a traitor, the estate was forfeit to the Crown. Penshurst Place came into royal hands, and Henry VIII stayed there when paying court to Anne Boleyn at Hever Castle nearby.

THE SIDNEY FAMILY

Edward VI granted the house and estate to the Sidney family in 1552. Sir Henry Sidney (1529–86) erected a new range and gatehouse to the north of the Barons' Hall. This included an arcade with Tuscan columns, completed in 1579 and perhaps England's earliest classical loggia. This new building incorporated one of the 14th-century defensive towers; the arcade was later glazed. Sir Henry also created magnificent gardens around the house.

Sir Henry Sidney, whose father was tutor to the future Edward VI, was a childhood friend of the King and grew up at court. He became a trusted servant of the Crown, serving both Mary I and Elizabeth I with distinction, and naming his own son, the celebrated Sir Philip Sidney, after Mary's husband, Philip II of Spain, who was the boy's godfather. Sir Henry's wife, Mary Dudley, was the sister of Queen Elizabeth I's favourite, Robert Dudley, Earl of Leicester. Elizabeth often visited Sir Henry's home, and the Queen Elizabeth Room, in which she held court when in residence there, is named in her honour.

Sir Philip Sidney, poet, soldier and courtier, author of *Arcadia* and *Defence of Poetry*, was born at Penshurst Place on 30 November 1554. After his death in a military encounter in the Netherlands at the early age of 31, he was given a state funeral in St Paul's Cathedral, becoming the first commoner to be accorded this honour (Nelson was next, in 1805). Sir Philip's brother, Sir Robert, inherited the house and built the Long Gallery, completed in 1601, as an extension to the staterooms. Lit by mullioned windows on both sides, it has elegant oak wainscoting and houses today, as in the early 17th century, many portraits of Sidney family members.

The house still remains in the hands of the Sidney family. Later owners have continued to modify the house, in particular remodelling the staterooms. In the second half of the 20th century, William Sidney, 1st Viscount De l'Isle, lovingly restored the house and estate.

Below: Penshurst's lavish Queen Elizabeth room. The Queen's great favourite, Leicester, was Sir Philip Sidney's uncle.

LEEDS CASTLE

A GIFT FOR QUEEN MARGARET

The full defensive potential of Leeds Castle in Kent was realized only in the late 13th century, when the River Len was dammed to form an artificial lake. By then, Leeds, a royal castle, had been standing on the site for about 200 years.

Before it was dammed, the Len naturally widened at this spot around two small islands. This caught the eye of a minister at the court of King Ethelbert IV of Kent, named Leede. After the Norman Conquest, William I granted the lands to Hamon de Crèvecoeur, whose son Robert built the first stone castle, which took the form of a keep and a gatehouse. Part of a cellar and some of the Gloriette Tower on the smaller northern island survive from this time.

Leeds Castle remained in the hands of the Crèvecoeur family until 1265, when the castle-builder's great-grandson was dispossessed after siding with the rebel baron, Simon de Montfort. Henry III then made a gift of the castle to Roger de Leyburn, whose son William sold it back to the Crown in 1298 to clear debts.

Below: Leeds Castle was much altered in the Tudor era, but some parts date back to the time of the Norman Robert de Crèvecoeur.

Above: Busts of Henry VIII and his three children, Mary I, Elizabeth I and Edward VI, are on display in the Queen's Gallery.

A CASTLE FOR QUEENS

Edward I and his first queen, Eleanor, loved the castle and often stayed there. He built a new curtain wall around the larger island, rebuilt the gatehouse on the northern island and added a chapel in the Gloriette Tower.

When Edward I remarried in 1299, he spent his honeymoon at Leeds Castle and then gave the beautifully situated fortress-palace to his new wife, Margaret of France. Their son, Edward II, by contrast, gave the castle to a leading courtier – Bartholomew de Badlesmere – who, in 1321, earned the King's wrath when his wife refused to allow Queen Isabella access to the castle. Edward besieged and took the castle, threw Lady Badlesmere in jail and subsequently beheaded Bartholomew.

Edward III also admired the castle, and between 1359 and 1377 was engaged in redecorating the royal apartments in the Gloriette Tower. His son and successor, Richard II, hired master mason Henry Yevele, builder of the nave at Canterbury Cathedral and designer of improvements at Westminster Hall, to carry out buiding work at Leeds Castle. Richard followed the royal tradition by giving the castle to his queen, Anne of Bohemia. He must also have liked the place himself because after her death in 1394 he spent a good deal of time there. In 1395, Richard received the French chronicler Jean Froissart at the castle.

Henry Bolingbroke, who deposed Richard II in 1399 and ascended the throne as Henry IV, gave Leeds Castle to his queen and second wife, Joan of Navarre. The couple stayed at the castle in 1403 to escape the plague in London.

IN THE HANDS OF THE TUDORS

Following Henry IV's death, Queen Joan was declared forfeit on charges of sorcery. She was confined in Pevensey Castle, and her stepson, Henry V, was

Above: Black swans live on the lake. They were a gift to British leader Sir Winston Churchill, who gave them to the castle.

free to give Leeds Castle to his beautiful French wife, Catherine of Valois. At Leeds Castle, after Henry V's death, Catherine fell in love with and secretly married Owen Tudor, a Welsh squire. After the secret of their marriage was revealed, Queen Catherine retired to a nunnery at Bermondsey, where she died in 1437, but the union with Tudor had far-reaching consequences, for her grandson by Owen, Henry Tudor, would win the crown in the Battle at Bosworth Field in 1485 and occupy the throne as King Henry VII.

The next royal to be associated with Leeds was Henry VIII, who spent lavishly on the place. He retained the fortifications, but his alterations to the royal apartments made Leeds more palace than fortress (see page 101).

CHAPEL ROYAL

When Edward I's beloved Queen Eleanor died in 1290, a grief-stricken Edward provided for mass to be said daily for her soul in the chapel he had added to the Gloriette Tower on the smaller northern island.

This benefaction – known as a chantry – was extended by Edward II, Richard II, Henry VI and Henry VII. The chapel itself was reconsecrated and made a Chapel Royal by the Archbishop of Canterbury, Donald Coggan, in 1978.

Above: The chapel has a serene atmosphere.

RABY CASTLE

STRONGHOLD OF THE NEVILLES

The powerful Neville family built Raby Castle, at Staindrop in Co Durham, in the late 14th century. Their stronghold stands on a place with venerable royal associations, reputedly the site of a palace belonging to Canute (r.1016–35).

The Nevilles were a significant Norman family who fought alongside William the Conqueror at Hastings and were rewarded with lands in the north of England. They acquired the manor of Raby through marriage in the 13th century, when Isabel Neville married the Lord of Raby, Robert FitzMaldred.

Among prominent early Nevilles was Robert Neville, who was killed at the 1319 Battle of Berwick. From 1334, another Neville, Ralph, served the English Crown as Warden of the Scottish Marches – a key position he shared with Henry Percy, 2nd Baron of Alnwick. The Neville and Percy families became fierce competitors for prominence and royal favour.

Above: Fortified mansion. Grandeur and comfort outweighed defensive effectiveness in the considerations of the builders at Raby.

NEW DEFENCES

Ralph's son, Sir John Neville, was granted a licence to crenellate and embattle all the towers, houses and walls at Raby by the Bishop of Durham in 1378. By this date the castle was well established, and doubtless fortified, but Sir John added new defences to his family stronghold, so that the castle had the key elements of a defensible fortress, with a moat, drawbridge, gatehouse and curtain wall 30ft (9m) high. But within the inner enclosure, the arrangement of towers and other fortifications was planned not to maximize defensive capabilities, but rather to emphasize both the power and the grandeur of the Neville family.

Below: In the 18th century, when this view of Raby was painted, the Vane family reworked the west wing and entrance hall.

THE NEVILLE GATEWAY

In the late 14th century, Sir John built the Neville Gateway in the western part of the castle, where the majority of the surviving medieval work is found and some of the walls are 20ft (6m) thick. The gateway is a celebration in stone of the family's ascent to power and pre-eminence: it bears the symbols of the Cross of St George (in reference to Sir John's acceptance as a Knight of the Garter in 1369) alongside the Nevilles' own saltire (St Andrew's cross) and a Latimer cross (because Sir John's second wife, named Elizabeth, was the heiress of the prominent Latimer family of Corby).

The gateway was the sole point of access to the inner court, and was originally fitted with a gate and drawbridge across the moat. From the gateway, a tunnel 70ft (21m) long leads to the inner court. Other elements surviving from the 14th century are the Chapel Tower (although this has an 18th-century doorway), the Servants' Hall and the splendid Kitchen Tower, which is almost entirely unchanged since its construction *c.*1360. The Great Hall may have been begun as early as 1320. Records show that in the mid-14th century, master mason John Lewyn was active at Raby, as he was at nearby Durham Cathedral.

Above: In the Barons' Hall at Raby, 700 knights gathered in 1569 to plot the ill-fated Rising of the North against Elizabeth I.

IMPRESSIVE TOWERS

Sir John's son, another Ralph, was an active builder at Raby and at another Neville property, Middleham Castle. In all, at Raby there were two gatehouses (an outer one, in the north, in addition to the inner Neville Gateway) and nine towers. Eight of the towers survive, including the majestic Clifford's Tower, 80ft (24m) in height. However, one in the southerly part of the castle was replaced by a dining room in the 1840s, when the south range was entirely rebuilt. At the south-east corner of the castle is the 11th-century Bulmer's Tower, a uniquely unusual five-sided 11th-century building, named after the Norman knight Bertram de Bulmer. The only other tower of this shape is found in Denmark.

LATER ALTERATIONS

The Nevilles fell dramatically from power and influence in 1569, and in the late 16th century, Raby Castle was forfeit to the Crown. In 1626, the castle and estate were bought by Sir Henry Vane, who built an arcade on the courtyard's eastern edge and added a five-bay façade on the central block. In the 18th century, his descendant Gilbert Vane employed the architect James Paine to produce the Hunter's Gallery and remodel the interiors of much of the west wing. In the 1780s, Sir Gilbert's son employed architect John Carr of York in the extraordinary project of refashioning the entrance hall so that a coach and horses could pass through it.

The 19th-century alterations by William Burn, a fashionable designer and remodeller of country houses, were unfortunately of the 'improving' early Victorian kind that swept away much that would have been of interest to later generations. In particular, Burn removed medieval vaulting from the Clifford and Bulmer Towers. Yet Raby Castle still makes an undeniably impressive impact, not least because of its size, but also because it retains a large number of authentic architectural elements surviving from the 14th century.

SITE OF CANUTE'S PALACE?

Raby probably stands on the site of a palace belonging to Canute, the 'Emperor of the North' and England's Danish king in 1016–35. The name of the settlement derives from the Danish 'ra' for 'boundary' and 'bi' for homestead. By tradition, Canute gave the estate to the monks of St Cuthbert, and the prior granted the land to Dolfin, a descendant of King Malcolm II of Scots. Dolfin's grandson was Robert Fitzmaldred, who married into the great Norman family of Neville (see main text). The Nevilles built on the association of their castle with Canute by inventing a bloodline showing they were descended from a niece of Canute himself. Raby tradition also claims that the oldest parts of Bulmer's Tower at the castle were built in Canute's time.

BODIAM CASTLE

CASTLE ON AN ISLAND

Of all the fortified great houses of the 14th century, Bodiam Castle in East Sussex probably has the best claim to being a truly defensible stronghold. It was clearly a comfortable and splendid dwelling, with elegant and well-designed residential quarters, but it also boasted four strong corner towers, a twin-towered gatehouse and wide water defences with a complex approach designed with defence much in mind.

The castle was built under a licence to crenellate ('for the defences of the adjacent county and the resistance against our enemies') granted to Sir Edward Dakygrigge by Richard II in 1385, at a time when the French had the upper hand in the English Channel, and at the height of English fears of an invasion. Sir Edward's manor of Bodiam stood in the valley of the River Rother, which at that time was large enough to be navigable by sizeable ships as far as Bodiam itself.

FRENCH DESIGN

Sir Edward built his fortified manor house at Bodiam from scratch, having abandoned the existing manor house nearby, which he had acquired through marriage, to create a compact castle. He based the design on continental fortifications he had seen first-hand when fighting in France under the command of Sir Robert Knollys during the reign of Richard II's predecessor and grandfather, King Edward III. The castle was rectangular. Four corner towers 60ft (18m) tall were linked by a defensive wall two storeys high, which included a square tower in the west and east walls, a vast gatehouse facing north and an additional postern tower situated in the south face.

BODIAM'S DEFENCES

The castle is, today, approached along a straight causeway from the north across the moat via a small octagonal island, but originally visitors – or, perhaps more

Above: The view of Bodiam across the moat from the south-east shows the postern tower (left, centre) in the two-storey south wall.

relevantly, attackers – had to approach from the west side of the moat and make a right-angled turn on the small island, all the while leaving themselves vulnerable to attack from the castle. Once on the octagonal island, the approach involved passing across a drawbridge to a barbican tower, then across another drawbridge to the castle's main gatehouse. The gatehouse itself was

BERKELEY CASTLE'S GREAT HALL

Above: Terraced gardens surround Berkeley Castle. From the gardens there are fine views of the country and the River Severn.

A majestic Great Hall was added to the 12th-century castle at Berkeley in Gloucestershire *c.*1340 by Thomas, 3rd Lord Berkeley. With large windows and a cavernous timbered roof, it stands 62ft (19m) long and 32ft (10m) high. Only 13 years earlier, the castle had been the scene of one of the most infamous events in English royal history: the murder in captivity of King Edward II, on 21 September 1327. Lord Thomas was cleared of responsibility for the deed and is remembered in both the Berkeley family and wider tradition as a man of compassion. However, closer investigation suggests that he must have known of the dark deeds and indeed sent news of the King's death to Queen Isabella and her lover, Roger Mortimer, Earl of March.

Above: A succession of monarchs, from Henry VII and Elizabeth I to George IV, has been entertained in the Great Hall.

fitted with three portcullises and three gates, as well as gun-holes, and 'murder holes' through which materials could be thrown at or poured down on anyone trying to attack the castle.

The castle came under attack twice. The first occasion was in 1483, when Bodiam's then owner, Sir Thomas Lewknor, had provoked the anger of Richard III. The King sent the Earl of Surrey to seek revenge, and Sir Thomas surrendered his castle without a struggle. Then, in 1643, during the English Civil War, Parliamentarian forces took the castle, again without a fight. The Roundheads left the outer castle intact, but caused severe damage within.

LUXURY WITHIN

Today, the castle's inner buildings remain in ruins, but it is possible to recreate a picture of the luxurious accommodation provided for Sir Edward Dalyngrigge in the 14th century. The public buildings included a large chapel, a Great Hall and a large Public Chamber. Sir Edward's elegant private chambers were in the east range's first floor and included a hall – complete with crenellated fireplace – giving access to two sleeping chambers, each with a garderobe, situated in the square tower on the castle's east wall. Sir Edward's private hall also gave access to a reserved side-chapel at first-floor level overlooking the altar in the main castle chapel. Thus, Sir Edward and his family could maintain their privacy while joining garrison soldiers at worship in the main chapel below.

RESTORATION DISCOVERIES

The castle at Bodiam was purchased and meticulously restored in the early 20th century by Lord Curzon, one-time Viceroy of India. Another indication of the level of luxury provided in this elegant fortified manor house was that, during restoration, Curzon found evidence of 33 fireplaces and no fewer than 28 lavatories, which were constructed in the curtain wall and gave directly into the moat.

Above: Easy access. On Bodiam's north face, a railed walkway now leads across the moat to the barbican and the gatehouse.

Below: The 60ft (18m) cylindrical corner towers of the four-sided castle at Bodiam each contain four storeys.

WESTMINSTER PALACE

HENRY III'S RESIDENCE

King Henry III (r.1216–72) was one of the greatest of England's royal builders. He spent £10,000 improving Westminster Palace, the royal residence first built alongside the Thames to the east of Westminster Abbey by Edward the Confessor (r.1042–66). Westminster was Edward's favourite palace and, in his time, as a result of his improvements, the finest in Europe (see page 27).

Henry's reign saw the building of the reputedly magnificent King's Great Chamber, or Painted Chamber, which measured 80 x 26ft (24 x 8m) and 31ft (9m) high, with a beautiful timbered ceiling and patterned floor tiles. Its walls were covered with superb murals by Masters William of Westminster and Walter of Durham, showing scenes from the Old Testament and the life of St Edward the Confessor. Nearby, Henry built new apartments for his queen, Eleanor, but these and the Painted Chamber were both destroyed in the fire that devastated the palace in 1834 – only the crypt of St Stephen's Chapel, the Jewel Tower and Westminster Hall, with its magnificent hammerbeam roof, survived the fire.

Above: The Jewel Tower is built from Kentish ragstone. Today it houses a collection of local archaeological finds.

THE JEWEL TOWER

The three-storey tower was built in 1365–6, probably by master mason Henry Yevele, to store the king's jewels, furs and other valuables. At the extreme southern edge of the palace complex, it was partially surrounded by a moat. It continued to be used as a royal store for valuables until the reign of Henry VII (r.1485–1509).

WINCHESTER PALACE

Winchester Palace, the London home of the Bishop of Winchester, was built in Southwark in 1109. Like Westminster Palace, it was improved in the later medieval period but largely destroyed by fire in the 19th century. The marriage reception for James I of Scots and Joan Beaufort was held there in 1424. Tradition has it Henry VIII met his fifth wife Catherine Howard there in 1540.

Right: The west wall, with its magnificent rose window, c. 1320, is the only part of the Great Hall to survive today.

THE HAMMERBEAM ROOF

The other surviving part of the palace is Westminster Hall, built by William Rufus in 1097. Significant alterations were made to the hall by Richard II from 1394 onward. Following designs by Henry Yevele, the walls were raised 2ft (0.6m) and refaced, and a magnificent hammerbeam roof, by Hugh Herland, was added. The roof, carved with angels and traceries, has a span of 69ft (21m), making it the largest timber roof in northern Europe, and soars to a height of 92ft (28m). Richard also built a gateway to the hall containing carved statues of English kings from Edward the Confessor onward.

EDINBURGH CASTLE

CASTLE ON A ROCK

During the reign of King David II of Scots (r.1329–71), major rebuilding work took place in Edinburgh Castle (see also page 106). The great volcanic rock on which the castle stands high above the city was a natural place for a fortified dwelling – and archaeologists have found evidence of settlement, as far back as the Bronze Age (2100–700BC). In the Norman era, Malcolm III (r.1058–93) built a stone castle on the rock. His queen, Margaret, died after hearing that Malcolm had been killed in an ambush in Northumbria; King David I (r.1125–53), her son, built the tiny Chapel of St Margaret in her honour in the castle precincts. This small, irregular chapel is the only part of the Norman castle that still survives today.

Below: Edinburgh Castle was a royal palace and military fortress until modern times.

DAVID'S TOWER

In the 14th century, Robert Stewart – grandson of Robert the Bruce, nephew of the reigning King David II, and himself the future King Robert II – built an L-shaped tower on the castle's northern side. Constructed in 1368–72 and almost 60ft (18m) high, the building, subsequently known as 'David's Tower', almost certainly contained royal apartments. Kitchens and offices were built alongside it in 1382–3. David's Tower is the first known example in Scotland of the tower house – a design pioneered by royalty that would become popular among the nobility. Historians cannot be sure of the exact layout of rooms within the tower, but above a vaulted ground floor they probably contained a first-floor suite for the king, comprising hall, private chamber and closet, with a similar suite for the queen on the floor above.

Above: St Margaret's Chapel is the oldest surviving building in Edinburgh. The tiny chapel holds only around 20 people.

The tower survived unscathed for around two centuries, but then its upper floors were destroyed in a 1573 siege during the reign of James VI of Scots, the future James I of England. The surviving part of the tower was then incorporated into the castle's Half Moon Battery, only to be rediscovered in the early 20th century.

IGHTHAM MOTE
A PICTURESQUE MANOR HOUSE

An idyllic manor house near Sevenoaks in Kent, Ightham Mote is arranged compactly around a courtyard and is enclosed by a stream-fed moat. The house retains a sturdy, well-worn and utilitarian beauty. The earliest buildings, including the massive Great Hall, date from the 14th century, but important additions, including a wonderfully decorated Tudor chapel, were made over the following 200–300 years.

IGHTHAM'S ORIGINS

The house's curious name comes from the nearby village of Ightham and that of the 'moot' (local council), which in medieval times met in the most prominent house in each locality. Its first named owner was Sir Thomas Cawne (d.1374), who lived in the house from *c.*1340. The earliest surviving buildings are those on the east side of the courtyard: the Great Hall, the old chapel with crypt, a kitchen and two solars or private chambers. Timber dating indicates that these rooms were completed *c.*1330, although there is some evidence that the crypt is a survival from an earlier house on the site. The moat and bridge were also laid out in the first half of the 14th century.

In the years 1487–1519, the house's then owner, Edward Haut, added south and west sides to the courtyard. Facing the bridge over the moat, he built a battlemented three-storey entrance tower or gatehouse – the only fortification on the site. On either side of the tower, he built two-storey residential quarters and added a similar two-storey range on the south side of the yard.

Right: The south-west front contains the central castellated gatehouse, accessed by a stone bridge across the moat.

TUDOR CHAPEL

In 1521–38, Sir Richard Clement, a notable figure at the court of Henry VIII, left his mark upon the house. Sir Richard added a new chapel on the north side of the courtyard in the form of an upper-floor timber room overhanging the moat with a cloister beneath. This beautiful Gothic chapel was fitted with a delicately carved tracery screen, six fine Dutch stained-glass windows, a hooded pulpit, linen-fold

Below: A stone urn stands on the lawn in the inner courtyard at Ightham Mote. The buildings behind are called the 'Elizabethan cottages' but in fact date to c.1475.

BROUGHTON CASTLE

Built *c.*1300 by Sir John de Broughton, Broughton Castle, near Banbury in Oxfordshire, is another fine example of the 14th-century fortified manor house. The house, protected by a wide moat, can be reached only by a single bridge across the moat and through a gatehouse.

Sir John de Broughton's manor house was sufficiently splendid to catch the eye of William of Wykeham, Chancellor of England and Bishop of Winchester, who purchased the property in 1377. His great-nephew Sir Thomas Wykeham added battlements to the gatehouse under a licence 'to crenellate and embattle' granted in 1406.

The Fiennes family, later Lords Saye and Sele, acquired the manor through marriage to Sir Thomas Wykeham's grand-daughter, Margaret, in 1448. In the Tudor period, Broughton Castle was substantially remodelled. During Charles I's reign, William, 8th Lord Saye and Sele, a leading Puritan and supporter of Parliament against the King, used Broughton as a meeting place for the King's opponents.

The family frittered away its wealth during the Regency period, but this had the unlooked-for and fortunate effect of subsequently saving Broughton from the 'improving' hand of Victorian architects. Building work was limited to repairs, begun in 1860 by Frederick, 16th Lord Saye and Sele, and continuing throughout the 20th century.

Broughton has won many admirers over the centuries: novelist Henry James called it 'the most delightful home in England' and it was used as the setting for *Shakespeare in Love* (1998) and *The Madness of King George* (1994).

Right: Broughton Castle's moat covers 3 acres (1.2ha). The house has a medieval Great Hall and fine plaster ceilings.

wall panelling and an arched ceiling with panels brightly painted with the Tudor rose, the arrows of Aragon (birthplace of Queen Catherine), the Beaufort portcullis and other emblems.

Below: This carved stone head is from the courtyard at Ightham Mote.

When it was finished, the chapel was somewhat reminiscent of a tournament pavilion of the kind used at events such as the outdoor peace summit, at the Field of the Cloth of Gold in France, organized by Cardinal Wolsey in 1520. Sir Richard also added stained-glass windows to the Great Hall, and window barge boards, once again decorated with Tudor symbols, to the oriel room.

The essential elements that give Ightham Mote its great charm were now in place. In later years, notable owners included Sir William and Dame Dorothy Selby, who, in 1611–41, added the drawing room and the rooms alongside. After 1889, Sir Thomas Colyer-Fergusson carried out widespread repairs.

AMERICAN PHILANTHROPIST

In the second half of the 20th century, the house was saved from possible demolition by an enlightened American businessman, Charles Henry Robinson of Portland, Maine. He purchased Ightham Mote and funded its renovation from afar, staying in the house during his visits to Europe. Upon his death in 1985, he left the house to the National Trust.

Below: There is a heraldic crest above the main entrance to Ightham Mote.

CHAPTER FOUR

CASTLES AND MANOR HOUSES

1400–1485

Sir Edward Bedingfeld began building the fortified manor house of Oxburgh Hall, near King's Lynn in Norfolk, under a licence to crenellate granted by Edward IV in 1482. The house's elegant design and the superb brickwork of its imposing twin-towered gatehouse make a very grand impression. Auguste Pugin called the house 'one of the noblest expressions of the domestic architecture of the 15th century'. This was a period that saw the rise of the brick-built tower and fortified house. Brick began to replace stone at a time when 'castles' were, in fact, houses built in the style of fortresses, and did not have to be defensible against siege engines. The great appeal of bricks was that they made possible details of surface patterning that could not be produced in stone; they were also cheaper than dressed stone and could be made on site.

One of the pioneers of the brick-built tower was the soldier and courtier, Sir John Falstaff, who began the splendid Caister Castle, in Norfolk, in 1432. At around the same time, Sir John's old friend and companion-at-arms, Ralph, Lord Cromwell, Treasurer of England under King Henry VI, erected a superb brick tower at Tattershall Castle, Lincolnshire. A decade later, another prominent figure at King Henry VI's court, Sir Roger de Fiennes, also Treasurer of the King's Household, began work on the elegant brick-built country house of Herstmonceux Castle in East Sussex. Then, later in the century, Sir John Wenlock rebuilt in brick at Someries Castle in Bedfordshire in the 1460s, and Thomas Rotherham, Bishop of Lincoln, commissioned a fine brick palace at Buckden, Huntingdonshire, in the 1470s.

Left: Castle in brick. Henry VI's treasurer, Sir Roger de Fiennes, spared no expense on his country mansion of Herstmonceux Castle, spending £3,800 on its construction.

TATTERSHALL CASTLE

SPLENDID BRICKWORK

Tattershall Castle was, like Bodiam Castle in Sussex, purchased and renovated by Lord Curzon of Kedleston upon his return from service as Viceroy of India. In the case of Tattershall, Curzon's intervention was very timely because when he bought the property, in 1910, its four superb carved-stone fireplaces had been taken out of the brickwork tower and were packed in boxes in London, waiting to be shipped to the United States. Lord Curzon reinstalled the fireplaces and devotedly refurbished the castle, which he declared 'the most splendid piece of brickwork in England'.

THE GREAT TOWER

The magnificent surviving Great Tower at Tattershall was erected by Ralph, Lord Cromwell, in 1432–8, as part of improvements to an earlier castle built *c.*1231 by Robert of Tattershall.

Above: Putting elegance and comfort before defence, Tattershall Castle contains sizeable windows fitted with heraldic stained glass.

Left: Both inside and out at Tattershall, Cromwell's Flemish and French craftsmen produced brickwork of the highest quality.

A prominent figure at court, Cromwell served as an adviser to Henry V before he was appointed Treasurer of England by Henry VI in 1433. At Tattershall, he clearly set out to build a lordly dwelling that befitted his newly won eminence.

Cromwell spared no expense to make his mark: his tower, which rose 100ft (30m) above the flat Lincolnshire countryside, was built using costly small red bricks, which were becoming increasingly fashionable. In the tower and nearby buildings at the castle, Cromwell's builders used one million bricks made in his local kilns.

The tower was not a military stronghold: it had ornate traceried windows and no fewer than three doors at ground level, and the corner turrets at parapet level were not defensively functional, since they were covered by mini-spires. In fact, it was designed for grandeur and comfort. It contained a vaulted basement beneath four residential floors, each of which held a great central hall with additional rooms and garderobes in the thick walls and the corner towers. On the ground floor was a Courtroom or Parlour, its carved stone fireplace beautifully decorated with heraldic devices of Cromwell's family. The first floor contained a Great Hall; the second provided an Audience Chamber and ceremonial area with magnificent moulded brick vaulting; and the third was the Lord's Privy Chamber or bedchamber.

Throughout, the castle, brickwork and stone carving were exquisitely finished, and, thanks to Lord Curzon's initiative in renovating and refurbishing the castle, these features can be seen and appreciated today.

DEFENCES

Ralph Cromwell lavished money on the comfort and appearance of his show-piece tower, but he did not entirely neglect the castle's overall defences. He added an outer moat to the building complex and constructed no fewer than three gatehouses and three bridges to guard the approach to the castle from the north.

Cromwell probably repaired and strengthened the 13th-century inner curtain wall, which contained eight drum towers and enclosed in the inner ward a separate Great Hall, as well as kitchens and a chapel. Little remains today except the superb tower.

Above: From the cellars to the battlements, there are no fewer than six floors in the great Square Keep at Tattershall Castle.

CAISTER CASTLE, NORFOLK

Sir John Falstaff, a veteran of the Battle of Agincourt and Henry V's military campaigns in France, and subsequently Governor of Maine and Anjou, rebuilt his family home at Caister, in Norfolk, in some style in 1432–46. His 'castle' was a rectangular brick country house, as lavishly fitted and furnished as a palace. The English chronicler William Worcester described it as a 'ryche juelle' ('rich jewel'). But it was also fortified and surrounded by a moat. It originally had four corner towers, but only one remains, an impressive five storeys, 100ft (30m) in height. Although the tower has machicolations and gun-holes, its large windows would have made it difficult to defend against a besieging force.

Right: The builder of Caister Castle is thought to have been Shakespeare's model for the character of Sir John Falstaff.

RETURN TO THE SQUARE KEEP

Architectural historians note that the square keep was not commonly built in England at the time of Lord Cromwell – the great English square keeps at the Tower of London, at Colchester and Rochester had been constructed three centuries earlier. They suggest that Cromwell may have been inspired to build in this way by the contemporary square keeps he saw in France, when on campaign with the English Army. The quality and style of the workmanship suggests that he imported the finest craftsmen from Flanders and France to work on the building.

LINLITHGOW PALACE

HOME OF THE SCOTTISH KINGS

King James I of Scots began the extensive rebuilding of the royal palace at Linlithgow, between Edinburgh and Stirling, in 1424. In that year, James returned to Scotland, aged 30, at the end of a prolonged 18-year exile in England that had begun when he was captured by pirates, while travelling to France, and handed over to England's King Henry IV. Under the terms of his release treaty, signed in 1423 with England's new king, Henry VI, James had to pay a ransom of £40,000. Nevertheless, James still found the necessary funds to undertake the reconstruction of Linlithgow, where a terrible fire a year later had devastated the earlier fortified dwelling.

Above: The Renaissance-style north façade at Linlithgow was built by James VI and may have been based on the Chateau de Blois in the Loire Valley, France.

QUEENS AND KINGS AT LINLITHGOW

According to Scottish royal tradition, in June 1513 Queen Margaret (Tudor), English-born wife of James IV, waited at Linlithgow for her royal husband to return from the Battle of Flodden Field, unaware that he lay dead with 10,000 of his fellow countrymen. The castle's north-west tower, in which she is said to have waited, is named Queen Margaret's Bower in her honour.

Later, Mary, Queen of Scots, was born at Linlithgow in December 1542, and after she returned to the Scottish throne following her long French exile she often stayed at the palace. Subsequently, Linlithgow began to become neglected, although Charles I stayed there in 1617 and again in 1633.

In 1745, Bonnie Prince Charlie stayed at the palace prior to his unsuccessful attempt to march on London. Subsequently, the Duke of Cumberland (son of England's King George II) stayed there with his army. When these troops departed on 1 February 1746, a fire left unattended started a devastating blaze that severely damaged the palace. Significant repairs were carried out in the 19th century.

Left: Mary, Queen of Scots, spent the first seven months of her life at Linlithgow Palace and often returned afterwards.

FIRST ROYAL BUILDING

King David I of Scots was the earliest royal builder at Linlithgow, erecting a manor house of timber in the mid-12th century. When Edward I of England invaded in the late 13th century, he and his trusted castle architect, Master James of St Georges, fortified David's palace with earthworks, ditches and wooden palisades, but stopped short of building in stone. Edward garrisoned the castle with the English troops needed for his Scottish campaigns. Subsequently, David II carried out rebuilding in the 14th century, but his work was swept away by the fire of 1424.

JAMES I'S CONTRIBUTION

James built an impressive stone entrance block on the east side of the surviving palace building. The raised entranceway was accessed by a ramp and drawbridge from the outer barbican. Above the entrance was the royal coat of arms and on either side were niches, believed once to have held statues of St Andrew and St James. The block also contained a first-floor Great Hall, measuring 100 x 30ft (30 x 9m). At one end were the royal kitchens, while at the other, perhaps, was a great stone fireplace, although in James's time there may have been a great chimneyless central hearth, as in English medieval halls such as Penshurst Place and Stokesay Castle.

The finished palace at Linlithgow took the form of a courtyard house, with four 'wings' around a central garden containing a fountain. Only the eastern front and part of the southern range were finished by James I, but there is evidence that the palace's courtyard was part of the plans from the start. Scholars believe that James, who was an accomplished artist as well as a learned man, may have played a significant part in designing Linlithgow himself. His project was never finished, but it appears to have been conceived as a palace, a royal dwelling, rather than a castle. James changed the entrance from the south to the east, constructing a very grand raised but unfortified gateway that could be viewed advantageously from that direction, across the waters of the adjacent Loch Linlithgow. The palace may have been planned as the Scottish answer to England's Sheen Palace, which James must certainly have visited during his long exile in England.

Above: The palace stands beside Linlithgow Loch. This reconstruction shows the complex shortly after its completion by James V.

Below: The courtyard fountain of c.1538. James V's queen, Mary of Guise, likened the palace to the best French chateaux.

THE PLAN COMPLETED

In the 15th and early 16th centuries, Kings James III and IV finished the work begun by James I, enclosing the courtyard by completing the southern range and then building on the north and finally the west sides. The west range contained some splendid royal apartments for James IV and his English queen, Margaret Tudor, daughter of Henry VII. James IV also made repairs and improvements to the Great Hall, to which he added a new roof, and built a new chapel.

In the time of James V, the main entrance was moved back to the southern range, and a new gatehouse built alongside it. James VI then made improvements to the northern range, including the addition of a fine Renaissance façade on the Long Gallery in 1618–24.

RAGLAN CASTLE
THE GRANDEST CASTLE IN WALES

The castle we see at Raglan was begun *c.*1430 by William ap Thomas, veteran of the Battle of Agincourt and later celebrated as 'the Blue Knight of Gwent', following his knighting by King Henry VI in 1449. William built the hexagonal keep known as the Yellow Tower of Gwent (*c.*1435-45), generally celebrated as being among the finest towers of the 15th century.

The Blue Knight was a follower of Richard, Duke of York, and his family's rise was accelerated by the success of the Yorkists, and in particular by Edward of York's coming to the throne as King Edward IV in 1461. By this time Sir William had died, but his son, another Sir William, was made Earl of Pembroke and Chief Justice first of South Wales, then of North Wales too. The younger Sir William completed the castle.

NORMAN CASTLE

Little remains of the early 12th-century motte-and-bailey castle that was built by followers of William FitzOsbern, Earl of Hereford, as the Normans pushed into Gwent. But it is likely that the Yellow Tower stands on what was the motte, or mound, of the Norman castle and that the castle's two enclosures, the Pitched Stone Court and the Fountain Court, occupy the land that was once the Norman castle's bailey.

YELLOW TOWER

The Yellow Tower of Gwent, so-called because it is made from a pale yellowish sandstone quarried locally at Redbrooke, has walls 10ft (3m) thick. It originally had four floors above the basement, but one level was lost when the castle was slighted in 1646 during the Civil War. Its ground-floor kitchen lay beneath a first-floor hall, which was surmounted by private and sleeping chambers on the levels above.

The tower was surrounded by an apron wall and a wide moat, and accessed only by a single drawbridge from the rest of the castle. It was a formidable stronghold in its own right, and certainly offered secure quarters to which the castle's defenders might retreat *in extremis*. Moreover, in an era of 'bastard feudalism', soldiers and retainers were bound to powerful lords by financial links rather than the ties of feudal loyalty, and the lords could not always be sure of the loyalty of the men they used to garrison them. As a result, they often fortified their own quarters within the castle, where they could, if the situation demanded, take refuge from their own garrison.

Above: The Moat Walk at the foot of the Yellow Tower was added c.*1600 by the Earl of Worcester. Niches in the wall once held statues of Roman emperors.*

Below: The Closet Tower stands to the right of the Great Gatehouse and contained a basement prison. The gatehouse, with its half-hexagonal towers, dates to the 1460s.

MACHICOLATION

The gatehouse at Raglan Castle included machicolation – a feature more commonly found in French than Welsh castles. A machicolated defensive wall has a projecting section with holes in the floor through which the castle's defenders could throw rocks or pour oil on attackers. Strictly speaking, the term 'machicolation' refers to the floor opening itself, which was usually between the corbels or supports of the projecting section of wall.

The younger Sir William was responsible for building the splendid Great Hall and accommodation ranged around the Fountain Court, which at one time contained a marble water fountain known as 'the White Horse'. The retainers' area was in a second courtyard, the Pitched Stone Court, further north.

Below: At the top of the Great Gatehouse towers the machicolations can be seen. The windows are narrow for purposes of defence.

STRONG DEFENCES

Raglan is an exception to the general movement away from castles to fortified country houses, for it was designed as a fortress proper – one of the last genuine castles ever built. In addition to the Great Tower, it has a curtain wall containing hexagonal towers and a machicolated gatehouse, which was fortified with three heavy double doors, two portcullises and a drawbridge. Throughout the castle, circular gun-ports were provided in the towers to strengthen defences.

In the Elizabethan era, William Somerset, Earl of Worcester, improved the Great Hall. Building in fine red sandstone that makes an appealing contrast to the prevailing yellow stone, he and his descendants carried out significant rebuilding, adding a magnificent Tudor Long Gallery, now ruined.

Above: This aerial view shows the Yellow Tower (near left), the Fountain Court (top left), and the Pitched Stone Court (top right) behind the Great Gatehouse.

CIVIL WAR

Edward Somerset, Marquis of Worcester, was a staunch Royalist, and the castle was the first to be fortified for Charles I during the Civil War. It was a major royalist centre during the war and the last castle to be surrendered to the Parliamentary army. The worth of Raglan's defences was proved by the fact that the surrender took place, in the lavish Great Hall, on 19 August 1646, only after several weeks of heavy bombardment, at the end of one of the war's longest sieges. The victorious Parliamentarians looted and plundered the splendid castle, slighted its defences and partially demolished the Yellow Tower. Raglan Castle has never been restored, and today remains a handsome, evocative ruin.

ST GEORGE'S CHAPEL
AND WINDSOR CASTLE

The magnificent St George's Chapel at Windsor Castle in Berkshire was begun by Edward IV in 1477. By then, Windsor had been a royal stronghold for over 400 years (see pages 153 and 224).

King Edward the Confessor held his court in his palace of Kingsbury at Old Windsor nearby, but after the Conquest William I built the original Windsor Castle, a motte-and-bailey fortification in a strong position on an escarpment overlooking the River Thames. He raised a wooden keep where the Round Tower stands today, atop a 50ft (15m) motte, and enclosed a 13-acre (5ha) bailey with stakes in a boomerang shape.

Above: St George's Chapel is widely considered to be one of Europe's finest late medieval buildings.

A ROYAL FAVOURITE

William II chose the castle for his Easter celebrations in 1097; Henry I built a chapel and royal apartments there and married his second wife, Adeliza of Louvain, at Windsor in January 1121. In the 1170s, Henry II rebuilt William I's original keep in stone, then reworked the defensive walls around the wards, adding square towers, and refashioned the royal apartments in the upper ward.

In 1216, the fortifications were fully tested when a baronial army besieged King John in the castle for three months. Although the castle held firm, Henry III added three round towers to the western wall. He also established St Edward's Chapel in the lower ward.

Edward III was born in Windsor Castle, in November 1312, and known as 'Edward Windsor'. In the 1360s, he extended and improved the castle, in particular building St George's Hall for the Knights of the Order of the Garter.

Below: The Choir in St George's Chapel. The banners of the knights of the garter hang above the garter stalls; beneath the banners are the knights' crests, helmets and swords.

ST GEORGE'S CHAPEL

Edward IV began the construction of a vast new chapel dedicated to St George, situated to the west of the earlier one. Master mason Henry Janyns carried out the project, overseen by Richard Beauchamp, Bishop of Salisbury. It was to contain the King's funerary monument. The chapel was unfinished at Edward's death in 1483, and work soon stopped.

The chapel was completed in the reign of Henry VII and became a burial place for British monarchs. No fewer than ten kings and queens are buried there.

NORTON CONYERS

THE HOUSE THAT INSPIRED *JANE EYRE*

Norton Conyers, a fine manor house near Ripon in Yorkshire, was developed by the Conyers, a Norman family granted land in the region after the Conquest of 1066. The house took its present form in the late 1400s, although the Dutch gables and carved doorway on the front are 17th century; the 15th-century brickwork is concealed by an 18th-century roughcast exterior. Norton Conyers appears to have been the inspiration for Thornfield Hall, Mr Rochester's house in Charlotte Brontë's novel *Jane Eyre.*

Above: Generations of prosperity. Tudor, Stuart and Georgian additions to the original 14th-century house take nothing away from the charm of Norton Conyers.

THE MAD WOMAN IN THE ATTIC

In 1839, when Charlotte Brontë was working as a governess for a family in Harrogate, she visited Norton Conyers and heard her host's account of how, in the 18th century, a mad woman had been locked away in the attic. In her novel *Jane Eyre*, published in 1847, Norton Conyers became Thornfield Hall and the mad woman the wife of the novel's Byronic hero, Mr Rochester.

Below: Charlotte Brontë. In 2004, just as described in Jane Eyre, *a blocked staircase was found at Norton Conyers.*

Norton Conyers stands in a landscaped garden enclosed by a grey stone boundary wall. Within, the impressive Great Hall dates from the 15th century, although its roof timbers have been hidden by a coved ceiling and the original wooden screens have been removed. Norton Conyers also boasts a magnificent 16th-century inlaid table in the hall.

CATHOLIC LORD DISPOSSESSED

The house takes the first part of its name from that of the Norton family, who came into ownership through marriage *c.*1370. However, Richard Norton cast his lot with the Catholic earls who plotted against Elizabeth I at Raby Castle, County Durham, in the doomed 1569 'Rebellion of the North'. As a traitor, Norton lost his property, which was forfeit to the Crown.

THE GRAHAMS TAKE OVER

Norton Conyers was later purchased by Sir Richard Graham, a member of the notable Scots Borders family, in 1624.

In 1644, family legend has it that a wounded Graham horseman rode back so fast from the Battle of Marston Moor that when he reached home his horse's hooves were red-hot. The animal carried its rider into the house because he was wounded, and left a hoof mark on the sweeping oak staircase of *c.*1630.

In 1679, the Grahams entertained the future King James II, then James, Duke of York, with his wife, Mary of Modena, on their way to Scotland. Sir Richard's descendants still own the house today.

Right: The main oak staircase at Norton Conyers, built c.*1630, showing some of the Graham portrait collection.*

OXBURGH HALL
A ROMANTIC MOATED MANOR

Oxburgh Hall has stylish defences – it lies within a square moat and has a gatehouse tower complete with battlements, arrow-slits and machicolations – but, as with many fortified manor houses, these features are more signs of status than effective elements of defence. For one thing, the moat is crossed by a fixed bridge rather than a drawbridge; for another, the arrow-slit arrangement means that defenders could not have provided effective cover fire from them. Moreover, the gate-tower has large windows. In addition, the Great Hall, even if sufficiently fortified to deter bands of marauders in the lawless late 15th century, would not repel well-equipped soldiers or withstand a siege.

The house, near King's Lynn in Norfolk, was begun in the 1480s by prominent nobleman, Sir Edward Bedingfeld, descendant of an originally Norman family. Sir Edward's ancestor, Sir Peter Bedingfeld, fought with honour alongside the Black Prince and King Edward III at the Battle of Crécy in 1346.

The fixed bridge across the moat leads through the arched entranceway at the foot of the tower into a central courtyard. Originally, the Great Hall stood on the south side of the courtyard, directly across from the tower, with two-storey residential buildings on the other sides. The Great Hall was demolished by Sir Richard Bedingfeld in 1775 to open up the courtyard to the moat and countryside beyond. Subsequently, two squat towers were raised at the south-west and south-east corners of the courtyard, filling part of the south side.

Above: The fixed bridge across the moat and Oxburgh Hall's twin-towered gatehouse can be seen at the left side of the picture.

Below: In addition to its superb brickwork and royal connections, Oxburgh Hall is celebrated for its French parterre gardens.

THE GATEHOUSE

The two towers of the gatehouse at Oxburgh Hall are topped with serrated battlements and decorated with horizontal brick mouldings. Within the gatehouse, a splendid brick-built spiral stairway rises from the ground-floor armoury to the roof. The first-floor chamber is known as the King's Room because it was occupied by King Henry VII when he visited Oxburgh in 1487. In a small side room on this floor are embroidered wall-hangings sewn by Mary, Queen of Scots, during her long captivity in England. She was assisted in this work by Bess of Hardwick (builder of Hardwick Hall). The second-floor chamber is named the Queen's Room.

During the reign of Mary I, Sir Henry Bedingfeld was in charge of keeping Princess Elizabeth, the future Elizabeth I, in custody, first in the Tower of London, and then under house arrest at Woodstock. However, Elizabeth showed that she bore no grudge to the family by visiting Oxburgh Hall in 1578.

HERSTMONCEUX CASTLE

FORMER HOME OF THE ROYAL OBSERVATORY

Sir Roger de Fiennes, Treasurer of the King's Household under King Henry VI, began building the vast and magnificent fortified manor house of Herstmonceux Castle, in East Sussex, in 1441. Along with Lord Cromwell of Tattershall Castle and Sir John Falstaff of Caister Castle, de Fiennes was a pioneer of brick building in 15th-century England. At Herstmonceux, he used Flemish brick and probably Flemish craftsmen to erect a handsome moated country mansion.

The place took its name from 12th-century English noblewoman, Idonea de Herst, and her Norman lord, Ingelram de Monceux. Situated just a few miles from the site of the Battle of Hastings, Herstmonceux was a place of note many centuries before Sir Roger began building there.

Below: According to local legend, the lands besides the moat at Herstmonceux are haunted by a lady in white, who is said to have been seduced, then killed, by Sir Roger.

STYLISTIC DEFENCES

The castle is rectangular in shape, with a polygonal (many-sided) tower at each corner, plus smaller towers spaced out along the length of the walls, and an impressive twin-towered gatehouse, 84ft (25.5m) high, boasting a double row of battlements and heavy machicolation. The gatehouse towers are fitted with gun-holes at ground level and arrow-slits further up. However, the castle was built for comfort and elegance, not as a fortress: the brick walls were far too soft and thin to withstand bombardment, and the turrets, machicolation, moat and battlements are for style, not for defence.

FROM PRIVATE TO PUBLIC

Sir Richard de Fiennes, son of Sir Roger, became Baron Dacre in 1458. The house later passed to the Lennard family through marriage. Then, in the 17th century, Thomas Lennard, 15th Lord Dacre, was made Earl of Sussex by King Charles II and married Anne, Duchess of Cleveland. He frittered away the family money, and the castle was sold.

Above: Sir Roger de Fiennes' arms are carved in stone above the arch in the splendid 84ft (25.5m) gatehouse.

A later owner, Robert Hare, dismantled much of the castle's interior and used the bricks from it in rebuilding Herstmonceux Place, a nearby house. The castle was rescued and renovated by Lt-Col Claude Lowther in the early 20th century. He rebuilt the south front in 1911–12. In 1948–88, the castle was the base of the Royal Greenwich Observatory, but later it was turned into an international study centre by the Queen's University, Canada.

HADDON HALL

HOME TO THE 'KING OF THE PEAK'

The handsome medieval manor house of Haddon Hall, near Bakewell in Derbyshire, has a splendid late 15th-century Dining Room and Great Chamber, both with fine original ceiling paintings. In addition, the house and estate contain a 14th-century Banqueting Hall and largely unchanged adjacent kitchens, Jacobean Long Gallery and terraced Elizabethan gardens. Much of Haddon Hall's charm and interest lie in the fact that it was uninhabited – and so unchanged – for around 200 years after the early 1700s, when the owners (from the 16th century, the dukes of Rutland) removed to their other, grander, house at Belvoir Castle. Then, in 1924, the Marquis of Granby, subsequently the 9th Duke, began a sensitive and careful restoration of the house of his ancestors.

Below: Sparse furnishings, richly carved wood panelling and fine plasterwork ceilings typify the rooms at Haddon Hall.

Above: Henry VII celebrates his marriage to Elizabeth of York. The royal couple are carved in the panelling of the dining room.

Haddon Hall stands in the Peak District National Park, on a hill overlooking the River Wye, on land granted by William the Conqueror to an illegitimate son named William Peverel. The oldest parts of the house, including sections of the boundary wall, the lower part of Peverel's Tower and the font and arches of the Chapel, date from the Norman period. The boundary wall was built under a licence of 1190, which forbade the use of crenellation and stated that the wall should be no more then 12ft (3.7m) high. The battlements on the walls and towers were added later.

BANQUETING HALL

This hall was built *c.*1370, and two windows and two gargoyles survive from the time of its construction. The oak screen and gallery are 15th century, and while the timber roof is a 20th-century one, it is a very skilful addition. Hanging in the hall is a tapestry of *c.*1470, of French *mille fleurs* design with the arms of England, which is believed to have been a gift from King Henry VIII. The kitchens alongside are fitted with well-used, centuries-old equipment, including a chopping block and a salting box.

MURALS AND MEDALLIONS

In the 15th century, fine murals were painted in the chapel: two of St Nicholas, one of St Anne and one of St Christopher carrying the Christ child across a river full of fish. These were

Below: The terraced gardens run down to the River Wye. They were restored in the 1920s to their appearance in Elizabethan times.

Above: A 15th-century mural in the chapel shows Saint Christopher's feet treading river waters as he carries the Christ child.

Right: Light floods into Haddon Hall's splendid Long Gallery through its expansive windows, creating a luminous promenade.

whitewashed by zealous Puritans in the 17th century, which protected the murals against decay. Also in the 15th century, a nine-panel alabaster reredos was built in the chapel and beautiful stained glass (dated 1427) installed.

At the end of the 15th century, Sir Henry Vernon built the Private Wing, including the Dining Room (originally known as the Parlour) and the Great Chamber above it. In the Dining Room, the painted ceiling (restored in 1926) includes black and red heraldic elements; in its wall panelling are carved medallions believed to represent Henry VII and his queen, Elizabeth of York.

'KING OF THE PEAK'

The celebrated oak-panelled Long Gallery, 110ft (34m) in length with beautiful oak panelling and carved walnut embellishments, was built by Sir George Vernon later in the 16th century. Sir George was celebrated for his hospitality and known as the 'King of the Peak'. Sir George's daughter, Dorothy, married John Manners, later Duke of Rutland. The house came to them, and the family lives there still.

GREAT HALL AT GREAT DIXTER

The cavernous Great Hall in the splendid timber-framed house of Great Dixter in East Sussex was built *c.*1440–54. Measuring 40 x 25ft (12 x 8m) and 31ft (9.5m) tall, it is one of England's largest surviving timber-framed halls. It has a splendid hammer-beam roof. Like Haddon Hall, Great Dixter was sensitively restored in the 20th century – in this case, by the architect Edwin Lutyens for owner Nathaniel Lloyd in 1910–11. Lutyens also designed a splendid topiary garden incorporating the manor's original farm buildings. Nathaniel Lloyd's sons, Quentin and Christopher, cared for the house and gardens respectively. Christopher, during whose period of care the gardens were internationally renowned and much visited, died on 27 January 2006.

Above: The porch at Great Dixter is 16th century or earlier.

PART TWO

TUDOR AND STUART

1485–1714

The Tudor and Stuart monarchs were among the great royal builders, creating lavish palaces in England and Scotland. The reign of Elizabeth I was an extraordinarily rich period for architecture, with the construction of 'prodigy houses'. The establishment of the House of Stuart, under James I and Charles I, saw the introduction of classical architecture to England.

Left: James V's Renaissance-style building at Holyrood Palace was carried out for his first wife, Madeleine de Valois, but she died before she could enjoy it.

ENGLAND TIMELINE, 1485-1714

Above: Hampton Court Palace is the most magnificent Tudor palace surviving today.

Above: Burghley House, one of the 'prodigy houses' built in the reign of Elizabeth I.

Above: Marlborough House was the London home of the 1st Duke of Marlborough.

1485–1579

*c.***1485** Cardinal John Morton, Bishop of Ely, builds the episcopal palace of Hatfield House, Hertfordshire.

1514–19 Cardinal Wolsey, Lord Chancellor, builds a magnificent Renaissance residence at Hampton Court Palace.

1537–41 James V remodels Falkland Palace to create Scotland's first palace in the continental Renaissance style.

*c.***1540** Lawrence Washington, ancestor of the first US President, George Washington, builds Sulgrave Manor in Northamptonshire on the site of the dissolved Priory of St Andrew.

*c.***1540** Henry VIII builds Deal Castle in Kent.

1540–45 Henry VIII builds Pendennis Castle near Falmouth in Cornwall.

1547–52 Edward, Duke of Somerset, builds the splendid Syon House in Middlesex.

1555 Sir William Cecil begins building Burghley House in Northamptonshire.

*c.***1565–75** Robert Dudley, Earl of Leicester, carries out grand rebuilding at Kenilworth Castle in Warwickshire.

1562 Sir William More begins the transformation of Loseley House in Surrey into a 'prodigy house'.

1567 Sir John Thynne begins building his great 'prodigy house' of Longleat House in Wiltshire.

1580–1629

1580–88 Sir Francis Willoughby builds Wollaton Hall in Nottinghamshire.

*c.***1590** Sir Edward Phelips begins building Montacute House in Somerset.

1587 Work on Burghley House, Lincolnshire, completed, for Sir William Cecil, 1st Baron Burghley.

1591–97 Elizabeth, Countess of Shrewsbury – 'Bess of Hardwick' – builds Hardwick Hall in Derbyshire.

1603–08 Thomas Sackville, 1st Earl of Dorset, rebuilds the elegant country house of Knole in Kent.

1605–14 Thomas Howard, 1st Earl of Suffolk, builds Audley End in Essex.

1607–08 Robert Cecil, 1st Earl of Salisbury, rebuilds Hatfield House in Hertfordshire.

1612 The leading Elizabethan 'surveyor' (architect), Robert Smythson, begins work at Bolsover Castle in Chesterfield, his last major house.

1615 Inigo Jones begins work on the Queen's House, Greenwich, based on an Italian Medici villa at Poggio a Caiano.

1616–25 Robert Lyminge builds Blickling Hall in Norfolk for Sir Henry Hobart.

1619–22 Inigo Jones builds the Banqueting House in Whitehall Palace.

1623 Inigo Jones begins work on the Queen's Chapel in St James's Palace.

1630–1714

1636–40 Major work by Philip Herbert, 4th Earl of Pembroke, at his Wilton House in Wiltshire includes a new south front designed by Isaac de Caus and Inigo Jones.

*c.***1675** Charles II spends £130,000 at Windsor Castle, building new state apartments, and redecorating St George's Hall and the King's Chapel.

1687–1707 William Cavendish, 4th Earl of Devonshire, entirely rebuilds Chatsworth House in Derbyshire.

1688–96 Charles Seymour, 6th Duke of Somerset, builds Petworth House on the site of a 13th-century castle in West Sussex.

1689 Sir Christopher Wren begins rebuilding Hampton Court Palace for King William III and Queen Mary II. In the same year rebuilding begins to transform Nottingham House, Kensington, into Kensington Palace.

*c.***1690** Ford, Lord Grey of Werke, builds Uppark, West Sussex.

1696–1702 Nicholas Hawksmoor designs Easton Neston in Northamptonshire, regarded by some as the first country house in the Baroque style.

1709–11 Sir Christopher Wren builds Marlborough House in London for John Churchill, 1st Duke of Marlborough, and his wife, Sarah, Duchess of Marlborough.

N
W
E
S
SCOTLAND
Belsay Hall
North Sea
Irish Sea
ENGLAND
Bolsover Castle
Chatsworth
Hardwicke Hall & Old Hall
Wollaton Hall
Belton House
Burghley House
The Wash
Felbrigg Hall
Blickling Hall
Caister Castle
Kenilworth Castle
Boughton House
Woburn Abbey
Audley End House
Sulgrave Manor
WALES
Tower of London
The Banqueting House, Palace of Westminster
Hatfield House
Mapledurham House
Syon House
Queen's House
Eltham Palace
Deal Castle
Windsor Castle
Hampton Court Palace
Hever Castle
Knole
Bristol Channel
Longleat
Loseley Park
Walmer Castle
Winchester Castle Great Hall
Goodwood House
Strait of Dover
Montacute House
Anthony House
Portland Castle
St Mawes Castle
Pendennis Castle
English Channel

SCOTLAND, WALES
AND NORTHERN IRELAND TIMELINES, 1485–1714

Above: Holyrood Palace is the official residence in Scotland of the Queen.

SCOTLAND, 1485–1714

1512 James IV of Scots builds a Great Tower at Rothesay Castle, Isle of Bute.
*c.*1530 George Gordon, 4th Earl of Huntly, begins major rebuilding of Huntly Castle, Aberdeenshire.
1536 James V of Scots completes major rebuilding of Holyrood Palace.
1537–41 James V's rebuilding at Falkland Palace creates Scotland's first Renaissance palace.
1538–42 James V builds a palace within Stirling Castle.
*c.*1580 Lord Edzell builds a courtyard mansion at Edzell Castle, Angus.
*c.*1585 5th Earl of Bothwell rebuilds Crichton Castle in the Renaissance style.
1594 The construction of Crathes Castle in Aberdeenshire is completed.
*c.*1595 9th Lord Glamis embarks on a remodelling of Glamis Castle, Angus.
*c.*1600 King James VI of Scots builds Dunfermline Palace.
1626 William Forbes completes Craigievar Castle in Aberdeenshire.
*c.*1675 Charles II rebuilds Holyrood Palace in Edinburgh.
1628 John Erskine, 3rd Earl of Mar, builds Braemar Castle, Aberdeenshire.
1640 Threave Castle, Dumfries and Galloway, surrenders after a 13-week siege.
1699 The decay of Tantallon Castle, E Lothian, begins when the Douglas earls of Angus sell it.

Above: Carew Castle stands on the tidal creek of the Carew River in Wales.

WALES, 1485–1714

*c.*1560 Sir Richard Clough builds Bachecraig, Denbigh, celebrated as the first classical country house in Wales.

*c.*1575 Sir John Perrot rebuilds Carew Castle in Dyfed.

*c.*1580 Sir John also rebuilds Laugharne Castle in South Wales. He was given the castle by Queen Elizabeth I in 1575.

1587–92 Sir Edward Herbert builds a splendid Long Gallery as part of major rebuilding at Powis Castle.

Above: Killyleagh Castle is the oldest occupied castle in Ireland.

NORTHERN IRELAND 1485–1714

1611 Capt Willam Cole rcbuilds Enniskillen Castle in Co Fermanagh.

1616 Rev Malcolm Hamilton builds Monea Castle in Co Fermanagh.

1620 Randall MacDonnell, 1st Earl of Antrim, builds a manor house within Dunluce Castle, Co Antrim.

1680 Springhill House, a 'Plantation' house, is built by William Conyngham in Co Londonderry.

WAY IN

CHAPTER FIVE

EARLY TUDOR PALACES AND COUNTRY HOUSES

1485–c.1550

At Hampton Court Palace in August 1546, Henry VIII made a bold statement of the glory of the youthful Tudor dynasty and his own regal largesse when he laid on feasts and entertainments for the French ambassador, a 200-strong body of French followers and 1,300 English courtiers. In the ten years *c.*1530-40, Henry had spent a massive £62,000 (around £18 million in today's money) on improving Hampton Court, already a glorious Renaissance-style palace built by Cardinal Thomas Wolsey in 1514-18.

At Hampton Court – and in a host of now ruined or demolished Tudor palaces – Henry's lavishly funded royal building expressed the magnificence of both Crown and state. Following his break with the Church of Rome and the establishment of the Church of England, the nation's greatest buildings were increasingly secular rather than sacred. This new wave of secular building was funded in large part by the Dissolution of the Monasteries, when in the 1530s Henry suppressed England's great religious houses and seized their lands and wealth. The Crown's loyal servants and Henry's associates – such as Sir William Compton, builder of Compton Wynyates, and William Sandys, builder of The Vyne – were rewarded with grants of land and office that made them rich. In their service, English masons, woodworkers and glaziers who would once have worked for the Church exercised their skills in building the fine country houses of the early Tudor period.

Left: The Gateway in the Tudor West Front at Hampton Court Palace was begun by Cardinal Wolsey and finished by Henry VIII.

COMPTON WYNYATES

AND THE VYNE

The delightful red-brick manor house of Compton Wynyates, in Warwickshire, was begun by Edmund Compton in 1481, just prior to the accession of the House of Tudor. Edmund's sturdy but good-looking country house was given some elegant additions, including a porch and some towers, by his son, the prominent Tudor courtier, Sir William Compton, between 1493 and 1528.

Above: In its idyllic setting, and with the soft glow of its bricks, Compton Wynyates is one of England's most attractive houses.

EDMUND COMPTON'S MANOR

The house's name has an uncertain derivation: 'Compton' certainly means 'dwelling in the coombe (valley)'; but 'Wynyates' may refer either to the vineyards that once were planted in the area or to the nearby gap in the hills ('wind gate'?), where a windmill was built.

The Compton family had lived in the area since the early years of the 13th century and built an earlier manor house that Edmund Compton redeveloped. He kept little but the moat and its drawbridge from the earlier house when he built a new dwelling of four wings, enclosing a courtyard, with walls 4ft (1.2m) thick, and an impressive Big Hall with a linen-fold panelling screen and a gallery. Edmund used attractive raspberry-coloured bricks that give the house an unforgettable glow against the greenery of the garden and the surrounding countryside. He dug a second, outer, moat – probably never filled with water – with its own drawbridge.

SIR WILLIAM COMPTON

Edmund Compton died in 1491 and his son, William, became a ward of the Crown. From the age of 11, William served at court as a page to Prince Henry, the future King Henry VIII, and in later life remained a great friend of that charismatic king. William fought, jousted and banqueted alongside his royal master, as well as romancing the ladies of the court. Henry knighted William at the Battle of Tournai, in 1512, and, as a sign of special favour, allowed him to add the royal lion of England to the Compton coat of arms.

At Compton Wynyates, *c.*1515, Sir William built a grand entrance porch and chapel, while adding a tower at each of the four corners of the house. The entrance porch was carved with the royal arms alongside the Latin inscription *Dom Rex Henricus Octav* ('My Master King Henry VIII'). He also installed the Big Hall's timber ceiling and great bay window, fitted with heraldic glass; both these came from the ruins of Fulbrooke Castle, near

Left: Rich in tradition and history, Compton Wynyates has fine gardens and flowering plants climbing its red walls.

Warwick, which he had been given by the King as a reward for his brave and loyal service.

KING HENRY VIII'S ROOM

Among the rooms at Compton Wynyates, King Henry VIII's Room is of particular interest. Here, the monarch stayed on several occasions, and the stained-glass window features the royal arms and those of Aragon (birthplace of Queen Catherine). In later years, Queen Elizabeth I slept in the same room in 1572, while King James I stayed there in 1617. James made Sir William Compton 1st Earl of Northampton. Charles I, a close friend of Spencer Compton, 2nd Earl of Northampton, also stayed here. The ceiling (of 1625) contains the monograms of all the room's royal residents.

LATER DEVELOPMENTS

During the Civil War, the Comptons remained staunch Royalists. The 2nd Earl fought at the battle of Edgehill in 1642 and was killed at the Battle of Hopton Heath in 1643. In June 1644, Compton Wynyates was besieged and taken by the Parliamentarian army. In 1645, the Comptons tried but failed to retake the house and then fled into exile, where they remained until the Restoration. In line with their usual policy of slighting royalist fortifications, the Parliamentarians took the action of filling in the house's moat.

In later years, Compton Wynyates was uninhabited. The house decayed and came close to complete ruin. Indeed, in 1768 Lord Northampton ordered its demolition, but his agent fortunately did not carry out his instructions. In the later 19th century, Compton Wynyates was restored and from 1884 was once again inhabited, by the 5th Marquess of Northampton and his wife.

Above: All who entered Sir William Compton's home walked beneath the motto 'My Master King Henry VIII'.

THE VYNE, HAMPSHIRE

The prominent Tudor courtier, William Sandys, built the manor house of The Vyne, in Hampshire, *c.*1500–20. It was built of attractive rose-coloured brick, with corner towers and tall windows across the main fronts, but had no moat or internal courtyard. Sandys became Lord Sandys in 1523 and was made Lord Chamberlain in Henry VIII's household in 1526. Henry visited The Vyne in 1510, 1531 and 1535, the third time with his new wife, Anne Boleyn. Lord Sandys died in 1540. Later owners of his house included Chaloner Chute (a Speaker of the House of Commons), who hired John Webb to build a classical portico, the earliest in an English country house, on The Vyne's north front (see also page 156).

Below: The placing of the original windows was more haphazard than the symmetrical arrangement of the later sash windows.

HAMPTON COURT PALACE
AND THE COURT OF HENRY VIII

One of England's finest royal buildings, Hampton Court is forever associated with the magnificent court of Henry VIII, although major changes were made in the 17th century during the reign of William and Mary (see pages 160–1). The palace came into royal hands as a gift from the statesman, Cardinal Wolsey, to his royal master, Henry VIII.

WOLSEY'S PALACE

In 1514, Wolsey, Lord Chancellor and Archbishop of York, obtained the lease of the building from the religious order of the Knights Hospitaliers of St John of Jerusalem. In five years of lavishly funded redevelopment, he transformed the Knights' relatively modest country retreat into a splendid and extensive palace. The eastern part of the kitchen range and the nearby Base Court, a guest courtyard surrounded by private accommodation for 40 or so visitors, remain essentially as they were in Wolsey's time.

Below: The 19th-century artist Joseph Nash imagines Wolsey entertaining his lord and king at Hampton Court Palace.

Above: The turrets flanking the gatehouse in the Tudor West Front at Hampton Court hold roundels with the heads of Roman emperors.

Recent archaeological research has shown that Wolsey's palace was laid out in a great geometric design that formed two eight-pointed stars, one beside the other. The magnificent design followed very closely the instructions in an Italian book of 1510, Paolo Cortese's *de Cardinalatu*, which described the dimensions and features of a perfect Cardinal's residence. Wolsey's flamboyant house was therefore England's first Italian Renaissance palace.

Above: Wolsey laid out the first gardens at Hampton Court, then Henry VIII began a major redevelopment of them in 1529.

In 1528, Wolsey was falling swiftly out of royal favour because he was unable to provide Henry VIII with a divorce from Catherine of Aragon. He attempted to halt this alarming slide by making a gift of his precious palace to Henry VIII. The ploy did not work: Henry happily accepted the gift of Hampton Court and almost at once launched his own major building projects there, but Wolsey's reputation was not restored.

Henry built extravagant royal suites, a beautiful chapel, an enormous Great Hall and 36,000sq ft (3,300sq m) of kitchens. He provided a vast lavatory complex that could be used by 28 people at one time, with water piped through 3 miles (5km) of lead piping. He laid out 1,100 acres (445ha) of hunting grounds, a large pleasure garden, tennis courts and a bowling alley.

ELTHAM PALACE

Another of Henry VIII's favourite residences was Eltham Palace, once a manor house in the Kent countryside, now enveloped by south London. Given in 1295 by Anthony Bek, Bishop of Durham, to the future Edward II, Eltham became a much-frequented royal

LOST PALACES OF THE TUDOR KINGS

Several other major Tudor palaces have been lost to posterity. Nonsuch Palace, near Ewell in Surrey, was so called because it was beyond compare – there was 'none such' anywhere else.

The Tudor palace at Greenwich was knocked down in the 17th century and replaced by the Queen's House and what is now the National Maritime Museum, designed by Inigo Jones and Sir Christopher Wren. The once-magnificent Richmond Palace, beside the Thames on the site of the former Sheen Palace in Surrey, collapsed into ruins.

Nothing remains of Baynard's Castle, which once stood near Upper Thames Street in the City of London. It was extended in the reign of Edward VI and frequented by Elizabeth I, but it burnt down in the Great Fire of London of 1666. Little also remains of Henry VIII's Bridewell Palace (once south of Fleet Street in London), or of his Whitehall Palace, also in central London, or of his Oatlands Palace near Weybridge in Surrey, where he loved to go hunting.

Below: A French chateau in Surrey. Henry VIII's Nonsuch Palace, near Ewell, was a magnificent sight in its Tudor prime.

Above: The cavernous Great Hall at Hampton Court, built by Henry VIII, has a magnificent hammer-beam roof.

house in the 14th century. The French chronicler, Jean Froissart, described Eltham as 'a very magnificent palace', and the poet, Geoffrey Chaucer, as Clerk of the King's Works, was in charge of improvements carried out during Richard II's reign. In 1475–80, Edward IV built the magnificent Great Hall, with its splendid hammer-beam roof.

Henry VIII's reign saw the building of a new chapel and royal accommodation, and the laying out of gardens, an archery range and a bowling green. Elizabeth I gave the royal apartments a new west front. But the palace began to fall into decline in the early 17th century, then was occupied and ransacked by Parliamentary soldiers during the Civil War. In the 1930s, the Great Hall was restored and incorporated into a splendid new Art Deco house built by Stephen and Virginia Courtauld (see page 236).

Right: The Great Hall of King Edward IV (c.1470) stands to the left of the Courtaulds' 1930s house at Eltham Palace.

HEVER CASTLE

THE HOME OF ANNE BOLEYN

The moated and fortified manor house of Hever Castle, near Edenbridge in Kent, was the childhood home of Anne Boleyn, mother of Elizabeth I. Henry VIII was a frequent visitor in the 1520s when he paid court to Anne.

THE BOLEYNS

The first fortified building at Hever was built *c.*1270: the outer defensive wall and forbidding three-storey gatehouse date from this time. A century later, Sir John de Cobham added battlements and a moat complete with drawbridge. In 1459, Sir Geoffrey Bullen, a former Lord Mayor of London, bought the castle. After Sir Geoffrey's grandson, Sir Thomas, married Lady Elizabeth Howard, daughter of the Earl of Surrey, the family (now calling itself Boleyn) rose to prominence. Thomas served Henry VIII as an ambassador and as Treasurer of the King's Household; he was made a Knight of the Garter in 1523 and Earl of Wiltshire in 1529. His two beautiful daughters, Mary and Anne, both served as ladies-in-waiting to Queen Catherine (of Aragon) and both caught the King's eye. Mary was Henry's mistress for a while, before she was eclipsed by Anne, who was beheaded three years after she became queen.

Above: In the early 16th century, Sir Thomas Boleyn, father of a future queen, built a Long Gallery at Hever Castle.

Above: In her youth, Anne served at court abroad. Margaret, Archduchess of Austria, praised Anne as "'bright and pleasant'.

Below: History breathes in the dining hall at Hever Castle, where Henry VIII paid court to the daughter of Sir Thomas Boleyn.

CHANGES OF OWNERSHIP

Two years later, on Thomas's death, Hever Castle was taken over by the Crown. It was soon the possession of another royal, for Henry VIII gave it to Anne of Cleves on their divorce in 1540, as he prepared to wed his fifth wife, Catherine Howard. After Anne's death in 1557, the castle reverted once more to the Crown until Mary Tudor made a gift of it to her courtier, Sir Edward Waldegrave. After many years of obscurity, the castle was bought in 1903 by the wealthy American financier William Waldorf Astor, who thoroughly renovated both house and estate.

MOCK TUDOR

As part of his restoration of Hever, Astor refashioned the adjacent farm buildings into a Tudor-style village, using 16th-century timber from the dismantled Tudor stables. He laid out the gardens in Italian style, complete with grottoes and marble pavements, and excavated a 35-acre (13ha) lake. He meticulously restored the interior of the castle. In the dining room, he fitted the door with a lock that Henry VIII had carried with him to secure his sleeping chamber when he travelled, and, alongside it, an almost identical modern replica.

LEEDS CASTLE

AND ITS TRANSFORMATION BY HENRY VIII

Henry VIII took a great liking to Leeds Castle in Kent, and carried out lavish improvements, transforming it from castle to fortified palace. The King was often in Kent, where he was entertained at Penshurst Place and visited Anne Boleyn at Hever Castle. Leeds Castle had well-established royal links, and had been favoured by kings and queens since Edward I honeymooned there in 1299 (see pages 64–5).

HENRY'S ALTERATIONS

Henry entrusted the work at Leeds Castle to Sir Henry Guildford, who became Comptroller of the Royal Household. He added a storey to the Gloriette Tower on the northern island, installing large windows in the royal apartments there. He erected the Maidens' Tower as space for the maids of honour and refashioned the 75ft (23m) Banqueting Hall, adding a large bow window. The hall now contains a portrait of Henry VIII, and a splendid tapestry of the Magi, *c.*1490.

Below: Henry VIII brought palatial luxury to Leeds Castle, in particular developing the Gloriette Tower and Banqueting Hall.

Above: The Queens' Bedroom was first used by Henry V's wife, Catherine de Valois. Anne Boleyn waited on Catherine of Aragon.

As well as investing heavily in the comfort of Leeds Castle, Henry VIII took care to maintain its defences, for he was always aware of the threat of foreign invasion. Towards the end of his reign, Henry gave Leeds Castle to Sir Anthony St Leger as a reward for his service as Ireland's Lord Deputy. The castle later belonged to John Culpeper, Chancellor of the Exchequer under King Charles I, and then to the Lords Fairfax. In the 20th century, the castle was restored by Lady Olive Baillie.

TUDOR STYLE

By the 1530s and 1540s, memories of the Wars of the Roses were beginning to fade, and the new style in building celebrated the 'Tudor peace' by using increasing numbers of ever-larger windows. One feature particularly characteristic of Tudor houses is the oriel window, which projects out from an upper floor, supported from beneath by a bracket.

Tudor architectural style also moved away from the pointed Gothic arch to a flattened arch, subsequently known as the Tudor arch. Doors were smaller and more ornate, and houses were increasingly fitted with coal-burning fireplaces and chimneys. Within, many houses were fitted with wood panelling, often oak carved to resemble folded cloth, which was later known as 'linen-fold panelling'.

THE TOWER OF LONDON
A ROYAL PRISON AND PALACE

In the medieval era, one king after another dug deep into Treasury funds to strengthen fortifications at the Tower of London, while also developing the site as one of the capital city's royal palaces (see also page 26). Henry VIII enjoyed staying at the Tower, as well as despatching his enemies to the prison quarters there. He and his father, Henry VII, enlarged and improved royal accommodation in the Tower enclosure, but they were to be the last English monarchs to use it as a royal residence.

MEDIEVAL FORTIFICATIONS

William Longchamp, Bishop of Ely, serving as regent while King Richard I was on Crusade, enlarged the Tower complex *c.*1190–1200, improving ditch defences to the north and east, building new sections of the wall and erecting the Bell Tower in the south-west. However, these new fortifications did not save Bishop William when the King's brother John besieged him there; through lack of provisions, the bishop was forced to surrender.

Above: This 15th-century manuscript illumination is the earliest detailed image of the Tower. It depicts the imprisonment of Charles, Duke of Orléans.

MAJOR EVENTS AT THE TOWER

1381 Richard II takes refuge in the Tower during the Peasants' Revolt.
1399 Richard II renounces the crown in the White Tower and is succeeded by Henry IV.
1465 and **1470** Edward IV holds court at the Tower.
1471 Henry VI is imprisoned and probably murdered in the Wakefield Tower.
1483 Richard III celebrates his coronation at the Tower; the 'Princes in the Tower', Edward V and his brother Richard, probably meet their end in the White Tower.
1485 Henry VII holds his victory celebrations at the Tower after winning the crown at the Battle of Bosworth.
1535–42 Henry VIII has many notable figures – including Sir Thomas More, Anne Boleyn, Thomas Cromwell and Catherine Howard – imprisoned in the Tower and then executed there.
1554 Lady Jane Grey, queen for nine days, is executed on Tower Green on the orders of Mary I; Mary's half-sister, Princess Elizabeth (the future Elizabeth I), is imprisoned in the Tower.
1601 Elizabeth I's former favourite, Robert Devereux, Earl of Essex, is the last person to be executed on Tower Green, having fallen out of favour with the Queen.

DEFENSIVE TOWERS

In the early years of Henry III's reign, the Wakefield and Lanthorn towers were built on the riverfront, providing royal accommodation for king and queen respectively, while the Great Hall was extended and improved. In *c.*1238–41, Henry III built a new defensive wall along the east, north and west sides of the complex, with nine defensive towers (including the Devereux, Martin and Salt towers at the corners) and a moat on the outside filled from the Thames. Henry's improvements, which cost more

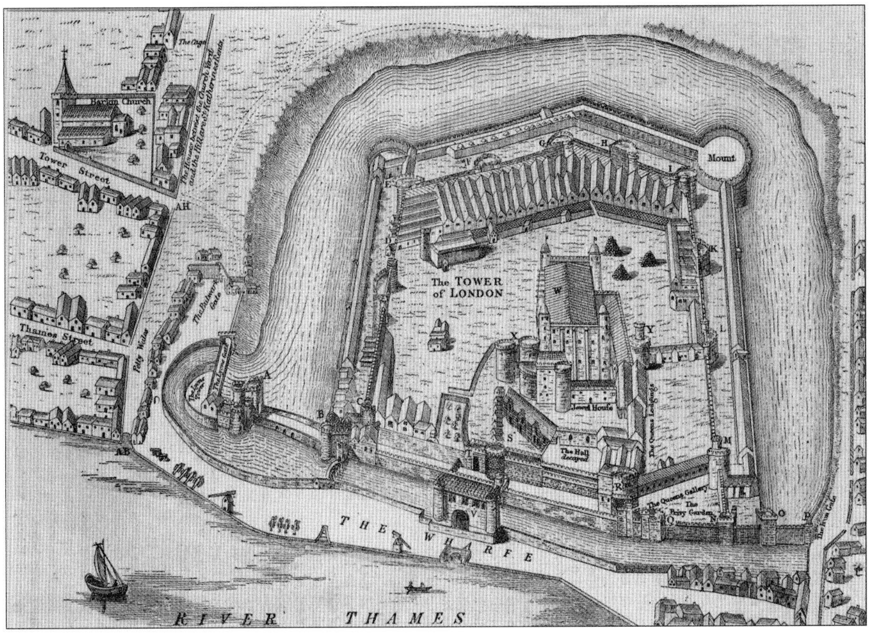

Right: This aerial view of the Tower was made in 1597, late in Elizabeth I's reign, by William Haiward and J. Gascoyne.

than £5,000, doubled the size of the Tower enclosure. He began regular use of the Tower as a prison and kept his extensive menagerie of animals there.

In 1275-85, Edward I further extended the enclosure, filling in his father's moat and building a second curtain wall to create concentric defences. Edward also built Beauchamp, Middle, Byward and St Thomas's towers, as well as a royal mint within the complex. Edward II did little further building work at the Tower, but he did move the royal accommodation from the Wakefield and St Thomas's towers to the Lanthorn Tower.

TUDOR IMPROVEMENTS

Henry VIII carried out extensive improvements to royal lodgings at the Tower. His father, Henry VII, had enlarged the royal accommodation in the Lanthorn Tower, providing a Tudor Long Gallery, a private room and a Library, as well as a garden. Henry VIII liked to stay in the improved Lanthorn Tower. He also built additional royal lodgings near the White Tower, erected the half-timbered King's House, which can still be seen today in the inner bailey's south-west corner, and rebuilt the Chapel Royal of St Peter ad Vincula (St Peter in Chains).

Meanwhile, Thomas Cromwell improved the defences of the fortified complex, and in the reign of Henry VIII the Tower saw many celebrated prisoners go to their deaths. In the space of just seven years, Sir Thomas More, Cardinal John Fisher, Anne Boleyn, Thomas Cromwell and Catherine Howard were all imprisoned in the Tower before their execution.

Above: Traitors' Gate – the riverbank water-gate at the foot of St Thomas's Tower – was built by Edward I in 1275–9.

Left: This view of the Tower from the river shows the Traitors' Gate in the centre foreground. All prisoners disembarked here and entered the Tower through this gate.

SULGRAVE MANOR
AND GEORGE WASHINGTON'S FAMILY

The sturdy, unpretentious manor house at Sulgrave, in Northamptonshire, was built in the early Tudor years by a direct ancestor of George Washington, the first President of the United States of America. Lawrence Washington, younger son of a prominent Lancashire family, was born *c.*1500. He became a wool merchant and bought the Priory of St Andrew, Northampton, from the Crown in 1539, following Henry VIII's Dissolution of the Monasteries.

Below: The compact south front of Sulgrave Manor, built of local limestone by Lawrence Washington, faces a pleasant garden.

THE ORIGINAL BUILDING

After his first wife, Elizabeth, died childless, Lawrence married Amy, daughter of landowner Robert Pargiter, and settled at Sulgrave, where he established Sulgrave Manor, which is a fine example of a smaller Tudor country house.

The house was built of local limestone, with a wide south frontage, a kitchen and buttery, a Great Hall, and above it a Great Chamber and two smaller private chambers. All these parts survive and can be seen today. Finds of what appear to have been Tudor-era foundation stones as much as 50ft (15m) west of the current house suggest that the original dwelling was considerably larger than the surviving house. The Great Hall has a stone floor, and its Tudor fireplace contains a salt cupboard carved with the initials of Lawrence Washington.

Above: George Washington, first President of the United States, traced his family roots to a Northamptonshire manor house.

'ER' AND STARS AND STRIPES

Lawrence added an entrance porch to the house's south front after 1558. Over the doorway he set in plaster the royal arms of England and the letters 'ER', to indicate 'Elizabeth Regina' in honour of Henry VIII's daughter Elizabeth I, who had ascended to the throne. The doorway spandrels were decorated with the Washington family arms: two stripes and three stars. Some people have suggested that this design was one of the inspirations for the 'stars and stripes' of the American flag.

Lawrence's eldest son, Robert Washington, who was born in 1544, subsequently inherited Sulgrave Manor, along with 1,250 acres (506ha) of farmland. Robert was George Washington's great-great-great-great-grandfather.

HELLEN'S, MUCH MARCLE

The charming country house of Hellen's in the Herefordshire village of Much Marcle near Ledbury was once known as Hellion's Home or Hellinham Castle. It was owned by the lords Audley, earls of Gloucester in the 14th century; a certain Walter Helyon leased the estate and gave his name to the house.

Hellen's lower and older wing contains a venerable Great Hall, refurbished after an 18th-century fire, with a chimney hood decorated with the emblems of the 'Black Prince', son of Edward III. According to tradition, this was fitted in the 14th century by James Audley, companion of the 'Black Prince'. The larger wing is Tudor and contains a splendid oak chimney-piece.

In the 16th century, the then occupier, a Roman Catholic named Richard Walwyn, decorated an upstairs room in this wing with gold and red brocade in honour of Mary Tudor, later Queen Mary I, who was staying nearby in Ludlow Castle. The fireplace is decorated with Mary's initials and coat of arms.

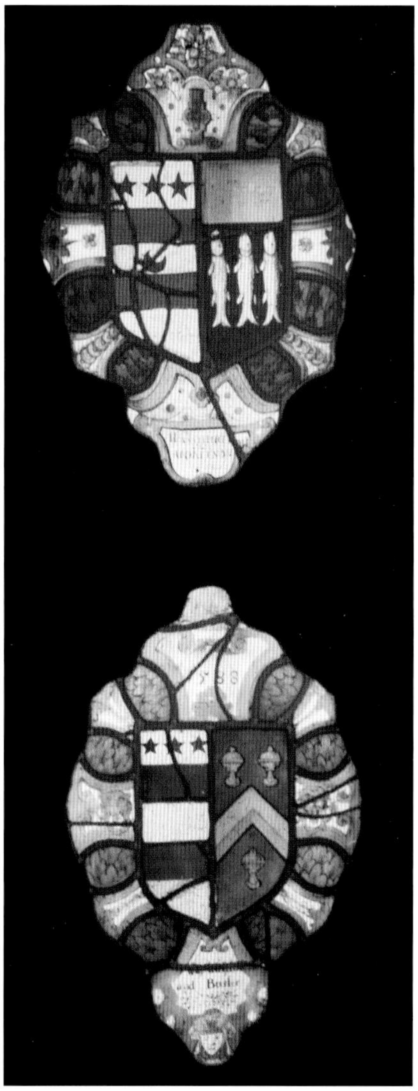

Right: These stained-glass panels feature the Washington and Kitson arms and the Washington and Butler Arms, 1588.

LATER ALTERATIONS

A north wing, set at right angles to Lawrence Washington's manor, was added *c.*1700 by the then owner, John Hodges. It contains the Great Kitchen and the Oak Parlour, on the ground floor, beneath two sleeping chambers, now known as the White Bedroom and the Chintz Bedroom. Another extension, the west wing, was built in 1929 when the house was being restored.

WASHINGTON'S DESCENDANTS

Lawrence Washington's grandson, another Lawrence, became a rector at Purleigh in Essex. But during the English Civil War, the staunchly royalist Reverend Washington was evicted by Parliament from his living, and died in poverty. His son, John, sailed to the English colony ofVirginia in 1656 and married Anne Pope from the Cliffs, a settlement in northern Virginia. They held an estate of 700 acres (385ha) at Mattox Creek Farm. Their eldest son, Lawrence, became a member of Virginia's House of Burgesses and had three children by Mildred Warner. The second, Augustine, was the father of George Washington, the first US President, born on 22 February 1732.

Below: The Great Bedchamber is part of the original manor house rather than the 18th-century extension. This picture is c.1910.

Below: Honouring the Queen. The royal arms of England and the initials 'ER' decorate the south porch, added c.1560.

EDINBURGH CASTLE
AND HOLYROODHOUSE

Edinburgh Castle was a well-established stronghold and royal dwelling by the latter years of the 14th century, when the future Robert II built David's Tower, containing royal apartments (see page 71). In the mid-1430s, James I built a new Great Chamber, probably alongside the royal accommodation in the Tower. His successor, James II, brought the great siege gun of Mons Meg to the castle, which assumed an increasingly important role as a royal artillery.

Left: Edinburgh Castle, on its rocky summit, proved too small for a sufficiently grand royal base, so Scotland's kings instead developed Holyrood Abbey into a palace.

GREAT CHAMBER, GREAT HALL

James IV extended the royal accommodation into the southern part of the rocky summit on which the castle stands, reconstructed James I's Great Chamber and built a Great Hall. These two buildings stand along the east and south sides of a courtyard (now Crown Square), with the 14th-century St Mary's Church along the north side (now the Scottish National War Memorial) and artillery buildings to the west. The extended Great Chamber had windows facing east, and must have provided fine views of the burgh below and the countryside beyond. The Great Hall was quite small, at 82 x 32ft (25 x 10m), because its size was limited by its location. It has large mullioned windows on the south side and a hammer-beam roof.

HOLYROODHOUSE

Holyrood Palace was originally part of a monastery. David I founded the Augustinian Priory of the Holy Rude in 1128, and after Edinburgh was made the capital of Scotland in the 15th century, the abbey guest house (Holyroodhouse) was increasingly used by the royal family, eventually eclipsing the castle as the city's foremost royal residence (see page 152). Set among gardens and orchards, it provided more space and comfort than the cramped royal palace of Edinburgh Castle, perched on its rocky summit above the burgh.

James II was born in Holyroodhouse in October 1430, held his coronation and marriage in the abbey church and was buried there in 1460. James IV built a new palace at Holyrood in 1501–4, but little or nothing survives of this palace, which was extensively rebuilt by James V. In 1528–32, he built a great rectangular tower with round corner turrets as a royal lodging. This impressive building is still standing today in the palace front. Then, in 1535–6, he rebuilt the west wing of James IV's palace, and adapted the north and south wings.

Below: James V built a Great Tower at the north-west corner of Holyroodhouse in 1528–32 and a new west front in 1535–6.

Below: The royal arms of James V of Scots sit proudly on the wall at Holyroodhouse. James was buried in the abbey in 1543.

FALKLAND PALACE
AND STIRLING CASTLE

Falkland Palace began as a castle built by the Macduffs, earls of Fife, probably in the 13th century. James II extended the castle and frequently visited it to hunt deer and wild boar. After 1458, when he granted a charter, it was known as Falkland Palace. James IV built a new palace complex, to the south of the royal castle, in 1501–13; then James V remodelled and rebuilt it, using French and Italian craftsmen, in 1537–41, to create Scotland's first palace in the continental Renaissance style.

James IV's palace was laid out around a courtyard, with a Great Hall on the north side, royal apartments on the east side, and a chapel and vestry to the south; entry was from the west, providing access to the adjacent burgh. James V remodelled the eastern block, building a new front that led on to the courtyard, entirely reconstructing the southern (chapel) section and adding an impressive gatehouse at its west end, designed to function as a new entrance. He also built, in 1539, a real tennis court, to the north of the palace. This can still be seen today and is Scotland's oldest court. James V's daughter, Mary, Queen of Scots, was a frequent visitor to Falkland Palace after her return to Scotland from French exile in 1561.

Below: At Stirling, James V's craftsmen brought the elegance of Italian-French Renaissance architecture to Scotland.

Above: Elements of the design at Falkland derive from that of the chateau at Joinville, built by the Duke of Guise in c.1530–40.

STIRLING CASTLE

At Stirling, James V built a magnificent Renaissance-style palace as part of the royal castle. The original castle was 11th-century and, as at Falkland, was extensively rebuilt by James IV, who built a vast Great Hall *c.*1498–1503, which measured 128 x 36ft (39 x 11m) and 54ft (16.5m) high, with no fewer than five fireplaces.

In 1538–42, his son, James V, built a lavish three-storey palace within the castle complex, containing apartments for himself and his queen, Mary of Guise. This included an extraordinary Royal Presence Chamber with a ceiling that originally had 100 carved oak heads, some of which survive. The building's principal façade contains tall, elegant windows and niches holding sculptured figures.

RENAISSANCE STYLE

The courtyard façades of the eastern (royal accommodation) and southern (chapel) ranges at Falkland Palace feature bays with medallion heads, dormer windows and statuary. Together, these make an elegant exposition of the latest French-Italian Renaissance style that would have appealed to James V's French wives – first Madeleine of Valois and then Mary of Guise. Scholars compare the bay design to those of the chateaux of Fontainebleu and Villers-Cotterêts, owned by Madeleine's father, the French king, Francis I.

DEAL CASTLE
COASTAL DEFENCES

Henry VIII built the low-lying artillery fort of Deal Castle, in Kent, as one of a string of coastal fortifications built around England's south coast in the later 1530s and early 1540s. Following his break with the Church of Rome, he feared invasion by the armies of a Franco-Spanish Catholic alliance brokered by the Pope.

SOUTH-COAST FORTS

Henry built three forts at Sandown, Deal and Walmer to cover anchorage off the Downs coast. They were built in 18 months using press-ganged labour and stone from local religious houses suppressed by the Dissolution of the Monasteries, including the former Carmelite priory at Sandwich. Earth bulwarks linked the three forts into a single defensive system. Today, little remains of the Sandown fort, and the defences at Walmer were later transformed into a splendid coastal residence, the official dwelling of the Lord Warden of the Cinque Ports, and the place where the Duke of Wellington, holder of this position, died in 1852. But the fort of Deal stands almost exactly as Henry VIII built it – with the exception of some battlements added in the mid-18th century.

Above: In the late 1530s, when he built these forts, Henry VIII was in his late 40s, less than a decade from his death (1547).

THE TUDOR ROSE

Deal Castle is best viewed from the air. It was designed with a central circular tower and two tiers of semicircular bastions, giving the whole the shape of a double clover-leaf or Tudor rose. The circular walls had the advantage of deflecting cannon shot better than flat ones with vulnerable corners. The fort stood within a wide and deep moat, crossed by a drawbridge. Its entrance was formidable, with a portcullis, five murder-holes giving on to the entrance passageway from above, and an extremely thick oak door studded with iron.

The castle was a vast gun fortification with more than 200 cannon and gun ports, yet it was designed to be garrisoned by just 24 men plus a captain. They were equipped to withstand a siege: the basement contained a well and storage areas for food and drink, while the ground floor housed a bakery

Below: Tudor rose or double clover? The coastal fort at Deal in Kent has an impressive outline when viewed from the air.

Above: At Pendennis Castle in Cornwall, the gun tower rises above the two-storey block containing the castellan's rooms.

and kitchen. Also on the ground floor were living quarters for the garrison, with more spacious accommodation on the first floor for the captain and also his senior subordinates.

Deal Castle fulfilled its intended primary role as a deterrent and was not attacked in the 1530s. In fact, the only military action it has seen in its entire history was in the English Civil War, when, originally garrisoned by Parliamentarians, it surrendered to Royalists, and then was besieged and recaptured with a loss of 80 Royalist lives in August 1648.

CORNISH STRONGHOLDS

Henry's coastal forts also included two handsome examples on Falmouth Bay in Cornwall: Pendennis Castle and St Mawes Castle, guarding the entrance to the River Fal estuary. Pendennis Castle was built in 1540–45: it was a keep within a curtain wall on Pendennis Head, with a smaller fortification, Little Dennis, on the rocks at the foot of the promontory. The keep combined a three-storey circular gun tower with a two-storey rectangular block that contained the accommodation for the castle governor. These buildings were enclosed by a low but stoutly defended curtain wall, and the entrance to the castle was via a drawbridge across a dry moat and guarded by a portcullis.

The headland was enclosed by an outer curtain wall, creating a 4-acre (1.6ha) enclosure, in 1598. This followed Spanish sea raids on Cornwall in 1595 and was carried out amid fears that plans were afoot for a second Armada on the tenth anniversary of the first.

Across the bay, St Mawes Castle consisted of a circular gun tower with three semicircular bastions around it so that, from above, the structure looked like a clover-leaf. Cannon were positioned on the roof of the tower and on the bastions, and also within the buildings to be fired through gun ports.

THE SIEGE OF PENDENNIS

Pendennis Castle was the last Royalist fort in England to surrender during the Civil War. Sir Thomas Fairfax and the Parliamentarian New Model Army arrived in Cornwall in early March 1646 and took St Mawes Castle without a fight on 12 March. But when he came to Pendennis Castle and demanded the surrender of the garrison, the 70-year-old castle commander, Colonel John Arundell, defiantly declared: 'The Castle was entrusted to my government by His Majesty.... my age of 70 calls me hence shortly.... I shall desire no other testimony to follow my departure than my...loyalty to His Majesty.... I resolve that I will here bury myself before I deliver up this Castle to those who fight against His Majesty.' The siege began, and remarkably the castle, although blockaded by sea and land, survived for nearly five months before surrendering on 17 August. Two days later, Royalist Raglan Castle in Wales also surrendered.

Below: St Mawes Castle was vulnerable to a land attack, but was in an ideal position for defending against invasion by sea.

SYON HOUSE
AND SUDELEY CASTLE

The splendid Syon House, now surrounded by London's westward sprawl at Brentford in Middlesex, was built during the reign of Edward VI by his uncle Edward, Duke of Somerset, Lord Protector. Somerset built a three-storey building with battlements and angle turrets around a central courtyard. His house stood on the foundations of the abbey church that had belonged to the convent on the site.

The Lord Protector also established one of England's first botanical gardens at Syon House, in the care of his personal physician, Dr William Turner.

Below: The 'Wizard' Earl built this superb 136ft (41m) Long Gallery at Syon House in the late 1500s. The sumptuous décor was designed by Robert Adam in the 1760s.

While working on the garden at Syon House, Dr Turner wrote *The Names of Herbes*, published in 1548. Dr Turner is believed to have planted the mulberry trees, introduced to England from Persia (modern Iran) only half a century earlier, that still thrive at Syon House.

A COLOURFUL HISTORY

The land on which Syon House was built had originally belonged to a Bridgettine convent, founded at Twickenham by Henry V in 1415. In the 1530s, the nuns' father confessor, Richard Reynolds, refused to accept Henry VIII's new status as Supreme Head of the Church of England and was brutally executed, his body later placed on the gateway to the abbey. Henry dissolved the Syon convent – named in honour of Mount Zion – and took possession of the building and lands in 1539. He incarcerated his fifth queen, Catherine Howard, at Syon House prior to her execution in 1542. After his death in 1547, Henry's coffin rested overnight at Syon *en route* from Westminster to Windsor. The next morning, the coffin was found to have burst open, and dogs were gnawing the royal corpse. Some people regarded this as divine retribution for Henry's desecration of the abbey.

Somerset was ousted as Lord Protector in 1549 and executed on trumped-up treason charges in 1552. His successor, John Dudley, Duke of Northumberland, took possession of Syon House. At Syon, Northumberland's daughter-in-law, Lady Jane Grey, agreed to the plan to make her queen on the death of Edward VI. When this scheme

SUDELEY CASTLE, GLOUCESTERSHIRE

The 15th-century Sudeley Castle in Gloucestershire was rebuilt in the late 1540s by Lord Thomas Seymour. Thomas was the brother of the Duke of Somerset, Lord Protector to Edward VI; their sister, Jane, had been Henry VIII's third wife, who had died giving birth to Edward in 1537, making the brothers the young king's uncles. In addition, Thomas married Henry VIII's sixth wife and widow, Catherine Parr, following the King's death.

Thomas and Catherine moved into Sudeley Castle, where they built a new set of rooms for Catherine's use. She gave birth at Sudeley to Lord Thomas's daughter, Mary, on 30 August 1548, but died of puerperal fever a week later and was buried in St Mary's Church near the castle.

After Lord Thomas Seymour's execution for treason in 1549, Sudeley Castle eventually passed into the hands of John Brydges, Lord Chandos, who entertained Elizabeth I at the castle three times.

Above: Sudeley Castle's 14 acres (6ha) of gardens have been lovingly redeveloped.

Below: Henry VIII, Elizabeth I and Charles I all paid visits to Sudeley. Charles's nephew Prince Rupert had his headquarters there in the Civil War.

failed, and Edward was succeeded by his sister, Queen Mary I, Northumberland, his son, Lord Guildford Dudley, and Lady Jane herself were all executed.

The Bridgettine nuns briefly came back from exile to live at Syon House under Mary I's rule, but in 1558 were banished once more. Then, in 1594, Syon House came into the possession of Henry Percy, 9th Earl of Northumberland, whose descendants still own the house today.

THE 'WIZARD' EARL

Henry redecorated Syon House internally, built new stables and erected a fine Tudor Long Gallery. Nicknamed 'the Wizard' because of his experiments with alchemy, he was a great scholar, friend of Sir Walter Raleigh and acquaintance of Shakespeare, Ben Jonson and Sir Edmund Spenser. However, on 4 November 1605, he entertained at Syon House a Roman Catholic cousin, Thomas Percy, who was implicated in the following day's 'Gunpowder Plot' to blow up the Houses of Parliament. Considered guilty by association, Northumberland was thrown into the Tower of London by James I, where he remained for 15 years.

His son Algernon, 10th Earl of Northumberland, commissioned Inigo Jones to design and build an arcade on Syon House's east side. The 10th Earl served as governor of Charles I's son James, Duke of York (the future James II); in 1646, the King's children stayed at Syon House to escape the London plague. The 10th Earl was a great patron of the arts, notably of the artists Sir Anthony van Dyck and Sir Peter Lely.

A NEW LOOK

A little over a century later, in the 1760s, the 1st Duke of Northumberland commissioned Robert Adam to redesign the interior of Syon House (see pages 196–7). He hired 'Capability' Brown to refashion the park. The Duke had inherited the estate through his marriage to the Percy heiress Elizabeth Seymour in 1750. He felt that Syon House, which he considered 'ruinous and inconvenient', needed thoroughly remodelling.

Below: Somerset built Syon House as a castle dwelling, with battlements and turrets. It sits in 40 acres (16ha) of gardens.

CHAPTER SIX

'PRODIGY HOUSES': THE AGE OF GLORIANA

*c.*1550–1600

In 1555, leading Elizabethan statesman Sir William Cecil began building a country mansion sufficiently grand to receive and entertain his queen, Elizabeth I. He spared no effort and no expense in creating the magnificent Burghley House in Lincolnshire. At around the same time, his fellow courtier and friend Sir Christopher Hatton was building a similarly extravagant house at Holdenby in Northamptonshire.

Cecil and Hatton were not unusual. Several Elizabethan noblemen sank their wealth into the creation of 'prodigy houses' – country palaces fit for the Queen. Sir William More rebuilt his manor house of Loseley House in Surrey, reputedly on the instructions of Elizabeth herself; the Queen's great favourite, Robert Dudley, Earl of Leicester, lavished funds on Kenilworth Castle in Warwickshire in order to welcome his royal patron there; Sir John Thynne built the magnificent Longleat House in Wiltshire; and Sir Francis Willoughby sank his fortune into the extravagantly ornamented Wollaton Hall in Nottinghamshire.

However, not all these houses achieved their objective. Sir William Cecil entertained Elizabeth and her court on 12 occasions at Burghley and his other houses. Elizabeth was entertained at Kenilworth Castle on several occasions, visited Longleat House even before it was finished and stayed at Loseley House at least twice. Yet, despite being a royal favourite, Sir Christopher Hatton – for all his devoted expenditure on Holdenby – was never honoured by a visit from the 'Virgin Queen'.

Left: A house, a prodigy – but not a home. Sir William Cecil was at court so much that he seldom lived at Burghley House.

BURGHLEY HOUSE

'E' FOR ELIZABETH

Sir William Cecil built his extravagant 'prodigy house' on the Burghley estate, which his father, Richard Cecil, had purchased after it had been seized from Peterborough Abbey on the Dissolution of the Monasteries under Henry VIII. Construction took 32 years, from 1555 to 1587.

During this period, Cecil proved an indispensable adviser to Elizabeth I, establishing himself as the leading politician of his day. Born in 1520, he had begun his career as secretary to the Protector, Edward Seymour, Duke of Somerset, during Edward VI's reign; on Elizabeth's accession in 1558, he was appointed Secretary of State, then made 1st Baron Burghley in 1571 and Lord High Treasurer in 1572.

PATRONS AND BUILDERS

The great houses of the Elizabethan era did not have architects in the sense in which we use the word. The people responsible for the shape the houses took were the master masons, the surveyors and their patrons, who commissioned the building. The patrons – renowned figures such as Sir William Cecil, Sir Thomas Thynne of Longleat House and Bess of Hardwick, who built Hardwick Hall in Derbyshire – were intimately involved in the design and construction process. The houses were often the three-dimensional stone embodiment of a 'device' or conceit: Burghley House was a giant 'E' to honour Elizabeth, while Hardwick Hall was a Greek cross doubled with a square placed upon it. Such a 'device' would have been the idea of the patron, in a sense their signature, an expression of their character, a statement of their intellectual and artistic prowess. The surveyors and master masons were charged with bringing these ideas into three solid dimensions. Among the surveyors, the greatest was Robert Smythson, who oversaw the building of many of the finest 'prodigy houses', including Longleat House, Hardwick Hall and Wollaton Hall.

Right: Statesman and patron. Men such as William Cecil saw a great house as a lasting expression of their character and wit.

A GIANT 'E'

Cecil was often absent from Burghley House, for his court and diplomatic responsibilities kept him very busy, but the building work was carried out largely according to his designs – with some assistance from a certain Henryk, an Antwerp mason. In *c.*1555–65, Cecil raised the east side of the house, then proceeded in 1577–87 to lay out the remainder of the house in the shape of a long courtyard, with a Great Hall at one end and a grand gatehouse at the other. The unusually high Great Hall was built with a splendid double-hammer-beam roof and notably elongated windows. Overall, the house took the form of a giant letter 'E' in honour of Elizabeth, although this touch can no longer be appreciated because the north-west wing was demolished in the mid-18th century.

Left: Burghley's size and roofline inspired Daniel Defoe's 1722 remark that it was 'more like a town than a house'.

Few other alterations have been made to the exterior of Burghley House since the completion of Cecil's work. It has splendid façades of hard 'Barnack rag', a limestone quarried nearby in Northamptonshire, with great expanses of glass in its transomed and mullioned windows.

Above: The George Rooms (so called because they were decorated for a visit by the Prince Regent) contain paintings by the great Italian baroque artist Antonio Verrio.

COMPLEX ROOFSCAPE

Burghley has a distinctive silhouette because its skyline is crowded with chimneys, cupolas and obelisks. Its lead roofing covers ¾ acre (over 3,000sq m). When English novelist, Daniel Defoe, visited Burghley House in 1722, he was particularly struck by the roof, which made Burghley look 'more like a town than a house...the towers and pinnacles, so high and placed at such a great distance from one another, look like so many distant parish churches in a town, and a large spire covered with lead, over the clock in the centre, looks like the Cathedral, or chief Church of that town'.

WEALTH OF ART

More than a century after its construction, Burghley's interior was transformed when Sir William Cecil's descendant, the 5th Earl of Exeter, embarked on a redecoration programme of the public and most important private rooms in the Baroque style. Exquisite plaster ceilings, probably designed by Edward Martin, and delicate carved wood panelling by Thomas Young and Grinling Gibbons were installed. A series of ceiling and wall paintings by the Italian artist Antonio Verrio adorn the suite now known as the George Rooms. His most spectacular work is in the Heaven Room.

The 5th and 9th Earls of Exeter, both great travellers and art collectors, amassed a remarkable collection of paintings now displayed in Burghley House. These include works by Pieter Brueghel, Rembrandt and Thomas Gainsborough, a portrait of Henry VIII by Joos van Cleve, portraits of the 5th Earl and of Antonio Verrio by Sir Godfrey Kneller, and a chapel altarpiece by Veronese.

GATES AND GROUNDS

In the late 17th century, Frenchman Jean Tijou added splendid wrought-iron gates to the principal gatehouse. In the mid-18th century, the 9th Earl of Exeter commissioned Lancelot 'Capability' Brown, both as an architect and to landscape the 300-acre (120ha) park. At this time, the house's north-west wing was demolished to allow better views of Brown's parkland from the south front.

Left: The vast kitchen at Burghley House dates back to Tudor times. It also contains 260 Georgian–Victorian copper utensils.

KENILWORTH CASTLE

ELIZABETH AND LEICESTER

In 1563, Elizabeth I granted Kenilworth Castle, a 12th-century Norman stronghold in Warwickshire, to her great favourite, Robert Dudley, Earl of Leicester. He built a gatehouse and elegant residential quarters to make the historic fortifications sufficiently grand for the Queen. She visited him at Kenilworth Castle in 1566, 1568, 1572 and 1575.

NORMAN ORIGINS

The original castle was built *c.*1122 by Geoffrey de Clinton, King Henry I's Chamberlain, on land granted to him by the King. Geoffrey built a simple motte-and-bailey castle, with a wooden tower enclosed by an earthwork bank. His works were remade in stone, probably by his son, Geoffrey de Clinton II, in the form of a two-storey stone keep with walls up to 20ft (6m) thick covering the original mound.

Above: This aerial view of the ruins of Kenilworth Castle shows the remains of the ornamental gardens laid out by Leicester.

Below: A reconstruction of the estate in the time of Elizabeth I. Leicester's Kenilworth was more country house than castle.

WATER DEFENCES

The castle passed into royal hands, and was greatly extended in 1210–15 by King John, who built an outer wall with defensive towers and a fortified dam that blocked several local streams to create a wide lake around the castle that covered 100 acres (40ha). The water defences played a key role in 1266, during the civil war between King Henry III and his son, Prince Edward, and rebel lords led by Simon de Montfort. The castle had been given to de Montfort by Henry, and when civil war broke out, de Montfort's supporters were besieged by a royalist force. The defenders held out for nine months, finally surrendering with honour. Castle-builders were impressed by the effectiveness of the lake in preventing attackers tunnelling into the castle or undermining its walls.

ONE HUNDRED KNIGHTS

In 1279, Kenilworth Castle was the scene of a famous jousting tournament held by Roger de Mortimer. In celebration of Arthurian chivalry, Roger established a 'Round Table' at the castle, and a company of 100 knights competed before an audience of 100 ladies on the lake dam.

SHAKESPEARE AT KENILWORTH

Above: Leicester and Elizabeth – an earl courts a queen in a summer garden. The Arcadian romance that inspired Shakespeare touches the English soul.

According to popular tradition, an 11-year-old William Shakespeare travelled from Stratford-upon-Avon to nearby Kenilworth Castle to witness the extravagant theatrical pageantry laid on by the Earl of Leicester for Queen Elizabeth in July 1575.

As part of the extravaganza, Elizabeth watched, and apparently greatly enjoyed, a performance of a play, *The Slaughter of the Danes at Hock Tide*, by an acting troupe named 'The Men of Coventry'; there were 'Arcadian' pageants featuring figures from classical mythology and English folklore. Some writers suggest that the magic of Shakespeare's play *A Midsummer Night's Dream* derives in part from his treasured memories of the Queen's visit to Kenilworth Castle.

The earls of Lancaster came into possession of the castle, and in 1389–94 Edward III's son John of Gaunt, 1st Duke of Lancaster, built a magnificent Great Hall and luxurious accommodation in the castle's inner ward. His grandson, Henry V, built a banqueting house at the end of the lake, or Great Mere. Henry VIII later rebuilt this house within the castle precincts.

Below: John of Gaunt's Hall (left) and Leicester's Buildings (right) sandwich the Saintlowe Tower (part of the Great Hall).

LEICESTER'S ALTERATIONS

After receiving the castle from Queen Elizabeth I, the Earl of Leicester created a grand entrance via a gatehouse to the north, added numerous windows to the keep, in the process of updating it to make it suitable for entertaining rather than siege defence, and built a residential suite (later known as Leicester's Buildings) to the south of the inner curtain wall. He also laid out a formal Elizabethan garden within the outer bailey.

In 1575, as part of her 'summer progress' around her kingdom, Elizabeth stayed at Kenilworth for 18 days, being entertained at Leicester's expense with pageants, jousting, dancing, theatrical shows, hunting and feasting. Leicester gave Elizabeth an entire wing and even had a garden laid out beneath her bedroom window when she complained of not being able to see the castle gardens from her private chambers. The visit reputedly cost Leicester £1,000 per day.

THE LOSS OF THE LAKE

During the Civil War, Parliamentary forces took the castle, and afterwards the north curtain wall and the keep's north wall were destroyed and the water defences drained. In later years, the castle crumbled into a romantic ruin, with only Leicester's gatehouse remaining habitable. The other major buildings, such as the keep and John of Gaunt's Great Hall, stood as evocative reminders of Kenilworth's importance in the Middle Ages and the Elizabethan age.

CRATHES CASTLE
AND THE SCOTTISH TOWER HOUSE

Built by the Burnett family in 1553–94, Crathes Castle in Aberdeenshire is a commanding example of the 16th-century Scottish tower house. In England, the long years of the 'Tudor peace' allowed wealthy merchants and landowners to concentrate on comfort and beauty rather than fortification, to build unfortified country houses rather than castles. But in Scotland, where times remained more turbulent, landowners built tower houses, which combined defensive capabilities with domestic comfort.

Crathes was begun by Alexander Burnett, descendant of the powerful, originally Anglo-Saxon, Burnard family, who were rewarded for service to King Robert I the Bruce with the barony of Leys and the position of Royal Forester in the Forest of Drum. Family legend has it that the Horn of Leys, an ivory hunting horn encrusted with jewels and now displayed in the High Hall of Crathes Castle, was given to a Burnett ancestor, also called Alexander, by the Bruce himself and came with the Forester's office. Crathes Castle was completed by yet another Alexander, great-grandson of the original builder.

GRANITE TOWER

Crathes Castle is a great L-shaped granite tower, its rooms piled one on top of another. The lower parts of the granite walls are plain, and rise, tapering inwards slightly, to finish in a 'fairytale' explosion of gables, corbels and turrets at roof level.

The design of the tower house was dictated partly by defensive needs and partly by the shortage of wood in Scotland. Large roofs required a great deal of timber, so the tower house enclosed a large amount of living space beneath a small roof. At Crathes, the roof covers 1,800sq ft (548sq m); stone vaulting rather than timber supports the whole of the first floor and most of the second. The High Hall, now floored with modern timber, originally had stone flags. Tower houses typically had a 'barmkin', or defensive wall, enclosing land at their base.

The tower at Crathes originally rose above a side wing erected to provide extra living space. This block was rebuilt as the Queen Anne Wing in the early 18th century by Thomas Burnett, who, as the father of 21 children, was in need of plentiful family accommodation. Thomas also removed the barmkin,

Below: Generations of Burnetts poured their energies into building Crathes Castle. The family lived there until 1966.

SCOTTISH BARONIAL STYLE

The Scottish tower house was one of the key inspirations for the 'Baronial style' in Scottish architecture that was in vogue from the early 1800s until *c.*1920. The Baronial style, which also drew key elements from Gothic Revival buildings, used towers with small turrets, stepped gables and crenellations to create the appearance of a 'fairytale castle'. Important examples of the Scottish Baronial style include Balmoral Castle, Skibo Castle in the Highlands and, in a modernized form, Castle Drogo in Devon.

Below: The Baronial-style Castle Fraser near Aberdeen was built by Michael Fraser, 6th Laird, beginning in 1575.

planting Irish yew hedges and an avenue of lime trees in its place. These plantings formed the basis of a beautiful garden developed by Sir James and Lady Burnett in the early 20th century. Unfortunately, Thomas's other legacy, the Queen Anne Wing, burned down in 1966. It was replaced by a modern two-storey range.

PAINTED CEILINGS

Crathes Castle is particularly notable for its original painted ceilings, seen to great advantage in the Chamber of the Muses, the Green Lady's Room and the Chamber of the Nine Worthies. The latter room, completed in 1602, features images of classical figures Julius Caesar, Alexander the Great and the ancient Greek hero, Hector; Old Testament figures Joshua, King David and Judas Maccabeus; and such legendary and historical figures as King Arthur, Charlemagne and Godfrey de Bouillon. An inscription translates as 'Good reader, tell me as you pass, which of these men the most valiant was?' The other ceilings are decorated with figures, abstract patterns, moral inscriptions and biblical and poetic quotations. Another fine ceiling, found in the Long Gallery, is panelled in oak and is unique in the whole of Scotland.

Right: The Chamber of the Nine Worthies at Crathes Castle has a thought-provoking decoration on its beautifully painted ceiling.

Below: The staircase at Craigievar Castle was too narrow for a coffin. So although William Forbes entered the castle by door, he finally had to leave by window.

HAUNTED ROOM

The Green Lady's Room at Crathes Castle is so called because it is said to be haunted by the ghost of a young woman dressed in green and carrying a baby in her arms. Legend has it that she was a noble guest at the castle who was made pregnant by a servant. An unfortunate event involving the child may once have taken place in the room, for an infant's skeleton was found by workmen beneath the hearthstone.

CRAIGIEVAR CASTLE

Near to Crathes Castle, also in Aberdeenshire, stands the handsome six-storey, pink-granite Craigievar Castle. Finished in 1626, it was built in an L-shape by a prosperous merchant named William Forbes, brother of the Bishop of Aberdeen.

William, known as 'Danzig Willie' because he had made his fortune in trading with that port (now known as Gdansk), had purchased the land and half-finished castle in 1610 from the Mortimer family. He poured his wealth into this magnificent romantic castle, which survives virtually unchanged today as another superb example of the Scots tower house.

LONGLEAT HOUSE
AND THE CLASSICAL RENAISSANCE

Longleat House in Wiltshire, one of the greatest of the 'prodigy houses', was constructed by Sir John Thynne *c.*1567–80. In 1575, Elizabeth stayed there during her great summer progress.

Thynne, a Shropshire farmer's son, born *c.*1512, had made his name and fortune during the reigns of Henry VIII and Edward VI. He served Edward Seymour, Earl of Hertford, later Duke of Somerset and Lord Protector in Edward VI's boyhood. Thynne was knighted by Somerset on the battlefield at Pinkie, where the Duke's English troops routed a Scots army under the Earl of Arran on 10 September 1547. When Somerset was disgraced and executed, Thynne was cast in the Tower of London for two years and fined £6,000.

The house in which Elizabeth stayed was Thynne's second on the site. He bought the Augustinian Priory at Longleat for £55 in *c.*1540 and began building there in 1546. His first house burned to the ground in 1567, but with typical tenacity he began rebuilding it. The design is Thynne's own, although to realize it he employed a number of surveyors, including Frenchman Allan Maynard and Englishman Robert Smythson – the latter subsequently responsible for Hardwick Hall.

Above: Tudor majesty. Longleat, celebrated as perhaps England's first classical country house, is largely unchanged externally.

Thynne created England's first house in the Italianate, or Renaissance, style. The layout was original: previously most English houses were built around a courtyard, with major rooms looking inwards on to this central space, or in the shape of an 'E', with two end wings and an entrance porch creating the form of the letter. Thynne, however, built a great cube, with all the major rooms facing outwards towards the surrounding park, and the inner courtyards functioning only to admit light.

Left: Longleat's interior is much altered. The sweeping Grand Staircase is part of the early 19th-century alterations carried out by Sir Jeffry Wyatville.

CLASSICAL FAÇADE

Longleat's square outline and decorative elements are derived from classical models. Its façade contains a large number of bay windows, a design inspired by French chateaux, and incorporates the first three classical 'orders'. Beneath the windows are round recesses to hold busts of Roman emperors. Cornices run between the floors, and at roof level there is a balustrade. On the roof are domed turrets intended to be used as intimate banqueting houses. Thynne used the best 'Bath stone' from a quarry at Box, which he bought for the purpose.

LATER ALTERATIONS

When Elizabeth visited in 1575, only eight years after Thynne had begun rebuilding following the fire, the house stood just two storeys tall. The third level, with Corinthian elements on the façade, was probably added after John Thynne's death, in May 1580, by his son, another John. Since then the exterior of Longleat House has survived largely unchanged, except for elements in the Baroque style that were added in the 1690s, when a doorway was built and four very fine statues were added to the balustrade.

Within the house, most of the rooms were altered in the 19th century; only the magnificent Great Hall survives largely as it was in Thynne's day. This cavernous room is 35ft (11m) high,

Above: Beauty well maintained. In 1689, Henry Thynne, brother of Lord Weymouth, wrote that the house's condition was 'so excellent it makes my mouth water'.

with a vast hammer-beam roof. The elegant carved chimneypiece, Minstrels' Gallery and screen were added around 20 years after Thynne's death, *c.*1600. The Small Gallery dates to 1663, and was built for a visit by Charles II and Queen Catherine just three years after the Restoration. It was Charles II who granted the Thynne family the title of Lord Weymouth. In the years after 1806, most of the other rooms at Longleat were redecorated by Sir Jeffry Wyatville (see page 213). Further sumptuous redecoration and remodelling was carried out in the 1870s by J.D. Crace.

In the surrounding park, formal gardens were established in the 1690s by George London (d.1714), who also worked at Hampton Court Palace. These were removed by Lancelot 'Capability' Brown, hired in 1757 by the then current Lord Weymouth to landscape the grounds.

BISHOP KEN'S LIBRARY

Longleat is also famous for its libraries. The family's book and manuscript collection was begun by John Thynne's uncle, William, a clerk in Henry VIII's kitchens. Perhaps surprisingly for one so parsimonious, John Thynne himself greatly expanded it, and by 1577 the collection at Longleat numbered 85 books and manuscripts – a large number for that time. Today, there are eight libraries at Longleat, including the beautiful Bishop Ken's Library, which runs on the top floor along the entire east front of the house. It is named after Thomas Ken, Bishop of Bath and Wells, who was a friend of the Lord Weymouth of his day, and retired to Longleat in 1691 after he was deprived of his bishopric for refusing to swear the required oath of allegiance to William and Mary.

IN THE MODERN ERA

Longleat House made its mark in the 20th century by becoming, in a blaze of publicity in 1947, the first privately owned stately home to be opened to the paying public. Thereafter, it continued to pioneer new ways of funding its upkeep: in the 1960s, a safari park was opened in the grounds and the house's name became associated with the lions that roam there. Longleat also has a splendid, very challenging 1½ acre (0.6ha) maze, designed by Greg Bright.

THE THREE 'ORDERS' AT LONGLEAT

Longleat's façade incorporated the first three classical 'orders', or column styles, of ancient Greece and Rome: the Doric, the Ionic and the Corinthian. The house follows the style established by ancient Roman builders of using the columns as decorative features on a façade, running them upwards from ground to roof level: Doric at ground level, Ionic in the middle and Corinthian on the second storey. Longleat is hailed as the first English house to employ the classical orders conspicuously revived in Italy during the Renaissance and advocated in the architectural literature of the 16th century.

Right: Note the round recesses beneath the windows. These were intended to hold busts of Roman emperors.

HARDWICK HALL

'MORE GLASS THAN WALL'

Famously declared to be 'more glass than wall', Hardwick Hall is celebrated above all for its west front, with its glittering array of symmetrically marshalled windows. This bold and overstated exterior conceals many subtle beauties within: its Long Gallery, at 166ft (50.5m) the second longest in Britain, and its elegant High Great Chamber, declared by Sir Sacherevell Sitwell to be 'the most beautiful room, not in England alone, but in the whole of Europe'.

Above: Elizabeth's family portraits decorate the suitably grand Long Gallery in the East Front. It has an elegant plaster ceiling.

BESS OF HARDWICK

Hardwick is an enduring monument to the pride and self-belief of its builder, Bess of Hardwick, who rose from fairly humble origins to a position of immense wealth and transcended the architectural fashions of the time to create a highly original house.

Bess, or Elizabeth, was born *c.*1520 to a squire of modest means. She made her first fortune through marriage at the age of 12 to Robert Barlow, a local man only two years older, who died within a few months of the wedding. Around 15 years later, she married Sir William Cavendish, a very wealthy gentleman who served as Treasurer of the Chamber at the court of Henry VIII. Sir William bought a house at Chatsworth in Derbyshire and rebuilt it in a grand manner befitting his station. His death, in 1557, left Elizabeth hugely wealthy and in possession of several fine properties besides Chatsworth. In 1560, she married Sir William St Loe, Captain of the Queen's Guard, and when he too died, *c.*1565, Bess was wealthier still.

Her fourth and final marriage, to George Talbot, 6th Earl of Shrewsbury, was her grandest. He too predeceased her, on his death in 1590 leaving an immense inheritance that made Bess one of England's richest women. At the age of 70, Bess, rich enough to leave her mark in some style, set about building Hardwick Hall close to the site of the Old Hall at Hardwick in which she had been born.

This new building, designed to Bess's exacting demands by Robert Smythson, veteran of Longleat House, was built in just six years (1591–7). It was intended to demonstrate in stone and glass how far Bess had risen. Proud of her Shrewsbury title, she had the initials 'ES' ('Elizabeth Shrewsbury') cut beneath a countess's coronet on the house's skyline.

IMPORTANCE OF SYMMETRY

The house took the form of a three-storey rectangular block, with six four-storey towers arranged around it. It relies for its effect on glass: there is

EMBROIDERED DECORATION

Even the grandest Elizabethan houses generally had little furniture beyond a few tables, chairs, cupboards and chests for storage. These palaces of the nobility were decorated within using panelling, plasterwork, tapestry and needlework. Hardwick Hall is particularly known for its magnificent embroidery on curtains, wall hangings, cushion covers, upholstery and bedspreads. A fine example is on the bedhead in the State Bedroom.

Left: The monogram 'ES' for 'Elizabeth Shrewsbury' appears in this embroidered velvet hanging from Hardwick Hall.

little surface decoration on the house's exterior and the windows have no borders, while the mullions and transoms are kept thin, emphasizing the reflective expanses of window glass. Bess and Smythson put symmetry above all else in the design of the façades; in places, changes in floor level cut across the inside of the great windows.

Within, the two-storey hall is set at an angle of 90 degrees to the main front rather than parallel to it, as was usual with medieval halls. A magnificent, meandering, superbly wide stone staircase leads up to the High Great Chamber. This extraordinary reception room was built to hang eight vast Brussels tapestries, showing the story of wandering Greek hero, Ulysses, that Bess had bought in 1587. They hang beneath a painted plaster frieze representing Diana, the chaste Roman hunting goddess, surrounded by animals, nymphs and trees. We know from surviving documents that the beautiful frieze was created by an otherwise unknown craftsman named Charles Williams, who was identified by Bess as a 'cunning plasterer'.

VAST LONG GALLERY

By the time Bess was building Hardwick Hall, the Long Gallery was a Tudor innovation that had become an essential feature of any great house. It was a kind of indoor promenade, used for the display of portraits and tapestries hung along the gallery walls and for the gentle exercise of guests as they walked up and down the immensely elongated room. At Hardwick, the Long Gallery extends along the entire east front. Lit by 20 tall windows, it is hung with beautiful Flanders tapestries and portraits of Bess, her husbands and children, as well as of various entrepreneurs, including Elizabeth I, Mary, Queen of Scots, the Earl of Leicester and others.

Above: Hardwick's unusual shape – a long three-storey rectangle with six four-storey towers – can be seen in this aerial view. The house stands in 300 acres (120ha) of park.

Below: Hardwick Hall's famous West Front. Each of the six rooftop pavilions has 'ES' ('Elizabeth Shrewsbury') carved into it.

MAPLEDURHAM HOUSE

THE REAL TOAD HALL

This handsome Elizabethan country house is the heart of the tiny Oxfordshire village of Mapledurham. It lies near the River Thames and has a remarkably well-preserved working 15th-century water mill on the estate. The house was built in 1588, the year of the Spanish Armada, by Sir Michael Blount, Lieutenant of the Tower of London. It incorporated parts of a 12th-century timber-framed manor house. Sir Michael's grandfather, Richard Blount, had purchased the estate in 1490.

Sir Michael chose warm, rose-red bricks for his house, and his craftsmen achieved attractive patterns in the brick-work. In its essential aspects, the house's exterior is unchanged since the Elizabethan era. The Blount family were Roman Catholics, and an interesting feature is the gable decorated with oyster shells at the back of the house – once an accepted signal that a house was a safe refuge for Catholics.

Above: Mapledurham is a fine example of the lesser Elizabethan country house.

ALEXANDER POPE

In the early 18th century, poet Alexander Pope, a friend of the Blount sisters, Teresa and Martha, was a frequent visitor to Mapledurham House. Pope played a part in the redesign of the grounds there, introducing William Kent to the family for the commission, which included introducing a 'ha ha' (a sunken boundary, here in the form of a concealed ditch) to create an uninterrupted view of the eastern approach, and to plant a natural-looking 'Pleasure Ground' to the north.

After the Catholic Relief Act of 1791 lifted most of the sanctions against practising Catholics that had been in place since Henry VIII's time, the Blounts built a pretty family chapel in Mapledurham House in 1797. They used the then popular 'Strawberry Hill Gothic style', so called after Horace Walpole's house at Twickenham of 1753–78.

Mapledurham originally contained a splendid Great Hall, but this was refashioned as an entrance hall in 1828. By the fireplace are two remarkable wooden deer, carved from a single tree.

TOAD HALL?

Kenneth Grahame, author of children's classic *The Wind in the Willows* (1908), lived close to Mapledurham House at Pangbourne and loved the nearby stretch of the River Thames. E.H. Shepard, who provided the famous illustrations for Grahame's book, is believed to have used Mapledurham House as the model for Toad Hall.

Below: Kenneth Grahame first wrote parts of his book in letters to his partially sighted son, Alistair.

Below: The original 15th-century roof and wall timbers survive amid 17th-century additions in the Mapledurham water mill.

LOSELEY PARK
AND QUEEN ELIZABETH'S PROGRESS

In 1562, leading courtier and trusted royal adviser Sir William More began to rebuild his Surrey manor house at the request of Elizabeth I herself. Like many Tudor landowners, he profited from the Dissolution of the Monasteries, building his 'prodigy house' using blocks of worked stone from the suppressed Cistercian monastery at Waverley Abbey nearby. This stone had first been used 450 years earlier, and must have given his house an established and age-mellowed appearance even when it was newly built.

Sir William constructed a dignified and handsome country house that has survived largely unaltered to the present day. Above the doorway he carved the motto *Invidiae claudor, pateo sed semper amico* ('Envy is barred, but friendship always welcomed'). Elizabeth evidently appreciated Sir William's hospitality and his company, for she visited Loseley House four times. Nor was she the last royal to do so, for James I was a guest of Sir George More on two occasions, and many years later, in 1932, Queen Mary also visited Loseley.

Above: The Holbein fireplace and the gilded ceiling make grand companions in Loseley Park's remarkable Drawing Room.

Above: Loseley Park's name is associated with the dairy products once made from the milk produced by its cows.

INNER BEAUTIES

The high-ceilinged Great Hall has a splendid oriel window with heraldic glass and Tudor panelling believed to have been removed from Henry VIII's peerless Nonsuch Palace. In the beautiful wood-panelled library, Elizabeth's initials and arms are carved in the overmantel.

The Drawing Room has a breathtaking and unique fireplace cut from a single block of chalk to a design by Hans Holbein and a superb gilded ceiling that was installed for the visits of James I. In return, James gave the More family a portrait of himself and Queen Anne of Denmark, which can be seen in the Great Hall.

Below: Tradition comes to the fore in the handsome Great Hall at Loseley, with its family portraits, antlers and fine furniture.

LATER ALTERATIONS

A new wing was added to Sir William's house *c.*1600, containing a gallery with extra rooms and a riding school. But this wing was demolished in 1820 after it had fallen into a poor condition. Then, in 1877, William More-Molyneux built a nursery wing on the house's south side.

The 21st-century occupants of the house, the More-Molyneuxs, are direct descendants of its 16th-century builder. Their estate of 1,400 acres (565ha) is partly occupied by a celebrated Jersey herd from whose milk the well-known Loseley Jersey ice cream was made. However, the Loseley dairy products are no longer made at the Loseley estate, the brand having been sold to Booker Plc in 1985.

CAREW CASTLE
AND THE WELSH COUNTRY HOUSE

The first stronghold on the site of Carew Castle, near Pembroke in South Wales, was an Iron Age Celtic fort. This was followed by a Norman timber and earthwork stronghold built in 1095 by Gerald de Windsor, a knight who held nearby Pembroke Castle from Henry I. Nothing remains of Gerald's fortress, but part of the east front probably dates from the 12th century. In the inner ward, the Old Tower was added in the early 13th century. A first-floor Great Hall, the Chapel Tower and the South-east Tower were erected in the late 13th century and the gatehouse was built in the early 14th century. This work was carried out by Sir Nicholas de Carew, who also raised a curtain wall to enclose the outer bailey.

Above: At Carew, the Elizabethan wing (with windows) is to the left; the rounded towers on the right are late 13th century.

SIR RHYS AP THOMAS

In the late 15th and early 16th centuries, Sir Rhys ap Thomas, an important Welsh ally of Henry VII who had acquired the castle in 1480 from a Carew lord, made many further improvements, adding a second Great Hall, stairs and splendid accommodation. It was in Carew Castle that Henry Tudor stayed in 1485, while passing through Wales on his way to the Battle of Bosworth, where he won the crown. On the battlefield, Henry knighted Rhys and made him Governor of Wales. In 1507, Sir Rhys threw a lavish celebration at Carew to celebrate the early triumphs of the Tudor dynasty.

SIR JOHN PERROT

Tudor courtier and statesman 'Good Sir John' Perrot received the lordship and castle of Carew from Queen Mary in 1558, and in 1559, at Elizabeth I's coronation, he was one of the four bearers of her 'canopy of state'. He rose to high position under Elizabeth, who granted him governorship of Carew, serving the Queen first as Lord of Munster and then as Lord Deputy of Ireland. He added a

Below: The solid rooms at Carew Castle were visited by Tudor royalty. Henry VII attended Sir Rhys's grand 1507 celebration.

Below: This interior view of steep steps and low doorways at Carew gives a sense of what life was like within a medieval or Tudor castle.

BACHECRAIG

The Tudor country mansion of Bachecraig near Denbigh is celebrated as the first classical house in Wales. It was built in the early part of Elizabeth's reign by the immensely wealthy Sir Richard Clough (d.1570). It was constructed on a grand scale, with continental ideas of proportion very much in mind: the chimneys, as well as the windows and other features, are carefully balanced for symmetry. Local legend has it that Sir Richard made a midnight pact with the Devil to supply the bricks he used for his house – and that these were fashioned from local clay, fired in an infernal kiln and supplied each morning, one day's worth at a time. Scholars believe that Sir Richard gained a reputation for dubious night-time work because he kept an astronomical observatory in the roof of Bachecraig and was often seen to be labouring there at night.

magnificent three-storey wing containing a majestic second-floor Long Gallery that ran for 130ft (40m). In its impressive, typically Elizabethan façade were two rows of big rectangular windows as well as two large oriel windows. Like the rest of this once-proud castle, it is now a sad ruin.

A man of fiery temper known for his 'majesty of personage', Perrot was rumoured at court to be an illegitimate son of Henry VIII, and, judging from his portraits, he certainly looked like the King. But his proud manner made him many enemies and he was convicted of high treason in 1591, before dying of natural causes the following year during imprisonment in the Tower of London.

LAUGHARNE AND POWIS

'Good Sir John' also refashioned and rebuilt the castle at Laugharne, in South Wales, into an Elizabethan country mansion after he was given the fortress by Elizabeth I in 1575. However, his work there apparently fell to ruin within a few years of his death in 1592, and most of what is visible today at Laugharne dates from the castle's earlier history.

Above: Laugharne Castle occupies a cliff, the site of a Norman ringwork, looking out across the estuary of the River Taf.

A COUNTRY HOUSE CASTLE

Powis Castle in central Wales was another military stronghold upgraded to become a fine Elizabethan country house. This attractive battlemented building, celebrated above all for its magnificent terraced gardens, has seen many refurbishments, most recently in the early 20th century. In the Tudor era, Sir Edward Herbert, who gained ownership of Powis in 1578 and whose family still live there, undertook extensive rebuilding and modernization work in 1587–95. All that survives today is the Long Gallery, although the castle still has several rooms with Elizabethan furnishings.

Below: Powis Castle stands on a commanding hilltop, its steep south-east approaches today occupied by gardens.

MONTACUTE HOUSE
AND WOLLATON HALL

In the 1590s, Somerset landowner Sir Edward Phelips began building Montacute House from beautiful honey-coloured limestone quarried at nearby Ham Hill. He employed a gifted Somerset master mason, William Arnold, who must take a great deal of the credit for Montacute, and who later worked at Cranbourne Manor in Dorset for Robert Cecil, 1st Earl of Salisbury.

Below: The end of the east front at Montacute House, with its curved Flemish gables, slender chimneys and large windows.

Above: The salvaged archway from Clifton Maybank makes a grand entrance in the centre of the west front at Montacute House.

Sir Edward needed a house grand enough to match his position, for he was a leading lawyer and politician in London. An MP from 1584, he was elected Speaker of the House of Commons in 1604. As a lawyer, he made the opening speech for the prosecution at the trial of Guy Fawkes after the discovery of the 'Gunpowder Plot' to blow up the Houses of Parliament in 1605.

THE ENTRANCE FRONT

With William Arnold, Phelips created a remarkable east entrance front at Montacute. The façade, 90ft (27m) high and almost 200ft (60m) across, is another Elizabethan 'wall of glass': it contains 39 mullioned windows, arranged in three perfectly symmetrical tiers. These straight horizontal lines are brought to life by the curves of the Flemish gables, the vertical lines of the slender chimneys on the roof above and a wealth of carved detail in the façade itself, including curved cornices on some of the windows and circular recesses that probably once held terracotta medallions. A delightful touch is

Above: An oak bedstead at Montacute is carved with the arms of James I and of Frederick V, Elector Palatine of the Rhine.

WOLLATON HALL, NOTTINGHAMSHIRE

The great Elizabethan surveyor Robert Smythson, who worked at Longleat House as well as Hardwick Hall, built the ravishing Wollaton Hall in Nottinghamshire for Sir Francis Willoughby in 1580–88. He used Italian master masons and probably worked to the designs of celebrated artist John Thorpe, based on those of Sir Francis himself. This elegant 'prodigy house' is highly ornamented: the four large corner towers are topped with pinnacles and the façades incorporate niches filled with the busts of great philosophers. In the centre of the house, the hall is elevated above the surrounding wings. Wollaton Hall is reputed to have cost the astonishing sum of £80,000 to build.

Left: At Wollaton Hall the central hall rises above the rest of the house; its four square corner towers rise to pinnacles.

the inclusion between the windows of the top storey of statues representing the 'Nine Worthies', here in the guise of Roman centurions. All the detail is in the same rich-coloured Ham Hill limestone as the main house.

A grass forecourt with side flowerbeds extends before the east front and is enclosed by a low wall. Two delicate corner pavilions have domed roofs and oriel windows on all four sides. Originally, a grand gatehouse stood in the centre of the front wall between the two pavilions, but it has been demolished.

Montacute contains the longest of all Elizabethan Long Galleries: the top-floor 'promenade' runs 172ft (52m) along the entire length of the house, and is 20ft (6m) across. Groups of connected rooms lead off either end of the gallery. Today it houses a splendid selection of 100 Tudor and Jacobean portraits from the collection of the National Portrait Gallery in London.

Aside from the Long Gallery, Montacute's finest room is certainly the Library, originally the Great Chamber. The panes of heraldic glass in the windows, the chimney-piece of Portland stone, a fine plasterwork frieze and the beautiful 16th-century wood panelling on the walls are all original.

WEST FRONT AND GARDENS

In 1786–7, Edward Phelips changed the entrance front to the west side. He salvaged a beautiful stone porch from a Tudor house at Clifton Maybank in Somerset that was being pulled down, and had it fitted into the centre of the front. The porch is made from the same stone as Montacute, and although it was made around 50 years before Montacute, its detail fits its new setting perfectly.

Ornamental gardens with elegant lines of yew trees lie to the north and south ends of the house. In the forecourt on the east front (the original entrance), are two flowerbeds planted in the 1950s to designs by Vita Sackville-West, poet, novelist and gardener.

Below: A late 19th-century watercolour shows one of the graceful domed pavilions in Montacute's formal east garden.

CHAPTER SEVEN

THE JACOBEAN COUNTRY HOUSE

*c.*1600–*c.*1650

In 1616, Inigo Jones, recently appointed Surveyor of Works to King James I, began work on the Queen's House in Greenwich for James's wife, Anne of Denmark. Jones had recently returned from a visit to Rome, during which he had studied ancient Roman buildings and the work of Italian Renaissance architects, including Andrea Palladio and Vincenzo Scamozzi. Jones introduced 'classical' architectural design – inspired by Renaissance and ancient Roman buildings – into England. As well as being England's first classical architect, he was a major influence on the 'Palladian' movement of the 18th century, in which architects returned to Palladio as a source of inspiration.
The elegant Queen's House was abandoned when Anne died in 1619 and only finished in 1635 for Charles II's queen, Henrietta Maria.
In the mean time, Inigo Jones had designed and built the magnificent Banqueting House in the royal palace of Whitehall and the Queen's Chapel, St James's, and worked on or supervised country houses at New Hall, Essex, Stoke Bruerne, Northamptonshire, and Chevening, Kent.
The career of Inigo Jones was a turning point in English architecture: the domestic tradition had come to a final flowering with acclaimed Jacobean houses such as Hatfield House, built in 1608–11; in contrast, the superb south front built in 1636–40 at Wilton House, Wiltshire, designed under Jones's supervision, showed a new way forward. It used a classical design, with devices such as the central window with carved figures that were taken directly from Jones's royal buildings in London, inspired in their turn by the designs of Scamozzi in Rome.

Left: Paintings by Sir Peter Paul Rubens were fitted in 1635 into the beamed ceiling of Inigo Jones's superb Banqueting House, Whitehall, completed in 1622.

KNOLE

HOME OF VITA SACKVILLE-WEST

The vast and historic country house of Knole, Sevenoaks, in Kent, was largely created by two men – Thomas Bourchier, a 15th-century Archbishop of Canterbury, and Thomas Sackville, 1st Earl of Dorset – in the early reign of King James I. This palatial house of grey Kentish ragstone with brown roof-tiles, so extensive that from a distance it resembles a village or small town, has remained largely unaltered since the sensitive external alterations and large-scale internal reworking carried out by Thomas Sackville around 400 years ago.

Sackville descendants have lived in Knole for over 400 years, and still inhabit part of the mansion today, although the house has been owned, managed and maintained by the National Trust since 1946.

Below: Knole's beautiful staircase, installed by Thomas Sackville, leads up to the equally grand Ballroom. Note the Sackville leopard atop the newel post (right).

HOUSE OF POETS

Thomas Sackville (1536–1608) was a poet and dramatist in his youth before settling into political life, and he co-wrote with Thomas Norton the first tragic play in English, *Gorboduc* or *Ferrex and Porrex*. The play, which describes conflicts among legendary rulers of ancient Britain, was performed on Twelfth Night 1561 in the Inner Temple Hall, London. Over the centuries, Sackville's house had many admirers. Edmund Burke declared it 'the most interesting thing in England'. Vita Sackville West (1892–1962) was born and lived there before her marriage to Harold Nicholson. Her sometime lover and close friend Virginia Woolf used Knole as the setting for her novel *Orlando* (1928). Vita herself used the house as the setting for a novel, *The Edwardians* (1930), and wrote a book about the house, *Knole and the Sackvilles*, published in 1922.

Right: Vita Sackville West loved the colours of Knole. She wrote, 'It is above all an English home ... It has the tone of England; it melts into the green of the garden turf.'

MEDIEVAL AND TUDOR PALACE

Thomas Bourchier bought the estate at Knole with its 13th-century house in 1456 for £266. Over the next three decades, he reconstructed and extended it into a grand episcopal palace with seven interconnecting courtyards, including two extensive quadrangles – the Stone Court and the Green Court – which stand one in front of the other at the entrance. In line with 15th-century practice, his house made at least a show of fortification, with extensive battlements on walls and towers, as well as two gatehouses. On the inner gatehouse, known as 'Bourchier's Tower', there is decorative machicolation.

Knole was the palace of five archbishops of Canterbury, from Thomas Bourchier to Thomas Cranmer. After Cranmer it passed to King Henry VIII in 1538, and was a royal palace for 28 years until Elizabeth I gave it to Thomas Sackville in 1566. The house was on lease until the year of Elizabeth's death, and so Sackville did not start his work on Knole until 1603, when he transformed the interior and made a series of well-judged alterations to the outer fabric that greatly accentuated its overall attractiveness.

SACKVILLE'S ALTERATIONS

To soften the house's fortress-like appearance, Thomas Sackville added mullioned windows and curved gables in the Flemish style, with decorative finials in the likeness of the leopards from the Sackville crest. In the Stone Court, he built a fine colonnade with a gallery above it.

Internally, he remodelled the Great Hall of 1460, adding a lower, plastered ceiling and a sumptuously carved oak screen. He added a beautiful timber Great Staircase, painted by artist Paul

Above: A great part of Knole's appeal lies in the fact that its exterior today looks largely as it did in the time of King James I.

Isaacson in yellows and greens, with a number of visual effects, including *trompe l'oeil* images of the balustrade on the walls, which were startlingly original at the time. The staircase, which has Sackville leopards above its newel posts, led to the Ballroom, where Sackville installed an extraordinary alabaster and marble chimney-piece and over-mantel made by Cornelius Cuer, royal master mason. This extravagantly grand room, which also features glorious painted oak panelling depicting mermaids and mermen, served as a reception chamber and dining room.

Sackville also built three grand galleries, including the Cartoon Gallery, with another splendid Jacobean ceiling and chimney-piece. The gallery takes it name from the copies of Raphael's cartoons (designs for paintings) made by artist Daniel Mytens, who was court painter to Charles I.

The cycles of time take solid form in this outstanding house. In addition to seven courtyards, for the days of the week, there are said to be 52 staircases, for the weeks of the year, and 365 rooms, for the days of the year. Many have commented on Knole's very English beauty and atmosphere. The poet and novelist Vita Sackville West, who grew up there, said Knole had 'a deep inward gaiety' and likened the house to 'some very old woman who has always been beautiful, who has had many lovers and seen many generations come and go ... and learnt an imperishable secret of tolerance and humour'.

LATER CHANGES

Since Thomas Sackville's changes, there have been some alterations to the house's furnishings and its decorative schemes, although the prevailing style remains Tudor and Jacobean. In the late 17th century, Thomas's great-great-grandson, Charles, 6th Earl of Dorset, added fine furniture and textiles. Then, around a century later, John Frederick, 3rd Duke of Dorset, installed many Old Masters that he had purchased during a Grand Tour of continental Europe.

Right: Thomas Sackville built the Cartoon Gallery in the 1600s, but the six copies of Raphael's cartoons were fitted in 1701.

HATFIELD HOUSE

HOME OF THE CECIL FAMILY

Robert Cecil, 1st Earl of Salisbury, had little choice when King James I 'suggested' that they swap houses. James would take for himself the beautiful Theobalds in Hertfordshire, built by Robert's father, William Cecil, Lord Burghley, and would give Robert the nearby royal palace of Hatfield.

The Tudor palace at Hatfield was built *c.*1485 by Cardinal John Morton, Bishop of Ely and later Archbishop of Canterbury under King Henry VII. Henry VIII seized it and used it mainly as a home, often effectively a prison, for his children. The future Elizabeth I spent most of her childhood at Hatfield, where she was told the news that her elder sister, Mary, had died, making her Queen of England. In her first act as Queen, Elizabeth appointed William Cecil her Principal Secretary, then held her first Council meeting in Hatfield's Great Hall.

The tower and Great Hall of the 15th-century palace are all that survive, for in 1607–08 Robert Cecil pulled down three sides of the original building as he set about constructing a new residence, devising his own floor plans and designs.

Below: A new direction? The tower, arcade, gables and forecourt point forward to the classical architecture of Inigo Jones – some say Jones himself designed the arcade.

ROYAL VISITORS

Like Burghley House and the other great 'prodigy houses' of the Elizabethan reign, Hatfield was designed to be a fitting venue for entertaining the monarch. A central block contained the main staterooms used for receiving and entertaining guests: there was a Great Hall in the centre, with a Long Gallery and four great rooms on the upper floor; the chapel stood at the side. This central building was flanked by two wings containing apartments for royal visitors: the queen in the west wing and the king on the east side. Terraced gardens were laid out complete with a lake and fountains, and with rare plants and trees imported from continental Europe by the botanist John Tradescant.

The house was completed in four years (1607–11), but Robert Cecil died the following year. In later years, his house was often visited by kings and queens, including James I, Charles I, James, Duke of York (the future James II) and Queen Victoria and Prince Albert.

Above: Among the many treasures at Hatfield is this genealogical chart that purports to trace Elizabeth I's descent from Adam.

CONTRASTING STYLES

The north and south front are in contrasting styles. The north front, of red brick with symmetrical lines of wide windows, providing an essentially flat surface varied by shallow bays, appears to be in a familiar domestic 'Tudor' style. The south front, however, has two projecting wings forming a forecourt,

Right: In an aerial view, the great size of the side wings for royal guests is clear. Salisbury laid out a vineyard in the extensive grounds, but the vines failed.

an elegant arcade in the Italian style, a delicate white tower and Flemish gables. Cecil's surveyor was Robert Lyminge and the master mason a certain Conn; Inigo Jones may have contributed to the stone forecourt on the south front. French, English and Flemish craftsmen were hired. They used bricks from the demolished wings of the Tudor palace, stone from Caen in Normandy and the finest marble from Carrara in Tuscany.

PORTRAITS OF A QUEEN

Hatfield House contains two of the most celebrated portraits of Elizabeth I. The first is the 'Ermine Portrait' by Nicholas Hilliard, so called because an ermine (an animal symbolic of royalty) is portrayed with the Queen; this hangs in the Marble Hall. The second is the 'Rainbow Portrait', probably by Hilliard's pupil, Isaac Oliver, but sometimes attributed to Marcus Gheeraerts the Younger. This is a veritable riot of symbolism, in which Elizabeth is shown wearing a gown embroidered with English wildflowers and holding a rainbow, symbolic of peace.

Below: The 'Rainbow Portrait' of Queen Elizabeth I.

Hatfield House contains two splendid examples of Jacobean style at its most flamboyant: the Grand Staircase, which is fitted with 'dog gates' to prevent animals going up, and is made of intricately carved oak, and the exuberantly decorated Marble Hall, which is often identified by architectural historians as the last great medieval hall in an English house. Also of note is the beautiful original stained glass, depicting Old Testament scenes, fitted in the chapel in 1609.

PROMINENT CECILS

Hatfield House has remained through the centuries in the hands of the Cecils, who, in the late 19th century, rose once again to great prominence – Robert Arthur Talbot Gascoyne-Cecil, 3rd Marquess of Salisbury, was leader of the Conservative Party and three times Prime Minister.

Below: The gardens at Hatfield House were restored in the Victorian era. They include herb gardens and orchards as well as terraces.

BOLSOVER CASTLE

SMYTHSON'S LAST HOUSE

Bolsover Castle, near Chesterfield in Derbyshire, was the last major house designed by the leading surveyor of the Elizabethan age, Robert Smythson. He began work at Bolsover for Sir Charles Cavendish in 1612.

The first castle on the site, a stone keep with a curtain wall, had been built by William Peverel (an illegitimate son of William the Conqueror) in the 12th century. But it was little more than a ruin by the mid-16th century, when it was bought by George Talbot, 6th Earl of Shrewsbury and fourth husband of Bess of Hardwick. He leased the castle in 1608 to his stepson, Sir Charles Cavendish. Sir Charles bought the house in 1613.

A FANTASY CASTLE

Sir Charles Cavendish and Robert Smythson built a delightful fantasy castle, an embodiment of Elizabethan-Jacobean ideals of chivalry. The tower keep, completed after Smythson's death in 1621, is today called 'the little castle'. It contains a series of elaborately decorated panelled rooms, with allegorical wall paintings and magnificent marble fireplaces. These rooms include the famous Star Chamber, Pillar Chamber, Elysium Chamber and Heaven Chamber. It gives on to a court with a central fountain (the Fountain Court). Tower and court occupy the site of William Peverel's original keep and inner bailey, and some parts of the walls of the Fountain Court are medieval originals.

The staterooms were in the Terrace Range, designed by Smythson and his son John, and included a Great Hall, very fine living quarters and a splendid 220ft (67m) Long Gallery. The Riding School range, designed by Robert Smythson's grandson, Huntingdon, has a superb timber roof of the early 1630s.

NEW OWNERS

In the Civil War, its owner, Sir William Cavendish, led the Royalist army at Marston Moor and following that defeat fled into exile. The castle was occupied by the Parliamentarians, but Sir William returned after 1660. Subsequently, the castle passed through the hands of various owners and residents until it was given to the state in 1945 by William Cavendish-Bentinck, 7th Duke of Portland. English Heritage is currently responsible for the castle.

ROBERT SMYTHSON

In a series of major building commissions between 1556 and his death in 1614, Robert Smythson achieved a creative blend of native English, Flemish and continental Renaissance architectural ideas. Although he was a figure of major significance for Elizabethan and Jacobean architecture, he lived before practitioners of his trade could claim great social standing. There is no surviving image of him, and we know little about him beyond the building projects on which he worked. His first house was Longleat for Sir John Thynne, begun when he was just 21. He was later surveyor on those jewels of the age, Hardwick Hall and Wollaton Hall.

Below: Bolsover Castle occupies a hilltop and commands fine views of the countryside – especially from the Terrace Range.

DUNFERMLINE PALACE
AND GLAMIS CASTLE

Before he became King of England, James Stuart, ruling as James VI of Scotland, established a fine royal palace at Dunfermline. The main part of the palace was originally a guesthouse in the Benedictine abbey founded by Queen Margaret and her son, David I; James also added a new building at Dunfermline, the Queen's House, for his wife, Anne of Denmark.

Royal connections to Dunfermline were well established. Queen (later Saint) Margaret was buried there, as was Robert I the Bruce, who had rebuilt the abbey's domestic buildings after they were ransacked by the army of Edward I of England. James I was born at the abbey, and James IV and James V stayed there.

James VI's palace was built around a courtyard, with the main range of royal apartments at the south-west, the new Queen's House to the north and the abbey buildings to the east. The main range incorporated parts of the medieval abbey guesthouse. The palace was the birthplace of Prince Charles (the future King Charles I, and the last monarch born in Scotland) in 1600. The palace is a ruin today, with only part of the outer shell of the south-west range surviving.

Above: Glamis Castle. The impressive main tower was constructed c. 1435. The oldest part is the east wing, built c. 1400.

Below: The remains of the south-west range at Dunfermline Palace. It once contained a large hall, with a kitchen and chamber.

GLAMIS CASTLE

The magnificent Banqueting Hall at Glamis Castle was built in the early 1600s as part of a substantial reworking of this largely 15th-century fortress by Patrick Lyon, the 9th Lord Glamis and 1st Earl of Kinghorne. The castle stands on the site of a building in which King Malcolm II was reputedly murdered; it was then a royal hunting lodge for many years and was the home of Janet Douglas, Lady Glamis, who was imprisoned and then burned at the stake as a witch. James V briefly seized the castle for four years. Mary, Queen of Scots, visited, and James VI came to stay often. In the 20th century, it was the childhood home of Queen Elizabeth, the Queen Mother; in 1930, she gave birth there to Princess Margaret, sister of Queen Elizabeth II.

AUDLEY END
A PALACE IN ALL BUT NAME

Above: Audley End, built to impress James I, became a palace when Charles II bought it as a base from which to attend horse-racing at Newmarket.

The country mansion of Audley End, near Saffron Walden, was built by Thomas Howard, 1st Earl of Suffolk, in 1605–14 to entertain King James I. Before its 18th-century alterations, it was more than twice the size it is today. Howard served as Lord Treasurer to the King and perhaps gave in to the temptation to divert funds towards the building of his house, for in 1619 he and his wife were imprisoned in the Tower of London, accused of embezzling thousands of pounds.

To create the grandest home in England of its day, Thomas Howard demolished an earlier house, Audley Inn, which had been erected by his grandfather, Sir Thomas Audley, in the middle of the 16th century. Sir Thomas himself had built on the site of a former Benedictine monastery, named Walden Abbey, given to him by Henry VIII in 1538 during the Dissolution of the Monasteries.

Below: The Great Hall. Note the Howard family crests in the plaster ceiling and the superb Jacobean carved wooden screen.

The new house, Audley End, built around two courtyards, has two porches on the front with separate entrances that led to separate suites of apartments for the king and queen. Within, the splendid Great Hall features a magnificent Jacobean carved oak screen, while the plaster panel ceiling is decorated with coloured crests of the Howard family.

Thomas Howard was rewarded with only one visit from James I, in 1614. James supposedly told his host: 'the building is too large for a King, but it might do for a Lord Treasurer'. In fact, Audley End became a royal palace between 1668 and 1701, when Charles II purchased it for the sum of £50,000 (it was repurchased by the earls of Suffolk). He stayed there in style and comfort when attending horse-racing at nearby Newmarket.

FORMAL GARDENS

Thomas Howard created vast, elaborate gardens with extended avenues of trees, and geometric arrangements of alleys and rectangular ponds. These designs led the eye along a main vista from the house's principal front, with another, lesser, vista at right angles.

FASHIONABLE ALTERATIONS

In the 18th century, after many decades of neglect, Sir John Griffin Griffin, 1st Baron Braybrooke, and a descendant of the earls of Suffolk, abandoned these gardens and hired Lancelot 'Capability' Brown to remake the grounds in the then fashionable landscape style. He also engaged Robert Adam to create a fine set of eight rooms, squeezed into the lower ground floor, refit the saloon, create a picture gallery, redecorate the chapel and build a number of garden monuments, including the Tea House Bridge that crosses the River Cam.

BLICKLING HALL

A JACOBEAN MANSION

Robert Lyminge, surveyor-architect for Sir Robert Cecil at Hatfield House, built the Jacobean mansion of Blickling Hall in Norfolk in 1616–25 for Sir Henry Hobart, Lord Chief Justice under King James I. Blickling's delightful entrance front uses many of the features of Hatfield, including a large clock tower, a prominent and decorated porch and ogival cupolas at the corners.

The new house was built on the site of an older Blickling Hall that had once belonged to Sir Thomas Boleyn, father of Anne Boleyn, queen of Henry VIII and mother of Elizabeth I. Unlike Hatfield House, Blicking Hall was constrained by its setting – indeed the yew hedges and the former moat (now a flower garden) are a good deal older than the Jacobean house. Perhaps because of these constraints, Lyminge decided to build a conventional courtyard house rather than adopt the fashionable H-shape used at Hatfield.

Below: The Long Gallery has been used as a library since the 18th century. Today it houses a collection of rare books.

Above: This detail of a musician is from the plaster ceiling of the Long Gallery.

HALL AND LONG GALLERY

The main entrance hall contains the majestic original Jacobean oak staircase, which was moved and extended when the hall was rebuilt in 1767 by a local architect, Thomas Ivory. His staircase splits into two at the main landing, while the original had one flight only, but the reconstruction is a work of great skill.

Blickling Hall's Long Gallery was one of the last but also one of the finest long galleries built in an English country house. It is 123ft (37m) long, and fills most of the house's east front. The room is a good deal wider than most long galleries, and has a magnificent plaster ceiling full of abstract and naturalistic designs, which was carved by Edward Stanyan in 1620. It houses a library of 12,000 volumes.

BIRTHPLACE OF A QUEEN?

The Great Hall at Blickling contains statues of Anne Boleyn and Elizabeth I, the former marked with the legend *Anna Bolena hic nata 1507* ('Anne Boleyn was born in this place in 1507'). Scholars believe that the claim is false. Although Anne's father, Sir Thomas Boleyn, once owned Blickling, he moved to Hever Castle in Kent around 1505, so unless Anne was born before her generally accepted birth date of 1507, she was born at Hever, not Blickling.

Below: The clock tower and ogival cupolas at the corners are among the features at Blickling Hall that recall Hatfield House.

THE QUEEN'S HOUSE, GREENWICH

'HOUSE OF DELIGHT'

Artist-turned-architect Inigo Jones's first major commission, after being appointed Surveyor of Works to King James I in 1615, was to design the Queen's House in Greenwich for James's wife, Anne of Denmark. Anne died in 1619, before the Queen's House was complete, but Jones returned to finish the work in 1635 at the request of King Charles I's wife, Henrietta Maria of France.

When Jones built the Queen's House it was part of the 15th-century royal palace of Placentia, birthplace both of Henry VIII (in 1491) and Elizabeth I (in 1533). This palace and its estate stood on the large riverside site now occupied by Greenwich Park, the National Maritime Museum and the Royal Naval College. Following the Restoration of the monarchy in 1660, Charles II set out to rebuild the Palace of Placentia to the designs of John Webb, an architect who, with Inigo Jones, pioneered the classical style in England. The only part of Webb's work that survives today is the east range of the King Charles block; the rest has been demolished.

Above: An Italian villa in Greenwich. The south front, with its colonnade of Ionic pillars, commands superb views of the park.

QUEEN'S CHAPEL, ST JAMES'S

Inigo Jones received the royal order to build the Queen's Chapel at St James's Palace in April 1623. It was planned as a Roman Catholic place of worship in which the intended wife of Charles, Prince of Wales, could hear Mass. Charles travelled to Spain with the Duke of Buckingham to woo the Infanta but failed in the mission, returning home empty-handed in October 1623. Instead, the chapel was used by Charles's eventual queen, Henrietta Maria of France, also a Roman Catholic. It is in the form of a double cube, with a gracefully curving coffered ceiling and at the east end an elegant arched three-light Venetian window – a much-used device in the Palladian revival.

ITALIAN INSPIRATION

Jones's design for the Queen's House was based on that of an Italian villa at Poggio a Caiano, built for Florentine statesman Lorenzo de Medici and completed in 1485 by Giuliano da Sangallo. Like Poggio a Caiano, the Queen's House consists of two main parts: one part stood within Placentia Palace and the second was in Greenwich Park, and they were connected by a covered bridge over the public road (moved in 1699 by Lord Romney, Ranger of the Royal Park) linking Deptford and Woolwich. Other key elements of the design derived from Jones's Italian model are the curved steps, terrace and widely spaced windows on the palace side of the building (the north front) and the open colonnade of six Ionic pillars along the park face (the south front). From the colonnade, which Jones called 'a frontispiece in the midst', there is a splendid view of the parkland.

FIRST OF JONES'S CUBES

Jones designed all the interiors. There were elaborate marble fireplaces and the rooms were adorned with carved wooden friezes. In the palace, or north, building he created a magnificent entrance hall, paved with black and white marble, its dimensions a perfect 40ft (12m) cube. This was the first of several cubes built by Jones – two side by side (a 'double cube') were used both in the Whitehall Palace Banqueting House and in the rebuilt south wing at Wilton House. In favouring these perfect dimensions, Jones was following one of the key tenets of Palladio, that houses should be designed in line with natural laws of symmetry, proportion and harmony. His entrance hall in the Queen's House was also the first instance in an English house of a hall designed for use as a reception room. Its ceiling was decorated with paintings by Orazio Gentileschi, representing the 'Arts of Peace'.

Above: From the river side, the neat Queen's House is dwarfed by Sir Christopher Wren's Royal Naval Hospital.

THE 'HOUSE OF DELIGHT'

Jones also installed England's first open-well spiral staircase, the Tulip Staircase, bringing all his delicacy to bear when he designed a balustrade of wrought iron decorated with the fleur-de-lys device as a mark of respect for the French-born queen. In the Queen's Drawing Room there hung a fine tapestry of Cupid and Psyche by Jacob Jordaens, perhaps after which she called the building her 'House of Delight'.

Below: This ceiling of the Arts and Sciences (1636) was painted for the Queen's House but later moved to Marlborough House.

After the Restoration, when Henrietta Maria, now the Queen Mother, returned to live there, the Queen's House was enlarged by John Webb as part of Charles II's large-scale plan to rebuild Placentia Palace. Nearby, Charles's new palace, the King's House, was begun on land beside the River Thames. It was never finished and later became the site of the Royal Naval Hospital, designed by Sir Christopher Wren.

STOKE PARK PAVILIONS

At Stoke Bruerne, Northamptonshire, Inigo Jones either designed or supervised the design of a country house for Sir Francis Crane. The house was never completed, and large parts were burned down in 1886, but two pavilions and colonnades have survived and can be seen today. The plan, with the central house connected to two pavilions by a graceful curving colonnade, was based on that of the mid-16th-century Villa di Papa Giulio in Rome, built by Giacomo Barozzi da Vignola for Pope Julius II. At Stoke Bruerne, the west pavilion contained a library and the east pavilion a chapel.

Below: One of two graceful pavilions designed by Jones for Sir Francis Crane's country house at Stoke Bruerne, Northants.

THE BANQUETING HOUSE, WHITEHALL

A MASTERPIECE OF CLASSICAL ARCHITECTURE

When King James I's Banqueting Hall in Whitehall Palace burned down in 1619 he commanded his Surveyor of Works, Inigo Jones, to replace it. Jones's Banqueting House, completed in three years by 1622, is his masterpiece. One of England's first and greatest classical buildings, it is the only part of the once extensive royal palace of Whitehall to survive today above ground. Contemporaries, however, seem to have found Jones's conception too grand and rather at odds with the rest of the Tudor palace. One response, in 1621, was that the hall was 'too faire and nothing suitable to the rest of the house'.

Above: Work of a master – Inigo Jones's Banqueting House façade facing Whitehall. Architects praise its vitality and harmony.

IONIC AND CORINTHIAN

The Banqueting House was designed not for dining but principally as a setting for state occasions, plays and the masques that Inigo Jones continued to design for the royal court. Indeed, its completion was celebrated with the performance of *The Masque of Augurs*, by Jones and Ben Jonson, on Twelfth Night 1622. The building's interior was Jones's version of a Roman basilica (hall): it consists of a vast 50ft (15m) double cube, and is ornamented with Ionic columns beneath a cantilevered gallery and Corinthian pilasters above.

This formidable interior space originally had a beamed ceiling, but the celebrated painted panels by Sir Peter Paul Rubens were fitted in 1635. The paintings are allegorical representations of James I's reign as a time of plenty and peace; Rubens had planned them at the time of building, but they were not finished until 1634.

Jones' façade for the Banqueting House also uses Ionic beneath Corinthian pilasters. Facing Whitehall, it was originally built using three colours of stone: brown for the basement, a dun colour for the upper walls and white Portland

Below: The Banqueting House survived in its original setting – as part of Whitehall Palace – for only 76 years, from completion in 1622 to the disastrous fire of 1698.

INIGO JONES: CLASSICAL PIONEER

The son of a London cloth worker, Inigo Jones first found royal employment as a painter at the court of Christian IV of Denmark and Norway. His work there gained him an entrée at the royal court in London, where he served Queen Anne (Christian IV's sister) from 1605 onward as a designer of costumes, scenery and effects for royal entertainments, or 'masques'. His first architectural work, commissioned by Robert Cecil, 1st Earl of Salisbury, was a design for the New Exchange in the Strand, London (demolished in the 18th century). Jones was then appointed Surveyor of Works, first to Henry, Prince of Wales, in 1610–12, and in 1615–43 to Kings James I and Charles I.

Above: Jones was a superb theatrical designer and one of England's greatest architects.

An admirer of classical Roman and Italian Renaissance architecture, Jones pioneered 'classicism' in English architecture, basing his designs on those of the Roman architect Vitrivius and his Italian followers Andrea Palladio and Vincenzo Scamozzi, and on study of Vitrivius's and Palladio's writings on architecture.

In addition to his major royal buildings in London, Jones contributed to the design and interior decoration of a number of country houses. He also designed and laid out London's first integrated square at Covent Garden and restored the old St Paul's Cathedral, though his reputedly superb work there was entirely lost in the Great Fire of London in 1666.

stone for the columns and the elegant balustrade. But it was refaced with Portland stone throughout during restoration by Sir John Soane in 1829.

WHITEHALL PALACE

In the 15th century, the Archbishops of York built as their London base a palace named York Place, which stood on the site of Inigo Jones's Banqueting House. When Cardinal Thomas Wolsey became Archbishop of York in 1514, he extended the palace, which, like Hampton Court, another of Wolsey's splendid residences, attracted the covetous eye of Henry VIII. In the late 1520s, his reputation failing and desperately trying to retain the King's favour, Wolsey gave York Place to Henry. Renamed Whitehall Palace it became Henry VIII's principal royal residence.

The King further extended and improved it, rebuilding a fine Privy Gallery that he had taken from another of Wolsey's houses, at Esher. He built a bowling alley, a tilt yard, a cockpit and real tennis courts and raised two great gateways over the roadway (from Charing Cross to Westminster) that ran through the palace complex. Within the many rooms of the palace, several walls and ceilings were painted by Hans Holbein, court painter from 1536.

The palace was later a favourite of Elizabeth I, although she made few alterations, and of Charles I. Most of this vast palace, which was said to contain 2,000 rooms, burned down in a single night in 1698 during the reign of William III and Mary II. Only Jones's Banqueting House was spared.

Right: Roman basilica updated – the great double cube of the Banqueting Hall. Note the Ionic columns beneath and the Corinthian pilasters above the gallery.

WILTON HOUSE

SEAT OF THE EARLS OF PEMBROKE

In the late 1630s, Philip Herbert, 4th Earl of Pembroke, built a magnificent new south front to his family's Tudor mansion at Wilton House in Wiltshire. Construction, carried out by the Frenchman Isaac de Caus, was supervised and directed by Inigo Jones, who designed seven magnificent staterooms for the interior.

Above: The east front (right) and the south front (left) at Wilton. The sedate exterior gives no hint of the riches within.

The original Wilton House was built by Sir William Herbert on land that formerly belonged to Wilton Abbey, which he was given by King Henry VIII in 1544. Sir William was related to the King by marriage, as his first wife, Anne, was the sister of Henry's sixth wife, Catherine Parr. In 1551, Henry made Sir William 1st Earl of Pembroke. At Wilton, Sir William built a fine courtyard house in the second half of the 1540s. The commanding tower in the centre of Wilton's east front is a survival from his splendid house.

WILTON'S SOUTH FRONT

The new south front of the 1630s was originally intended as the right half of a much longer façade, which was to have had a portico with six Corinthian columns at its centre; this was probably never carried through because the Civil War intervened. De Caus's original plan of this projected design, which still survives, was improved, perhaps by Jones, with the addition of towers at each end.

DOUBLE CUBE ROOM

While the building's facade has a classical, Italianate appearance, its extraordinary interior exhibits the influence of French style. The most celebrated of Jones's staterooms is the lavishly decorated Double Cube Room. This is not, in fact, the original room built in the 1630s, since a fire in 1647 or 1648 severely damaged the central part of the wing and the room was rebuilt and redecorated *c.*1648–53 by John Webb, under the direction of Jones, who was

Below: In de Caus's original design, the south front as we see it was just the right half of a longer façade with a central portico.

A COLLEGE OF THE 'LEARNED AND INGENIOUS'

Wilton House was the scene of great events in the Elizabethan and Jacobean periods, when Mary, Countess of Pembroke (wife of Henry Herbert, 2nd Earl of Pembroke) was a great literary hostess. The writer John Aubrey declared: 'In her time, Wilton House was like a college, there were so many learned and ingenious persons'. Mary was herself a poet and her brother was Sir Philip Sidney, who often stayed with her and wrote the bulk of his prose romance *The Arcadia* there before 1581. Christopher Marlowe, Edmund Spenser, Ben Jonson and John Donne certainly visited Wilton; some writers believe Shakespeare himself was a guest of the Countess of Pembroke and that *As You Like It* had its first performance at Wilton House on 2 December 1603, with James I in the audience.

then over 70 years old. The room is called Double Cube because of its dimensions: 60ft (18m) long by 30ft (9m) wide and 30ft (9m) high. It is decorated with expanses of fruit and flowers carved in wood and then gilded and fixed to the white walls. The chimney-pieces are of intricately carved Italian marble; the coved ceilings are equally ornate. On the walls hang portraits by Sir Anthony van Dyck of the Herberts and the royal family. The room is today furnished with lavish gilt mirrors, and red velvet chairs and sofas designed in the 18th century by William Kent and Thomas Chippendale. Beside it is the similarly lavishly decorated Single Cube Room, a perfect 30ft (9m) cube. The latest thinking is that the fire did not reach this room, and therefore it appears today as it was decorated in the 1630s. The lower panels on its walls retell the story of Philip Sidney's *The Arcadia*. In World War II, remarkably, the Double Cube Room was a military operations centre in which the D-Day landings were planned.

Above: The Double Cube Room. Credit for its decorative scheme should go to Jean Barbet and John Webb – especially Webb, who redecorated it after the 1647–8 fire.

Below: Wilton's Palladian bridge was the original of the three country-house bridges in this style. It was copied at Stowe (1738) and Prior Park, Bath (1756).

PALLADIAN BRIDGE

Wilton House is also celebrated for its Palladian-style bridge across the River Nadder, which flows through the grounds, built in 1737 by Henry Herbert, the 9th Earl of Pembroke. With its temple portico, it is one of three almost identical bridges of this period; others are to be found at Prior Park, Bath, and Stowe, Buckingham.

In the 9th Earl's time, also, the gardens were landscaped in the 'picturesque style'; then, in 1779, Lancelot 'Capability' Brown was brought in to redesign them. At the start of the 19th century, Wyatt opened up the interior of the house by adding Gothic cloisters and building a new entrance via the north forecourt.

WILTON'S POPULARITY

Wilton House was a great favourite of James I, and across the centuries it remained close to the heart of national life, visited frequently by the reigning monarch. It so impressed Daniel Defoe that he wrote 'One cannot be said to have seen anything that a man of curiosity would think worth seeing in the country and not have been at Wilton House'.

More recently, the house and grounds have become a star of the screen. Major productions filmed at Wilton have included *The Madness of King George*, *Mrs Brown*, *Sense and Sensibility* and the 2005 version of *Pride and Prejudice*.

'PLANTATION CASTLES' IN ULSTER

BALFOUR, ENNISKILLEN, MONEA, TULLY AND KILLYLEAGH

In 1618, Scottish Protestant lord, Sir James Balfour, built Castle Balfour at Linaskea in County Fermanagh on the site of a fortress belonging to the Maguires, the leading family of Fermanagh since 1300. Sir James got the Maguire land as a beneficiary of James I's 'Plantation' of Ulster — the introduction of Protestant Englishmen and Scots into this rebellious and strongly Catholic part of northern Ireland.

Castle Balfour, now ruined, was built in the style of contemporary Scottish strong-houses, on a T-plan with stair turrets and parapets.

Another Maguire stronghold was rebuilt at nearby Enniskillen, County Fermanagh, by Captain William Cole – like Balfour, originally a man of Fife – in 1611. While living in a makeshift timber house, Cole reworked the ruined medieval fortress, adding a strong defensive wall and raising a new dwelling. He built a distinctively Scottish water-gate to guard the entrance from the adjacent Lough Erne. It has twin turrets with conical roofs. Stylistic similarities suggest that Enniskillen and Balfour castles may have been rebuilt by the same Scottish masons.

Above: Enniskillen's substantial twin-turreted gate was built to guard against a waterborne attack across Lough Erne.

SCOTTISH PROFILE AT MONEA

Castle Balfour and Enniskillen Castle are just two of several fortifications in Northern Ireland built or refashioned by Scottish or English incomers, who received their lands as part of the Plantation of Ulster. Near Enniskillen, the substantial Monea Castle was built *c.*1616 by Scottish churchman, Malcolm Hamilton, later Archbishop of Cashel. The rectangular three-storey stronghold, now ruined, was 50ft (15m) tall and 20ft (6m) wide, enclosed by a 300ft (91m) defensive circuit wall 9ft (2.7m) in height. On its west front stood two cylindrical towers with square rooms projecting diagonally at attic level – a distinctive profile probably copied from that of Claypotts Castle near Dundee in Scotland. The castle had a single entrance in the most northerly of these towers, with a spiral staircase leading to the well-lit main reception rooms, with big windows and window-seats, on the first floor and then to the bedrooms on the second floor.

Later, the castle was the residence of Gustavus Hamilton, Governor of Enniskillen and 1st Viscount Boyne. Hamilton was financially ruined during the Williamite Wars, during which he

DUNLUCE: A MANSION WITHIN A CASTLE

In *c.*1620, Randal McDonnell, 1st Earl of Antrim, constructed an elegant manor house with gables and large mullioned windows within the fortifications of a 13th-century castle at Dunluce, County Antrim, on a basalt rock above the sea. He was the son of Scottish adventurer, Sorley Boy McDonnell, who captured the castle in *c.*1560 from members of the locally powerful McQuillan clan and, after being evicted, retook it from an English garrison. In 1586, Sorley Boy was made Constable of the Castle by Elizabeth I, but his loyalty was not beyond question – two years later, he reputedly gave refuge to survivors from a Spanish Armada galleon, which had foundered on Atlantic rocks below the castle; he also armed his castle with cannon taken from the ship.

Randal McDonnell married Lady Katharine Manners, the widow of great court favourite the Earl of Buckingham, and brought her to live at Dunluce. They equipped their mansion lavishly – with the finest tapestries and, it is said, a pair of curtains from Hampton Court Palace. Its remains can be seen today within the castle walls, alongside the columns of an extraordinary sandstone loggia that Sorley Boy erected, along the lines of one built by the Earl of Bothwell at Crichton Castle near Edinburgh.

Above: At Killyleagh, the original 17th-century towers are rather lost amid the mid-19th-century Scots Baronial reworking.

was Brigadier General of William III's army. After his death in 1691, his family remained in residence at Monea for some time, but eventually were forced by money difficulties to sell the castle.

TULLY CASTLE

Another Scottish planter, Sir John Hume of Berwick, built Tully Castle near Blaney village in County Fermanagh, overlooking Lower Lough Erne, in 1612-15. The village and area took the name Blaney from that of Sir Edward Blaney, who, as Lord Deputy in the service of King James I, had been despatched to Fermanagh to oversee and arrange the Plantation.

Tully Castle consisted of a defended enclosure or bawn, with four projecting rectangular corner towers, plus a two-and-half-storey fortified building. Today it is a substantial and picturesque ruin because it was captured and burned by Rory, scion of the Maguire family, during an attack on Christmas Day 1641 that was part of the bloody rebellion of that year by Irish Catholics. In the attack on Tully Castle, 16 men and 69 women and children were killed, although the Hume family survived.

ROUGHAN CASTLE

Near Newmills in County Tyrone, Andrew Stewart built Roughan Castle in *c.*1618. His father was another Scottish nobleman and benificiary of the Plantation, Lord Castlestewart, who had founded Stewartstown, near Newmills. The three-storey castle has a 20ft (6m) central tower and four round corner towers. In the rebellion of 1641, the castle was held by Andrew Stewart's descendant Robert Stewart, who, after marrying into the O'Neill family, took the side of the rebels.

KILLYLEAGH CASTLE

Another beneficiary of the Plantation was Sir James Hamilton of Ayrshire, who was granted large territories in County Down that had previously belonged to the O'Neill clan. He built Killyleagh Castle, with a round tower and conical roof, on the site of a 12th-century fortification raised by Norman adventurer-knight John de Courcy. The round tower survives on the south corner of the castle front; it is balanced by an identical tower on the north end of the front, added in the late 17th century following damage in the civil war. The castle was reworked in the Scottish Baronial style in the mid-19th century by Archibald Hamilton.

Above: The ruins of Monea Castle give a good indication of its former grandeur – and show off the distinctive design of the tower.

Right: Monea Castle in its prime, c.1620. This view shows its distinctive round towers with square rooms projecting at attic level.

CHAPTER EIGHT

RESTORATION STYLE

*c.*1660–*c.*1714

During the years of the Commonwealth and Protectorate, many of England's leading Royalists were forced to abandon their country houses to live in exile in Europe. During these years, they were impressed by French, Italian and Dutch styles of architecture, decoration and garden design. When they returned with Charles II at the Restoration of the Monarchy in 1660, many brought with them continental tastes for elaborate decoration. Craftsmen such as the French metalworker Jean Tijou, the Dutch-born woodcarver Grinling Gibbons, and the Danish sculptor Caius Gabriel Cibber, worked on magnificent interiors for discerning patrons at houses such as Chatsworth, Petworth and Belton, for Charles II in his superb staterooms at Windsor Castle and, after the 'Glorious Revolution' of 1688, for William III and Mary II at Hampton Court Palace. Their work adorned Great Apartments – suites of grand reception rooms, which, in the 17th century, replaced the Great Hall as the principal feature of the great house and palace. These staterooms attempted to mirror the splendour of the chateaux and palaces of continental Europe, especially that of Louis XIV at Versailles. European taste and, in particular, Louis's great palace complex – a resounding expression of his absolute rule – also had an influence on the laying out of pleasure grounds around country houses and palaces in these years. At Hampton Court Palace, for example, both Charles II and, later, William and Mary created elaborate water and floral decorations in the French style.

Left: The originally Tudor Chatsworth House, completely rebuilt in grand style by the 4th Earl of Devonshire in 1687–1707, stands in a beautiful position beside the River Derwent.

PETWORTH HOUSE
AND GRINLING GIBBONS

Petworth House was built in 1688–96 by Charles Seymour, 6th Duke of Somerset, incorporating part of a 13th-century castle that belonged to the Percy earls of Northumberland. The Duke's great house, which stands on the edge of the West Sussex town of Petworth, is renowned particularly for its association with artists and contains a room of woodcarving generally agreed to be the masterpiece of the great craftsman Grinling Gibbons.

Petworth House is often cited as a rare example of direct French influence on the English great house. Horace Walpole declared it to be 'in the style of the Tuileries', the royal palace that once stood alongside the Louvre in central Paris. Petworth's original west entrance front is thought to have featured a central dome, with a series of elaborate urns around its cupola, while statues were arranged on the balustrade running across the entire front. This arrangement can be seen in a picture of the house *c.*1700, now at Belvoir Castle. However, the central dome was destroyed and the west front damaged in a fire of 1714. During restoration, the house was given a plainer appearance.

Even so, nine of the west front's 42 tall windows (three in the centre and three at each end) have busts and carving above them in a French style. The famous deer park at Petworth was landscaped by 'Capability' Brown in the 1750s.

ENTRANCE HALL

Within, the house contains nine interconnecting staterooms arranged along the front, facing the park, and behind them nine equally grand rooms along the east, or town, side of the house. In the centre of the west front is the Marble Hall, originally the entrance hall, with a floor of white, green and black marble, a fireplace at its north and south ends and elaborate carving by John Selden around the doors and fireplaces and above the cornice. (Selden worked on the estate for the Duke, yet, despite the superb quality of his work, is little known aside from Petworth House.) In the 19th century, the entrance was moved from the park side to the house's other main front, on the east side facing the town.

GRINLING GIBBONS ROOM

Further along the front to the north is the Grinling Gibbons Room. In this large space, 20ft (6m) high, 24ft (7m) wide and 60ft (18m) long, Gibbons provided fantastically carved frames for seven portraits – including a large central one of Henry VIII, copied from the celebrated original of Hans Holbein. Gibbons' limewood-carving of flowers, fruit, leaves, musical instruments, birds, baskets and other intricate objects is wonderfully detailed and delicate.

MASTER OF WOODCARVING: GRINLING GIBBONS

Born in Rotterdam, in 1648, to an English father, Gibbons had made his name in London as a wood carver by the early 1670s. He produced woodcarvings for Charles II at Windsor Castle and, in the 1680s–90s, made the carvings for Petworth House while also completing work at Hampton Court Palace and Kensington Palace, as commissioned by William III and Mary II. He was appointed Master Carver at the Royal Court in 1693. He also did exquisite work at St Paul's Cathedral, carving choir stalls and a fine organ screen, as well as working in stone on the exterior of Sir Christopher Wren's building (completed in 1710) and making a bronze statue of James II, now outside the National Gallery, London.

Above: Gibbons' delicate work had an enduring influence on country house decor.

Below: Grinling Gibbons' carving on the picture frames at Petworth House is marked by a breathtaking realism and delicacy.

CHAPEL

The chapel at Petworth House is a survivor from the 13th-century castle of the Percy earls. To this, in 1690–2, the 6th Duke added a plaster ceiling together with stalls, altar rail and gallery in gilded wood.

CAPTURED ON CANVAS

In the 1750s, Alicia Maria, Countess of Egremont, lavishly redecorated the sitting room now known as the White and Gold Room. This is probably the room painted by J.M.W. Turner in his celebrated picture *Drawing Room at Petworth*, now held by the National Gallery, London. This is one of a famous series of paintings by Turner, who visited several times in the 1830s as a friend of the 3rd Earl of Egremont.

FRENCH INFLUENCE AT BOUGHTON

At the same time that Petworth House was being built, the main north front at Boughton House, Northamptonshire, was constructed in a French style by the francophile Ralph, 3rd Lord Montagu, who had served as Charles II's ambassador to France in 1669, 1676 and 1677. The front has a protruding pavilion at each end and between these a ground-floor loggia (arcade) that Montagu called 'the cloisters'. Above the arcade was the five-room Great Apartment floored with parquet in the style of Versailles.

Lord Montagu was a colourful and notable character: Jonathan Swift declared him to be 'as arrant a knave as any in his time', while William Congreve dedicated his play *The Way of the World* to him in 1700. Lord Montagu received William III in the splendid surroundings of Boughton House in 1695. He also built a fine town house, Montagu House, in London, which subsequently became the first home of the British Museum. In 1705, Queen Anne made Lord Montagu Marquess of Monthermer and 1st Duke of Montagu.

Above: A regal French style in Sussex. The great west front at Petworth House faces the park and contains nine grand state rooms.

Right: Gibbons' work in situ. *Horace Walpole said the Gibbons Room at Petworth was 'the most superb monument of his skill'.*

HOLYROODHOUSE PALACE

SCOTTISH ROYAL RESIDENCE

In the 1530s, James V raised a conical-turreted rectangular tower at Holyroodhouse in Edinburgh containing royal apartments (see page 106). The palace served as the principal residence of Mary, Queen of Scots, and witnessed the murder of her secretary, David Rizzio, at the hands of men led by Mary's husband, Lord Darnley. In the reign of Mary's son, James VI of Scots and I of England, the palace fell into decline but was renovated in time for the Scottish coronation of James's son and successor, Charles I. During the Civil War, Parliamentarian forces were housed in the palace, which was badly damaged by fire.

CHARLES II'S RECONSTRUCTION WORK

During the 1670s, Charles II initiated a major reconstruction of the Palace of Holyroodhouse. Directed by Sir William Bruce, who was appointed Surveyor-General and Overseer of the King's Buildings in Scotland, and implemented by Robert Mylne, the King's Master Mason in Scotland, Charles's programme involved raising a southern tower on the entrance front to match the splendid northern one built by James V, and erecting a range between the towers with a fine Doric portico at the entrance. Fine classical façades were added to the inner quadrangle, with an elegant arcade at ground level.

The first floor contained the royal apartments, fitted with impressive plaster ceilings – especially in the West Drawing Room – and elegant wainscoting. In the Long Gallery, the Dutch artist Jacob de Wet painted 110 portraits of Scottish kings, both real and legendary, from Fergus I to Charles II, who commissioned the work. Charles also made the Holyrood Abbey Church the Chapel Royal for the palace. Charles, however, saw none of this fine work, as he did not once visit Holyroodhouse.

LATER DEVELOPMENTS

During the brief reign of Charles's successor, the Roman Catholic James VII of Scots and II of England, the King adapted the chapel so it could be used for Roman Catholic rites. In later years, his grandson 'Bonnie Prince Charlie' stayed at Holyroodhouse Palace for a few weeks in 1745, during his attempt to win the throne back for his father, but after the collapse of the '45 revolt no royal stayed there until Queen Victoria in the 19th century. Renovated in Victorian times and by George V, the Palace has regained its position as Scotland's foremost royal palace. It is Queen Elizabeth II's official residence when she visits Scotland each year.

Above: Charles II and James, Duke of York. James was deposed before he could enjoy the alterations he made at Holyroodhouse.

Below: Charles II's rebuilding at Holyroodhouse transformed the building into an elegant palace in the classical style.

WINDSOR CASTLE
AND CHARLES II

Above: This reconstruction shows St George's Hall in the 1670s – as decorated by Verrio and Gibbons for Charles II.

Windsor Castle (see also page 82) was Charles II's favourite royal residence outside London, and he undertook a major rebuilding scheme there in the 1670s. Using Hugh May as architect, Antonio Verrio as principal artist and Grinling Gibbon for decorative carving, Charles built new state apartments and redecorated St George's Hall and the King's Chapel at an overall cost of £130,000. Much of this splendid work was remodelled in the 19th century by George IV and Sir Jeffry Wyatville (see page 224), but elements of the 1670s' alterations survive in the King's Dining Room, in the Queen's Presence and Audience Chambers and (outside) in the Long Walk, lined with elms for its 3 mile (4.5km) route from the south entrance of the castle to Windsor Great Park.

THE UPPER WARD

Externally, Hugh May rebuilt the castle's upper ward in a largely classical style. Its east front, for example, had four massive towers and a central *piano nobile* accessed by two staircases. Internally, the lavish state apartments attempted to replicate some of the magnificence of Versailles. They are identified by some architectural historians as the first English apartments in the Baroque style and were the inspiration for sets of similarly magnificent staterooms at houses such as Burghley and Chatsworth. The king and queen had separate suites of apartments, including drawing rooms, audience chambers and bedchambers; the queen also had a ballroom. Gibbons' naturalistic carving of game birds, flowers, fruit and fish adorned the walls, which were also wainscoted; 13 ceiling paintings by Verrio represented the triumphs of the King and the Church of England.

Below: Charles II laid out the imposing Long Walk, lined with elms, approaching Windsor Castle across the Great Park.

ST GEORGE'S HALL

Charles's redecorated St George's Hall also featured grand historical-allegorical paintings by Verrio, depicting scenes from the history of the Order of the Garter, together with Charles II enthroned in grandeur. The hall was fitted with a gilt throne made by John van der Stein and Louis von Opstal.

GIBBONS' WORK IN EVIDENCE

Some of Gibbons' carving survives today in the Waterloo Chamber, which was created by George IV in the 1820s. In addition, the Royal Chapel contained wooden stalls carved in the shape of laurel and palm by Gibbons; the walls were decorated with a set of Verrio murals depicting Christ's miracles, while the ceiling celebrated the Resurrection. Behind the altar was a version of the *Last Supper* and columns derived from Gian Lorenzo Bernini's Baroque-style *baldechino* (canopy) in St Peter's, Rome.

AN UNFINISHED PALACE

Charles II began a grand new royal residence at Winchester to replace the medieval castle and palace there. Building was begun in 1682 to designs by Sir Christopher Wren that aimed to replicate the glory of Versailles on English soil. At Charles's death in 1685, the shell of the building was complete. But thereafter work was stopped by James II, and Wren's building was never fitted out internally. The 'palace' was later used as a military barracks before burning down in 1894.

CHATSWORTH

'PALACE OF THE PEAK'

Chatsworth's superbly grand appearance, lavish interior, magnificent works of art and splendid gardens in a wonderful setting combine to make it one of the finest – and perhaps the most famous – of all England's stately homes. The house, which stands in the glorious countryside of the Derbyshire Peak District, is celebrated as 'the Palace of the Peak'. (See also page 225.)

The first major house at Chatsworth was built in the mid-16th century by Elizabeth Cavendish (later 'Bess of Hardwick', builder of Hardwick House) and her second husband, Sir William Cavendish, Treasurer of the Chamber at the court of King Henry VIII. This house was completely rebuilt in 1687–1707 by William Cavendish, the 4th Earl of Devonshire.

A long wing was built to the north of the 4th Earl's elegant house in the 19th century by yet another William Cavendish, 6th Duke of Devonshire, to the designs of architect Sir Jeffry Wyatville.

Above: Garden diversion. The cascade installed in 1696 created interesting sound effects, as well as being a visual delight.

REBUILDING CHATSWORTH

The 16th-century house stood on the same site as the one we see today, on a terrace beside the River Derwent, and like its successor it was built around a central courtyard. In 1687, the 4th Earl began with the intention of rebuilding only the south front of this house, but when he found that this improvement showed up imperfections in the other parts of the house, he was persuaded to move on to another part, and then another. He intended each improvement to be the last, but in the end, over the course of 20 years, he rebuilt Chatsworth entirely, one section at a time.

The new south and east wings were designed by William Talman, then an unknown architect. Talman grew increasingly frustrated by the Earl's autocratic behaviour, particularly his habit of changing his mind and tearing down

Below: Baroque aesthetics? This riot of figures is a detail from one of Laguerre's exuberant ceilings at Chatsworth.

JEAN TIJOU

The supremely skilled metalworker, Jean Tijou, was a French Huguenot who came to England as a religious exile after 1685. He did exquisite work at Hampton Court Palace and its gardens and made screens and grilles for St Paul's Cathedral, as well as working at Chatsworth, Burghley House, Castle Howard and Easton Neston. The 'Golden Gates' he provided at Chatsworth are matched by his intricate gilded iron gates at Burghley House.

A KENNEDY AT CHATSWORTH

In 1944, William, Marquess of Hartington, eldest son of the 10th Duke of Devonshire and heir to Chatsworth House, married an American bride, Kathleen Kennedy, whose brother John F. Kennedy would in 1961 become the 35th President of the United States. William was killed in action that same year, and his young wife lived only four years as the Marchioness of Hartington before herself dying in an air accident in 1948. Her portrait is displayed in the Sketch Galleries at Chatsworth House; she is buried at the churchyard of St Peter in the village of Edensor on the Chatsworth estate – in the same graveyard as the 6th Duke of Devonshire and Joseph Paxton.

building work that had already been completed. The relationship was soured further by prolonged disputes over payment, which resulted in Sir Christopher Wren being despatched to Chatsworth in 1692 to make a judgement on how much the building had cost to that date: his arbitration was the sum of £9,025 16s 6¾d. As a result of this quarrel, Talman was not involved in the rebuilding of the west and north fronts. The west front was probably designed by Thomas Archer, while the north front may have been the work of the Earl himself (from 1694, the 1st Duke of Devonshire) or perhaps was created by John Fitch or even Wren.

LAVISH INTERIORS

The interior of the new house was lavishly decorated and fitted out by the finest craftsmen. Louis Laguerre painted the chapel frescoes (which have remained unaltered since 1694) and, together with Antonio Verrio and Ricard, decorated the ceilings of the staterooms and staircase. These rooms are arranged on the top floor of the three-storey house and provide marvellous views of the park outside. The great stone staircase has a fine wrought-iron balustrade by Frenchman Jean Tijou; a second staircase rises beneath a coved ceiling by Sir James Thornhill, who also painted the illusionist decoration in the Sabine Room. In the State Music Room, the Dutch artist, Jan van der Vaart, painted another widely celebrated *trompe l'oeil*: an image of a very realistic violin hanging on a door.

THE GARDENS AND PARK

The extensive gardens and parkland we see today were largely created in the 18th century by 'Capability' Brown and in the 19th century by the 6th Duke, his architect Sir Jeffry Wyatville, and his gardener Joseph Paxton (later designer of the Crystal Palace in London). However, the Great Cascade, the stepped waterfall that descends the slope behind the house, was designed in the 1st Duke's time by Thomas Archer in 1696. Waters from the moorland above feed into a 'Cascade House' and then run down the slope for around ¼ mile (0.4km) over steps varying in size and shape, which alter the sound made by the water as it falls. When the Great Cascade was built, Chatsworth's grounds contained formal terraces and parterres designed by the foremost landscape gardeners of their day: George London and Henry Wise.

Below: Chatsworth probably looks at its most beautiful when the rich hues of its stonework are set off by autumnal leaves.

FELBRIGG HALL

AN ARCHITECTURAL CURIOSITY

In the L-shaped country house of Felbrigg Hall, near Cromer in Norfolk, a Jacobean wing of 1621–4 meets at right angles with a classical wing of *c.*1680. Two architectural languages, the first native English, the second classical in origin, though only 60 years apart, meet here in curious juxtaposition.

Above: Two houses in one at Felbrigg. This view shows the Jacobean wing, with the classical wing just visible facing to the left.

LYMINGE'S JACOBEAN WING

The first Felbrigg Hall was medieval. Thomas Windham demolished all except the cellars when he commissioned Robert Lyminge to build a new house.

Lyminge's Jacobean wing has seven bays, including the central porch, and a homely rustic appearance, being built of a combination of flint, brick and stone. Within, the house originally contained a hall and kitchen on the ground floor, a bedchamber and private saloon on the second floor and a Long Gallery along the length of the third floor. Although these rooms have been restructured in the intervening years, the actual façade remains largely untouched.

SAMWELL'S CLASSICAL WING

In 1675–86, Thomas Windham's son, William, built a contrasting classical wing, which was designed by gentleman architect William Samwell, with fine red brickwork, 16 tall windows and six small dormers in the roof. It connects with the Jacobean wing at the corner, but the two wings make no concessions to each other.

PAINE'S REMODELLED ROOMS

In 1749–56, William Windham's grandson, William Windham II, commissioned the architect James Paine to remodel the three main rooms on the ground floor of the 1680s wing. One, originally the entrance hall, he made the Dining Room; a second was the Drawing Room; the third, called 'the Cabinet', he fitted with red damask on the walls as a backing for a collection of paintings brought back by his patron from a continental Grand Tour.

In an upstairs room, Paine created a fine Gothic library to house William Windham II's large book collection. It is considered a splendid example of the early Gothic Revival style.

ENGLAND'S FIRST CLASSICAL PORTICO

The Vyne in Hampshire, built by Tudor courtier Lord Sandys, was owned during the Commonwealth period by Chaloner Chute, the Speaker of the House of Commons. In *c.*1654, he commissioned John Webb to build a classical portico on the house's north front, which was the first structure of its kind in the country.

Below: The first classical portico in an English country house looks out across the lake in the grounds of The Vyne.

NOTTINGHAM CASTLE

A DUCAL MANSION

William the Conqueror first established a timber fortress in Nottingham in the year after the Conquest. In 1170, Henry III built a stone castle on the same elevated site, establishing Nottingham Castle as the most important and formidable royal castle in the Midlands. Finally, William Cavendish, 1st Duke of Newcastle, and his son Henry, 2nd Duke, erected a ducal mansion on this historic site in 1674–9.

The castle witnessed numerous important events in the medieval period. In 1194, King Richard I the Lionheart used siege machinery to take the castle from his brother John (the future King John), who had seized power while Richard was on Crusade. Then, in 1330, Edward III broke into the castle through a 300ft (91m)- long subterranean passageway, surprising his mother, Queen Isabella, and her lover, Roger Mortimer, Earl of March, who together were the effective rulers of the country, although Edward wore the crown. Mortimer was executed in London. The passageway, known as Mortimer's Hole, can be seen in the grounds. In 1485, Richard III rode out from Nottingham Castle to Bosworth Field, the battlefield on which he lost his crown to Henry Tudor, the future Henry VII and father of Henry VIII.

Right: An artwork reconstruction shows clearly the size of the original Nottingham Castle – and its imposing situation.

IN AND OUT OF ROYAL HANDS

In 1623, James I granted the castle and its adjacent parkland to Francis Manners, 6th Earl of Rutland. In the Civil War, Nottingham Castle was a rallying point for King Charles I, who raised the royal standard there in 1642. It was later garrisoned for Parliament under the command of Colonel John Hutchinson. His troops repulsed several royalist attempts to capture the castle. Then, after Charles I's execution in 1649, the stronghold was demolished on the orders of Parliament.

'PROSPECT HOUSE'

The mansion the 1st and 2nd Dukes built on the site of the original castle, was a 'prospect house': perched on its high rock, it had superb views over the town and parkland. The house had two wings. The staterooms for grand receptions were on the first floor. In the early Hanoverian years, Thomas Pelham, the then Duke of Newcastle, was twice prime minister (1754–6 and 1757–62).

In the 19th century, the mansion was severely damaged when, in 1831, rioters protesting in favour of parliamentary reform broke into the house and started a great fire. (Its owner, Henry, 4th Duke of Newcastle, was a well-known opponent of reform.) The conflagration reduced the building to a shell, but it was restored and refurbished as an art gallery in 1878.

Below: Nottingham Castle – a ducal mansion rather than a fortress. Its elevated position gives it superb views of the city.

BELTON HOUSE

'A GLORIOUS HOUSE'

The elegant Belton House, near Grantham, was built in 1685–8 for Sir John Brownlow, High Sheriff of Lincolnshire. It is ranked as one of England's finest examples of a late 17th-century country house.

We know disappointingly little about Sir John Brownlow himself. He wed his cousin and fathered five lively daughters, and apart from being High Sheriff of Lincolnshire, he was twice MP for Grantham. Belton House was sufficiently grand for Sir John to entertain William III there in 1695, but two years later he took his own life.

Above: The south (right) and west fronts at Belton House. Note James Wyatt's elegant neoclassical doorway of 1777.

CHRISTOPHER WREN AS ROYAL ARCHITECT

Sir Christopher Wren is celebrated above all for his design of the rebuilt St Paul's Cathedral (and 52 other London churches). Yet he was also a significant royal architect, serving as the monarch's Surveyor of Works from 1669 to 1718, for Charles II, James II, William III and Mary II, Anne and George I. Wren was influenced not only by the classical architecture of Inigo Jones and John Webb in England, but also by the magnificent Louvre and Versailles palaces, which he saw on a trip to France in the 1660s. He was Professor of Astronomy at Oxford University and a founder and President of the Royal Society (an elite scientific body in London), and thus brought a vast intellect and a fresh outlook to his architectural work. He provided designs for rebuilding Whitehall Palace, designed a new palace (never finished) for Charles II at Winchester, made alterations to the Queen's Chapel, St James's, and added a small block of new staterooms there. Wren also designed the Royal Naval Hospital in Greenwich, in addition to substantial work at Hampton Court Palace and Kensington Palace. His range was wide: some claim him as an architect of the monumental Baroque (there are certainly elements of this style in some of his church designs), while others prefer to emphasize his more conventional work, which was carried out in a classical Renaissance style.

Left: Sir Christopher Wren, associated forever with the dome of St Paul's Cathedral, may have designed Belton House.

His architect is not known, although possible names mentioned by historians are William Winde, William Stanton and even Sir Christopher Wren. The design was closely based on that of Clarendon House on Piccadilly, London. This building, designed by Sir Roger Pratt for Edward Hyde, Earl of Clarendon, was highly regarded by contemporaries (Pepys called it 'the finest pile I ever saw in my life ... a glorious house'), but it was demolished in 1683 after the Earl's fall from favour and flight to France.

MELLOW STONE EXTERIOR

The H-shaped house at Belton has two near-identical façades: to the south is the main entrance and to the north the garden front. Thirteen large windows arrayed in two symmetrical lines of seven fill the main section of the front, between protruding end wings that are each two bays wide.

The north front has been unchanged since building, but on the entrance front James Wyatt added a neoclassical doorway with pilasters (flattened columns) and entablature (decorative carving above the columns) in 1777. The house is built of ashlar dressed stone from the quarry at nearby Ancaster, which has weathered delightfully over the years to give the house a mellow look.

INTERIOR GRANDEUR

The interior is lavishly decorated with woodcarving and stucco work. The Marble Hall and Saloon have exquisite limewood carving by the great Grinling Gibbons; the chapel has a wonderfully carved original reredos (ornamental screen) that may also be by Gibbons. The chapel is virtually unaltered and it and the Chapel Gallery also contain fine plaster ceilings modelled by Edward Goudge. The wall panelling in the Chapel Drawing Room is delicately painted to simulate marble.

ALTERATION AND RESTORATION

Upstairs, the Tyrconnel Room is a rare example of a late 18th-century painted floor: it features the arms of the Brownlow family amid decorative foliage. In *c.*1776–7, James Wyatt built the splendid library, which has a barrel-vaulted ceiling.

In the early 19th century, Sir Jeffry Wyatville added a fine staircase to Belton House and created the elegant Red Drawing Room, which has a wonderful *trompe l'oeil* frieze together with panels of crimson damask set in the wainscoting. The room is hung with a wealth of pictures, including a number of works by Van Dyck, Titian and Rembrandt.

Outside, Wyatville built an orangery and fountain and laid out an Italian garden. Later in the 19th century, the 3rd Earl of Brownlow sensitively restored Belton House, in particular rebuilding the balustrade and cupola on the roof.

THE 'LADY ARCHITECT' OF WESTON PARK

Elizabeth, Lady Wilbrahim, rebuilt Weston Park in Shropshire in the 1670s. She designed in the classical idiom – visitors can see her copy of Palladio's *First Book of Architecture* annotated with notes for redesigning the house. But her house also exhibits French influence, in its semicircular pediments, and Dutch style in its combination of brick and stone. She inherited the medieval house that stood on the site, and then acquired wealth through marriage to Sir Thomas Wilbrahim in 1651. This remarkable woman also designed the parish church and stables at Weston Park.

Weston Park contains a magnificent art collection, including works by Holbein and van Dyck. It stands in an estate of 1000 acres (404ha), in parkland landscaped by 'Capability' Brown in 1765; in the 1770s, James Paine built a Temple of Diana in the grounds.

Above: Weston Park was designed by Elizabeth, Lady Wilbrahim, in the 1670s in the Palladian style.

In the 19th century, it was often visited by Prime Minister Benjamin Disraeli, who had an intense platonic relationship with Selina, Countess of Bradford, wife of the house's then owner, the 3rd Earl of Bradford. A collection of 1,100 letters from Disraeli to the Countess is displayed at the house. In modern times, the house was the venue for the G8 summit of world leaders in 1998.

ROYAL CONNECTIONS

Belton House sits in 36 acres (14ha) of fine formal and semi-formal gardens and a large landscaped park. The house remained in the hands of Sir John Brownlow's descendants until 1984, when it passed to the care of the National Trust. George III visited, as did Edward VIII before his abdication, at a time when the then Lord Brownlow was Lord-in-Waiting to the King. The library at Belton contains a display of objects associated with Edward VIII.

Left: Belton's 19th-century orangery, Italianate fountain and garden were designed by Sir Jeffry Wyatville.

HAMPTON COURT, KENSINGTON PALACE
AND THE WORK OF SIR CHRISTOPHER WREN

In 1689, William III and Mary II commissioned Sir Christopher Wren to rebuild Hampton Court Palace. Wren's intention was to sweep away the Tudor palace (see pages 98-9), retaining only the Great Hall, and to create a majestic Renaissance-style country residence grand enough to rival Louis XIV's palace at Versailles. In the event, due to lack of money and time (William and Mary were impatient to see results), Wren built only new sets of apartments for the King and Queen.

Above: Detail of Wren's windows in the new east front at Hampton Court.

Above: William's and Mary's initials are intertwined on a Hampton Court façade.

THE FOUNTAIN COURT

The apartments were around a new courtyard, the Fountain Court, which Wren raised on the site of the former royal lodgings. The building work also created a new east front for the palace. The King and Queen, who ruled as joint monarchs, were to have separate sets of rooms accessed by separate grand staircases.

Below: In red brick with Portland stone dressing, the east front at Hampton Court is a handsome example of Anglo-Dutch style.

Work began in 1689 and was completed by 1694. The new buildings featured the finest stone carving by Grinling Gibbons and Caius Gabriel Cibber, as well as splendid ironwork by Jean Tijou. However, following Mary's death that year, William halted the work before the interiors were decorated. In 1698, after the destruction of Whitehall Palace in a vast fire, William ordered the resumption of work at Hampton Court. The interior decoration, under the supervision of William Talman and with the King's personal involvement, continued until 1702. The ceilings above the staircase and in the King's staterooms were painted by Antonio Verrio.

HAMPTON COURT GARDENS

Charles II had laid out a long 'canal' or elongated pond before the east front of the palace in 1668. William III filled in part of the 'canal' to create a parterre (a display of ornamental flowerbeds), designed by the Huguenot Daniel Marot. Working with the garden designer George London and with William Talman as architect, William also laid out a Privy Garden in the area between the palace and the River Thames and the Bushy Park Avenue to the north of the palace. The gardens contained splendid ironwork gates by Jean Tijou and architectural ornament by Cibber and Edward Pearce.

The Privy Garden was meticulously restored in 1991–5 with great concern for historical accuracy.

THE MOVE TO KENSINGTON

Asthma-sufferer William III was advised by his doctors to move away from the smog-polluted atmosphere produced by countless coal fires around Whitehall Palace. He found it easier to breathe the country air at Hampton Court, but in winter he suffered even there on account of the mists rising from the Thames. His search for a conveniently situated winter residence ended at Kensington, then well outside London.

THE NEW PALACE

William bought Nottingham House, a relatively modest Jacobean mansion built in about 1605 and owned by Daniel Finch, 2nd Earl of Nottingham, for around £20,000. Sir Christopher Wren enlarged it by adding a pavilion on each corner; he also moved the entrance to the west front, where he raised a two-storey portico and an entrance courtyard accessed through a clock-tower gateway.

The rebuilding began in July 1689 and was carried out very quickly, for William and Mary were in a great hurry to move in. In their haste, strict supervision of the site must have been lacking, for during that November part of the King's staterooms collapsed, killing eight labourers.

KENSINGTON GARDENS

Some 26 acres (10.5ha) of formal gardens at Kensington Palace were created by Queen Mary and Henry Wise. During Anne's reign, a big Baroque orangery was built by Sir John Vanbrugh. In about 1730, the Round Pond was created in Kensington Palace Gardens for Caroline, wife of George II, and the gardens were opened to the public *c.* 1830.

Left: The Great Staircase at Kensington Palace was later painted by William Kent.

Right: No flourishes. John Evelyn thought Kensington Palace 'a very sweet villa'.

Above: Marot's formal east front gardens, which replaced Charles II's canal, remain one of the glories of Hampton Court.

EASTON NESTON
AND NICHOLAS HAWKSMOOR

Designed by Nicholas Hawksmoor, star pupil of Sir Christopher Wren, in 1696–1702, Easton Neston is often seen as a forerunner of the English Baroque style.

The patron, Sir William Fermor, 1st Lord Leominster, originally offered the job to Sir Christopher Wren, to whom he was related by marriage, around 1680. Then, or shortly afterwards, Sir Christopher designed two wings for the house, which were built, but the main house itself was not designed or constructed – probably because money was short. However, in 1692, after Fermor had made an advantageous marriage, he turned again to the project, and Wren recommended Hawksmoor, who designed and constructed Easton Neston unsupervised. Because the other major houses he was involved with (Castle Howard and Blenheim Palace) were undertaken in collaboration with Vanbrugh, Easton Neston is remembered as the only country house that this remarkable architect built alone.

PILASTERS AND COLUMNS

Hawksmoor's house is a small-scale palace. Built from the finest cream-coloured Helmdon stone (also used at Blenheim Palace and Stowe), Easton Neston is rectangular, with three storeys on the two main façades: first a ground floor, then two equal upper storeys each containing eight tall windows. At the four corners and between all the windows, pilasters (decorative features of attached pillars or columns) rise the entire height of the façade. On the entrance front, two rounded Corinthian columns, one on either side of the door, rise to a round-topped pediment cut with the Fermor arms and motto *Hora e sempre* ('Now and forever'). Above the door, in line with the top-storey windows, is an arched 'Venetian window', while at roof level a balustrade is adorned with urns on top of each of the pilasters. The windows on the shorter sides of the house reveal the fact that it contains two 'mezzanine' floors for servants between the main floors of the house, making five storeys in all.

Above: In 1876, this engraving of Easton Neston and part of the grounds was printed in the Illustrated London News.

NICHOLAS HAWKSMOOR

Like his mentor, Sir Christopher Wren, Nicholas Hawksmoor is remembered above all as a church architect. Hawksmoor worked with Wren on the rebuilding of St Paul's Cathedral, built several superb London churches and designed the towers on the west front of Westminster Abbey. He also played a major role in building Castle Howard and Blenheim Palace, in addition to Easton Neston.

Born around 1660 in Nottinghamshire, Hawksmoor began working for Wren by 1680. His career advanced swiftly: before his 40th birthday, he was working alongside Vanbrugh at Castle Howard. For many years his work was overshadowed by that of Vanbrugh and Wren, but today he is increasingly seen as a highly original and gifted architect who combined the classicism of Wren with the Baroque of Vanbrugh. Hawksmoor also designed a new quadrangle at All Souls College, Oxford University, combining a classical interior with a Gothic exterior. He died in London in 1736.

Left: The West Front at Westminster Abbey. The lower part was built in the 15th century, the towers added by Hawksmoor.

GRANDIOSE PLANS

Hawksmoor drew plans for a large and elaborate forecourt at Easton Neston. He suggested building two side wings to house stables on one side and servants' rooms on the other, and a splendid colonnade flanking the entrance. He did build the entrance piers (which are still standing) and the stable block (quickly demolished), but otherwise these grandiose plans did not come to fruition.

INTERIOR ALTERATIONS

The interior of Easton Neston has been changed somewhat since Hawksmoor built it – notably the Drawing Room was elaborately decorated with intricate

Above: Hawksmoor's design for Easton Neston exudes stately elegance. His grand plans for a dramatic Baroque-style use of space with a forecourt and side wings were, unfortunately, not brought to fruition.

plasterwork in the mid-18th century and his large hall divided in two in the late 19th century to make a dining room alongside a smaller hall. However, the other main rooms remain unchanged, and on a bright day are flooded with light through the tall windows that rise almost from floor to ceiling, as does the elegant staircase with Tijou-style balustrade in wrought iron.

CHANGE OF OWNERSHIP

Easton Neston remained in the hands of Sir William Fermor's descendants for a little over three centuries, always as a private home and never open to the public. But the costs of renovation following a fire in July 2002 severely tested the family finances, and in 2005 Lord Hesketh sold the house and part of its 3,319-acre (1,343ha) estate to St Petersburg-born US-based fashion businessman, Leon Max.

A BAROQUE BUILDING?

In contrast with other leading architects of his day, Hawksmoor made no voyages to see Italian and French buildings at first hand, and his classical influences all came via the study of reproductions in books. Architectural historians see elements at Easton Neston derived from the mid-16th-century palaces built by Michelangelo in the Piazza del Campidoglio on the Capitoline Hill in Rome. But, especially in Hawskmoor's large-scale courtyard design that was never built, continental influences prevail. There are also traces of the Baroque – the dramatic and exuberant monumental style more fully expressed in later houses, such as Castle Howard and Blenheim Palace, on which Hawksmoor worked with Sir John Vanbrugh. Easton Neston can be seen as a forerunner of these buildings, an early flowering of the English Baroque. It also anticipates the Petit Trianon at Versailles, built in 1762–8 by Ange-Jacques Gabriel for Louis XV's mistress, Madame de Pompadour.

Below: Easton Neston's owner in the 1930s, Thomas Fermor-Hesketh (1st Baron Hesketh), stands between his daughters.

MARLBOROUGH HOUSE

AND THE CHURCHILLS

Above: 'Strong, plain and convenient' – and, with Hampton Court, another example of the Anglo-Dutch strain in Wren's output.

Marlborough House, alongside St James's Palace in Pall Mall, London, was built in 1709–11 to plans by Sir Christopher Wren for John Churchill, 1st Duke of Marlborough, and his wife, Sarah, Duchess of Marlborough and close friend of Queen Anne. The Duchess was the driving force behind the project, arranging a lease on the land, selecting Wren as architect – rather than Sir John Vanbrugh, who was then engaged by the Duke on Blenheim Palace – and, indeed, overseeing the final stages of building herself.

The dignified, originally two-storey house was, as the Duchess requested of Wren, 'strong, plain and convenient'. The design may have been drawn by Wren's son, also called Christopher, with his father's guidance. Its red bricks came from Holland, and had been carried as ballast in ships returning from taking supplies to the Duke of Marlborough's armies in the Low Countries.

The house contains the grand two-storey Saloon with paintings by Louis Laguerre of the Duke's triumph at the Battle of Blenheim. The ceiling features a painting by Orazio Gentileschi, originally in the entrance hall of the Queen's House, Greenwich, but removed to Marlborough House at the start of the 18th century with Queen Anne's approval. The magnificent Ramillies Staircase, with black marble steps, ascends beneath paintings by Laguerre of scenes from another of the Duke's great battles, Ramillies.

The Duke of Marlborough died in 1722 and his body lay in state in Marlborough House prior to his funeral in Westminster Abbey. The Duchess died after a long widowhood at Marlborough House in 1744. Sir William Chambers extended the house in the 1770s, increasing it from the original two to three storeys.

A ROYAL PALACE

In 1817, the land and the house that stood on it reverted to the Crown. Marlborough House was the London residence of Edward, Prince of Wales (the future Edward VII), and his wife, Princess Alexandra of Denmark, from 1863 to 1901 and was immortalized in the popular name for the Prince's raffish friends, the 'Marlborough House set'. The future George V was born at Marlborough House, in 1865, and lived there while Prince of Wales in the 1900s.

Later, it was twice the home of widowed queens, first of Edward VII's widow, Alexandra, in 1910–25, and then of George V's widow, Mary, in 1936–53. In 1965, the house became home to the Commonwealth Secretariat and the Commonwealth Foundations and today is used for international conferences.

JOHN CHURCHILL, 1ST DUKE OF MARLBOROUGH

The 1st Duke of Marlborough is renowned as one of England's greatest generals. His reputation rests on the series of great victories he won over the army of Louis XIV of France, most famously at Blenheim (1704), Ramillies (1706) and Oudenarde (1708); the Baroque masterpiece of Blenheim Palace in Oxfordshire was begun as a gift from Queen Anne and country in gratitude for the first of these. Before these years of greatness, he had survived disgrace, including imprisonment in 1691, when he was suspected of plotting to restore James II to the throne.

Above: John Churchill by Christian Linke.

UPPARK

AN ELEGANT COUNTRY HOUSE

The delightful country house of Uppark near Petersfield in West Sussex commands a breathtaking view of the South Downs. It was built *c.*1690 for Ford, Lord Grey of Werke, who was created Earl of Tankerville in 1695. Some authorities identify the architect as William Talman, who was dismissed around this time by Sir William Cavendish, 1st Duke of Devonshire, from Chatsworth House.

AN ELEGANT DWELLING

Uppark was built on the site of an earlier house in a well-established country park belonging to the lords Grey. It has an elegant brick and stone south façade of nine bays, and the arms of a later owner, Sir Matthew Fetherstonhaugh, affixed to the pediment that rises over the central upper-floor windows. Of particular interest are the highly decorated modillions, or brackets, that support the roof cornice and the pediment.

Uppark is also celebrated for its elegant 18th-century interiors, installed by Sir Matthew and his wife, Sarah. The principal rooms include a Saloon that recalls in its lavish decoration the Double Cube Room at Wilton House.

LADY HAMILTON

An Uppark resident of note in the late 18th century was Emma Hart, later better known as Lady Hamilton, wife of Sir William Hamilton and mistress of Horatio, Lord Nelson. In 1781, aged around 18, Emma lived at Uppark as the mistress of Sir Harry Fetherstonhaugh. The table in the dining room is the one on which Emma is said to have danced naked for Sir Harry and his friends.

Above: The splendid brick and stone south front at Uppark, with the Featherstonhaugh arms in the pediment.

A PHOENIX FROM THE ASHES

Following a disastrous fire, which gutted the house in 1989, Uppark became a virtual laboratory for the latest techniques in meticulous architectural restoration. As part of this restoration by the National Trust, the gardens were remade in line with the 18th-century designs of Humphry Repton.

Left: Gilded opulence. The lavish interiors of Uppark provided an arena for gracious living.

THE HOUSEKEEPER'S SON

The novelist H.G. Wells, author of *The Time Machine* and *The War of the Worlds*, spent some of his early years at Uppark, where his mother, Sarah Neal, was a ladies' maid and housekeeper in the 1870s–80s. At the time, Wells was trying to make his way in the world, and returned a number of times to Uppark after failed placements as a draper's apprentice, a chemist's assistant and a teacher. Wells wrote in his autobiography that 'the place had a great effect on me'; and he certainly took full advantage of Uppark's splendid library.

PART THREE

THE MODERN ERA

1714–TODAY

Many of the great houses of the 18th and 19th centuries served as magnets for the leading architects, designers, painters, sculptors and garden planners of the age. For much of this period, royal residences were overshadowed by the great country homes of the aristocracy, but later monarchs built on a much grander sale – notably at Buckingham Palace and Carlton House.

Left: Buckingham Palace. The Duke of Buckingham's town house became a royal residence in 1762 and was transformed into a palace by John Nash after 1826. Its east front was remodelled by Sir Aston Webb in 1913.

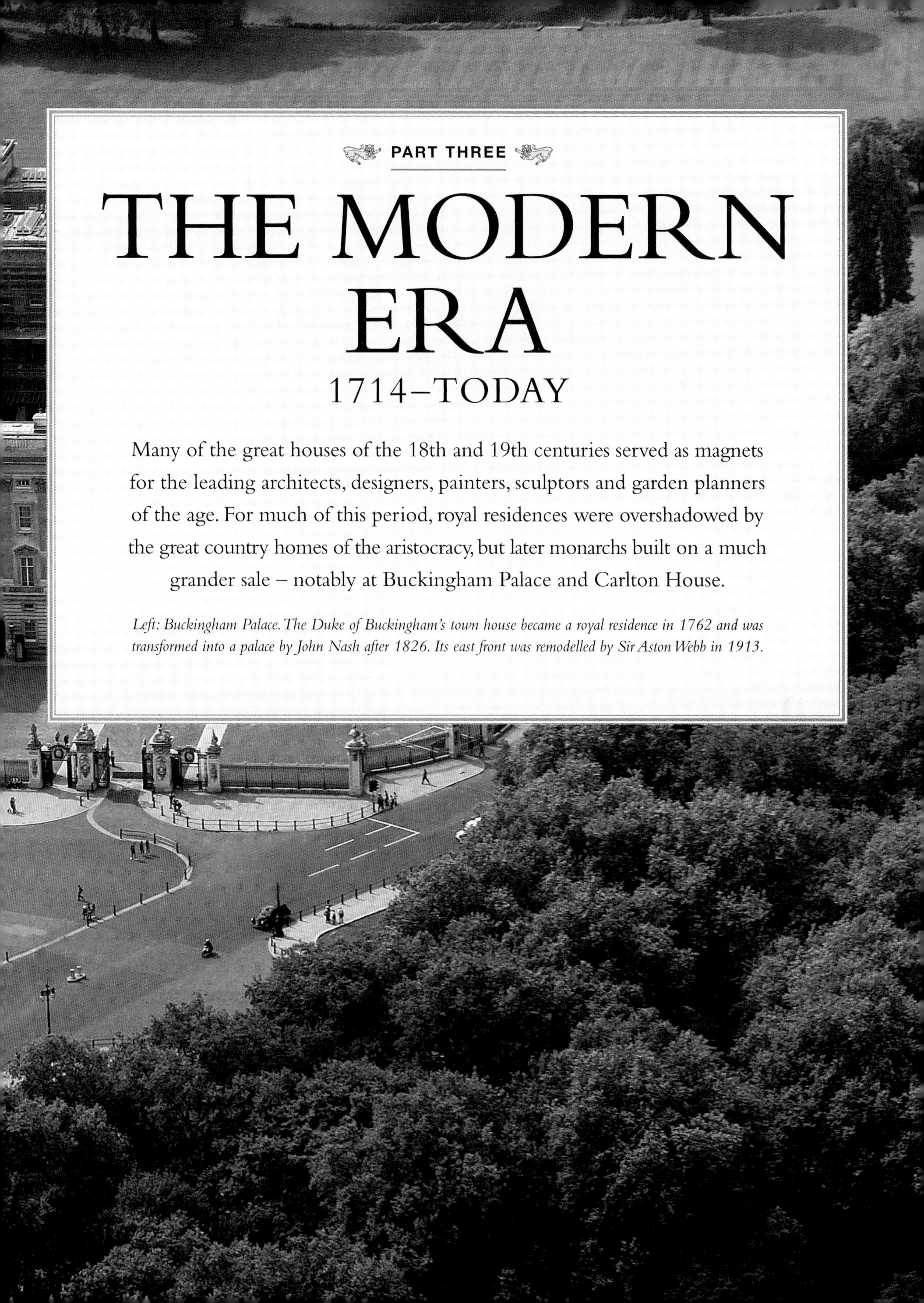

ENGLAND TIMELINE, 1714–TODAY

Above: Blenheim Palace is one of Sir John Vanbrugh's masterpieces.

Above: George IV and Wyatville rebuilt Windsor Castle in Gothic Revival style.

Above: Castle Drogo, Devon, Lutyens' extraordinary 20th-century castle.

ENGLAND, 1714–99

1715 Colen Campbell begins Wanstead House in Essex.
*c.*1720 Castle Howard nears completion.
1722 Blenheim Palace in Oxfordshire, close to completion.
1722 James Gibbs builds Ditchley Park, Oxfordshire, for the 2nd Earl of Lichfield.
1723 Campbell completes Mereworth Castle, Kent, based on a villa by Palladio.
1725 The 3rd Earl of Burlington builds Chiswick House (now in west London).
1734 William Kent begins building Holkham Hall, Norfolk.
1734 Kent builds the south portico, Stowe House, Buckinghamshire.
1747 Horace Walpole begins rebuilding his villa at Strawberry Hill, Middlesex.
1751–57 'Capability' Brown landscapes the park at Petworth House, Sussex.
1758 Robert Adam begins work at Kedleston Hall, Derbyshire.
1762 Robert Adam begins work on the interior of Syon House, Middlesex.
1762 George III buys the future Buckingham Palace as a family house.
1764–79 Robert Adam rebuilds Kenwood House in Hampstead.
1781 George III buys the Dutch House in Kew, south-west London.
1783 The Prince of Wales begins refurbishment of Carlton House, London.
1788 James Wyatt completes work on Heveningham Hall, Suffolk.

ENGLAND, 1800–1899

1803 John Nash builds Cronkhill in Shropshire.
1805 Sandridge Park built in Devon, another Nash house.
1806–14 North front of Longleat House, Wiltshire, rebuilt by Jeffry Wyatt.
1810–20 Robert Smirke builds Eastnor Castle in the Norman Revival style.
1815–23 John Nash builds the Royal Pavilion, Brighton.
1823 **onwards** George IV and Jeffry Wyatville rebuild Windsor Castle in the Gothic Revival style.
1826 George IV begins the conversion of Buckingham House into a palace.
1837–45 Anthony Salvin builds Harlaxton Hall in Lincolnshire.
1842–49 Highclere Castle is rebuilt by Sir Charles Barry.
1845–51 Prince Albert builds Osborne House, Isle of Wight.
*c.*1850 Anthony Salvin rebuilds Alnwick Castle, Northumberland.
1855 Paxton begins building Mentmore Towers, Buckinghamshire, for Baron Mayer Amschel de Rothschild.
1862 The future Edward VII buys the Sandringham estate in Norfolk.
1873–76 Pugin rebuilds Carlton Towers, Yorkshire, in the Victorian Gothic style.
1870 Buckler begins lavish rebuilding of Arundel Castle, West Sussex.
1874–79 Destailleur builds Waddesdon Manor, Buckinghamshire.

ENGLAND, 1900–TODAY

1900–03 At Elveden Hall, Suffolk, Lord Iveagh builds the marble Indian Hall.
1911 New east forecourt and Victoria Memorial at Buckingham Palace.
1912–30 Edwin Lutyens builds Castle Drogo, Devon, for Julius Charles Drewe.
1913 East front of Buckingham Palace refaced in Portland stone by Aston Webb.
1931–36 Courtaulds restore the 15th-century Great Hall at Eltham Palace, and build a superb Art Deco house.
1958–62 Phillimore builds Arundel Park for the Duke and Duchess of Norfolk.
1961–62 Patrick Gwynne builds an ultramodern country house at Witley Park, Surrey.
1963–65 The unusual country house of Stratton Park, Hampshire, incorporates the surviving Doric portico of a ruined 'Greek Revival' house.
1967–71 Raymond Erith and Quinlan Terry build Kings Walden Bury, Herts.
1971–73 John Dennys designs Eaton Hall, Cheshire, in the Modern style. In 1989 the house is refaced in a more traditional guise.
1976 Elizabeth II buys Gatcombe Park, Gloucestershire, for Princess Anne and Captain Mark Phillips.
1980 Duchy of Cornwall buys Highgrove in Gloucestershire, for Prince Charles.
2003 Quinlan Terry's Ferne Park, Dorset, wins acclaim.

N
W
E
S
SCOTLAND
Banburgh Castle
Alnwick Castle
Seaton Delaval Hall
North Sea
Muncaster Castle
Castle Howard
Harewood House
Irish Sea
Brodsworth Hall
Heaton Hall
ENGLAND
Chatsworth
The Wash
Kedleston Hall
Nottingham Castle
Holkham Hall
Blickling Hall
Sandringham
Houghton Hall
Rousham House
Weston Park
Elveden Hall
Arbury Hall
Upton House
Stoke Park Pavilions
Althorp
Woburn Abbey
Eastnor Castle
Ditchley Park
Stowe House
WALES
Hellens
Sudeley Castle
Waddesdon Manor
Knebworth House
Blenheim Palace
Hughenden Manor
Cliveden
Eltham Palace
Windsor Castle
Bristol Channel
Prior Park
Highclere Castle
Polesden Lacy
Stourhead
Petworth House
Clandon Park
Port Lympne
Wilton House
Uppark
Arundel Castle
Strait of Dover
Castle Drogo
Beaulieu
Osborne House
Norris Castle
The Royal Pavilion
Carisbrooke Castle
St Michael's Mount
English Channel
Kenwood House
Kensington Palace
Osterley Park
Chiswick House
Buckingham Palace
Westminster Palace
Syon House
Kew Palace
Marble Hill House
Strawberry Hill
LONDON
Hampton Court Palace

SCOTLAND, WALES
AND NORTHERN IRELAND TIMELINES, 1714–TODAY

Above: Balmoral Castle was Prince Albert's fantasy Highland castle.

SCOTLAND, 1714–TODAY

1746–89 Inveraray Castle, Argyll, rebuilt to the design of Robert Adam.

1777–92 Robert Adam works on the refurbishment of Culzean Castle, Ayrshire.

1815 William Wilkins's Dalmeny House, Lothian, is built in the Tudor Revival style.

*c.*1825 Architect William Burn's Carstairs House, Strathclyde, is built in the Elizabethan Revival style.

1855 Prince Albert completes Balmoral Castle, Grampian, in the Scottish Baronial style.

1891 A Scots Baronial east wing is added to Glamis Castle in Tayside.

1901–05 Manderston near Duns, Berwickshire, one of the finest of Edwardian country houses, is built by John Kinross for Sir James Miller.

1912 Lt-Col John MacRae-Gilstrap begins the restoration of 13th-century Eilean Donan Castle near Dornie.

1952 The Queen Mother buys and restores the Castle of Mey in Caithness.

*c.*1955 Edward Bruce, 10th Earl of Elgin, rebuilds the 17th-century Culross Abbey House in Fife.

1955 The Queen Mother adds a new wing to Birkhall near Balmoral.

1960 Claud Phillimore designs Abercairney at Crieff in Perthshire.

1938–70 Restoration of Kisimul Castle, Isle of Barra, by Robert MacNeil.

Above: Castell Coch, Wales, was remodelled by the 3rd Marquess of Bute and Burges.

WALES, 1714–TODAY

1749–52 Picton Castle interior remodelled by Sir John Philipps.
1770 Cresselly House built for John Bartlett Allen.
*c.*1825 Thomas Hopper builds Penrhyn Castle in the Norman Revival style.
1866 William Burges rebuilds Cardiff Castle for the 3rd Marquess of Bute.
1875 Burges rebuilds Castell Coch, near Cardiff, for Lord Bute.
1977 John Taylor builds Castle Gyrn in Wales – a country house in castle form.

Above: Castle Coole, a fine Irish neo-classical house, was built by James Wyatt.

NORTHERN IRELAND, 1714–TODAY

1790–98 James Wyatt builds Castle Coole for the 1st Earl of Belmore.
1819 Thomas Hopper begins work on Gosford Castle, Co Armagh.
*c.*1835 Edward Blore rebuilds Narrow Water Castle in the Tudor Revival style.
1867–70 Belfast Castle is built in the Scots Baronial style.
1824 The Argory, Moy, a neoclassical house, built for Walter McGeough.

CHAPTER NINE

THE BAROQUE AND PALLADIAN STYLES

*c.*1714–*c.*1760

Soldier, playwright and London socialite, John Vanbrugh, had no experience of building when, in 1699, in association with Nicholas Hawksmoor, he began to draw up designs for the grand and exuberant Castle Howard in Yorkshire. Starting from scratch as an architect, his revolutionary great house – a group of buildings full of energy and movement – was designed to be seen as a vast sculpture against garden structures and ornaments in a great landscape. It was the first major statement of the Baroque in English architecture.

The often sensuous and dramatic Baroque style in art and architecture had developed from *c.*1600 in continental Europe, particularly in the strongly Roman Catholic countries of Italy and Spain. As it spread to Protestant countries, including England, it found expression in monumental and highly ornamented buildings set in grand, picturesque landscapes. Vanbrugh went on, with Hawksmoor, to design and build another great Baroque house, Blenheim Palace.

However, to some early 18th-century architects and patrons, the Baroque style seemed overblown. These men looked back to more sober classical buildings designed almost a century earlier by Inigo Jones, under the influence of the Italian Renaissance architect and theorist, Andrea Palladio. Led by Colen Campbell, Richard Boyle, 3rd Earl of Burlington, and William Kent, the Palladian movement resulted in the building of more restrained houses on the villa plan, such as Campbell's Mereworth Castle and Wanstead, Lord Burlington's Chiswick House and Kent's Holkham Hall.

Left: Castle Howard's crowning glory is its majestic dome and lantern. Vanbrugh and Hawksmoor added the feature to their design after building had begun in 1699.

CASTLE HOWARD

VANBRUGH'S MASTERPIECE

The immensely proud Charles Howard, 3rd Earl of Carlisle, had the opportunity to make a grand architectural statement when his centuries-old family mansion, Henderskelfe Castle in Yorkshire, was severely damaged by fire in 1693. He called on one of the leading architects of his day, William Talman, to draw up plans. But the men quarrelled over the architect's proposed charges, and Lord Carlisle dismissed Talman. Then he made an astonishing decision, entrusting the vast project to John Vanbrugh, a rising playwright and man-about-town in London. Vanbrugh had already proved himself a brilliant man, but there was clearly no way of knowing whether he could apply his abilities to architecture.

Vanbrugh turned to his friend, the architect Nicholas Hawksmoor, for help and also worked closely with Lord Carlisle himself on the house. Credit for the exuberant Baroque masterpiece they created is usually given to Vanbrugh but should really be shared by all three. The first designs were made in 1699, and building – using a delightful pale yellow local stone – began in 1700.

Below: Vanbrugh's Temple of the Four Winds was unfinished at his death in 1726. It was completed in 1738. Francesco Vassalli decorated the inside with scagliola.

Above: Beauty, energy, exuberance, drama. Thanks to renovation, Castle Howard still has the magnificent profile its creators envisaged. The Atlas Fountain (foreground) was added by the 7th Earl in the 1850s.

ENGLAND'S FIRST DOME

The main entrance front faces north. Beneath an imposing dome, its grand central block is faced with Corinthian pilasters and contains elegant arched doorways and windows; statues and urns occupy niches and stand on the balustrade. The magnificent dome and lantern, the first in England, was completed by 1706, predating the dome of St Paul's Cathedral, London, by two years. However, the dome visible today is actually a meticulous 20th-century reconstruction, built after the original dome was destroyed in a fire of 1940.

EAST AND WEST WINGS

Wings to the west and east were intended to extend forward to create a grand forecourt. The east wing was built by Vanbrugh and Hawksmoor, and beyond it is a second service enclosure, the Laundry Court. The original design called for a similar structure on the west side, but the western wing was not built, because Lord Carlisle lost interest in the project. (The west wing we see today was added in 1759 in the Palladian style by Sir Thomas Robinson.)

The south, or garden, front also makes dramatic use of Corinthian pilasters: here smaller ones on the single-storey wings echo the large and impressive ones on the two-storey main block. The whole front has a rusticated basement with square windows that contrast with the arched ones above them.

THE ESSENCE OF THE BAROQUE

Inside, the hugely impressive entrance hall is 52ft (16m) square and is lit from the lantern in the dome, which rises to a height of 70ft (21m) overhead. Two staircases and four stone corridors lead off, creating a sense of movement through a dramatic use of architectural space that exemplifies the finest qualities of the English Baroque.

The hall frescoes and the decoration within the dome were painted by the Italian artist Giovanni Pellegrini in 1709–12. The fireplace and Niche of

Bacchus were made of *scagliola* (a combination of marble and plaster) by Italian craftsmen Bagutti and Plura in 1711–12. It is one of the earliest examples in England of the craft, which became very popular later in the century.

The largest of the other rooms is now the Long Gallery in the west wing, though prior to a fire in 1940 some of the many staterooms on the south front were grander. Left unfinished for 50 years, the gallery was completed by Charles Tatham *c*.1810. This wing also contained the main bedrooms.

Above: Eighteenth-century promenaders admire Castle Howard's south front.

DESIGNING THE GROUNDS

In the early 1720s, with the house inhabitable but the west wing not started, Lord Carlisle became more interested in setting out the gardens and park with pavilions and 'rustic' buildings than in completing the house to the original designs. Vanbrugh and Hawksmoor continued to work on these projects at Castle Howard until their deaths, in 1726 and 1736 respectively.

In the grounds, Vanbrugh designed the domed Temple of the Four Winds, originally known as the Temple of Diana and partly based on Andrea Palladio's Villa Capra near Vicenza (the same house that inspired Colen Campbell's Mereworth Castle). The temple was built in 1723–38.

The cylindrical mausoleum for the burial of Lord Carlisle and his descendants, the grandest in Britain, was originally designed by Hawksmoor in 1729, although his plan was significantly altered in the 1730s by others, including Sir Thomas Robinson and Lord Burlington. In addition to the vaults, it contains a chapel with a graceful domed ceiling. It was finished in the 1740s. Hawksmoor based his design on that of the 1502 Church of St Pietro in Montorio in Rome, designed by Donato Bramante for Pope Julius II.

The grounds also contain an obelisk, erected in 1714, at the head of the drive where the great lime avenues intersect; a pyramid designed by Hawksmoor in 1728; a gatehouse that was originally a freestanding 'pyramid arch' designed by Vanbrugh in 1719, but which had wings added by Sir Thomas Robinson in 1756–8; and mock fortifications in the style of medieval town walls, erected near the gatehouse in the 1720s.

DRAMATIC SETTING

Building these structures in the grounds was part of the architects' original conception, for they wanted to create the most dramatic of settings for their imposing house. Horace Walpole, connoisseur and creator of Strawberry Hill at Twickenham, visited Castle Howard in 1772. His reaction would doubtless have delighted Hawksmoor, Vanbrugh and Lord Carlisle, for he enthused about its sublime environs as much as the house itself: 'Nobody...had informed me that I should at one view see a palace, a town, a fortified city, temples on high places, woods worthy of being each a metropolis of the Druids, vales connected to hills by other woods, the noblest lawn in the world fenced by half the horizon, and a mausoleum that would tempt one to be buried alive; in short I have seen gigantic palaces before but never a sublime one.'

THE ENGLISH BAROQUE

The word 'baroque' denoted works of art that ignored the accepted proportions or rules. Paintings, sculpture and architecture by great Baroque artists, such as the Italian Gian Lorenzo Bernini, were sensuous and dramatic, aiming to appeal to the soul by way of the senses. When the style was taken up in Protestant northern Europe, it tended to be more formal and restrained, appealing to viewers through its monumental size, surface ornamentation, the geometric arrangement of its constituent parts and its interaction with its setting, be it the streets around a London church or a picturesque country park around a stately house. Some historians see the English version of the Baroque as springing fully formed from Vanbrugh and Hawksmoor at Castle Howard; others argue that it had its antecedent a little earlier in Hawksmoor's Easton Neston.

BLENHEIM PALACE
AND THE MARLBOROUGHS

In 1705, Queen Anne gave the royal manor of Woodstock near Oxford to John Churchill, 1st Duke of Marlborough. The land was to be the setting for a great mansion, a lasting tribute from a grateful queen and country for Marlborough's victory over a French-Bavarian army in August 1704, at Blenheim, in southern Germany.

To build the great house that would become known as Blenheim Palace, the Duke chose John Vanbrugh. In doing so he overlooked the more obvious claim of Sir Christopher Wren, Surveyor of the Queen's Works and the choice of Marlborough's strong-willed and powerful wife, Sarah. As a result, Vanbrugh and the Duchess got off to a bad start, and they were at odds throughout the building, much of which took place while the Duke himself was away at war.

With Nicholas Hawksmoor, Vanbrugh set out to build a monument to the Duke's great victories and the age of Queen Anne, a Baroque mansion that placed enormous emphasis on style and grandeur. The Duchess, however, wanted a country house designed for comfort.

ROYAL DISFAVOUR

Building began in 1705. The arguments between Vanbrugh and the Duchess were compounded by major problems in paying for materials and labour: costs were supposedly to be covered by the Queen and the state but money was often not forthcoming, particularly after the Marlboroughs lost favour with the Queen and retreated into continental exile in 1712. Work at Blenheim ceased that year, with the workforce owed £45,000. After Anne's death in 1714, the Duke and Duchess returned and work resumed on the house. But after a major row with the Duchess, Vanbrugh resigned in fury in 1717, and Hawksmoor worked on alone. The great house was largely completed by 1722, the year of the Duke's death, but this brought no end to the animosity between the Duchess and Vanbrugh. In 1725, he was even refused entrance by the Duchess when he attempted to visit with the Earl of Carlisle to view his work.

Above: Aristocratic breeding. Churchill (left), with wife, Lady Sarah, and five children.

THE GREAT COURT

Everywhere at Blenheim, the scale is vast. The house's main entrance stands beneath a towering portico bearing the Duke's arms on the pediment, amid the extravagantly ornamented splendour of the Great Court. On either side of the portico are curved arcades; the four corners of the 480ft (145m) wide central block are topped with extraordinary towers bearing pinnacles 30ft (9m) high carved by Grinling Gibbons. Tuscan colonnades connect the house to the service and stable courts. Enclosed by these side wings, the Great Court is no less than 300ft (90m) deep.

A long straight drive leads directly into the Great Court, but modern visitors enter through the East Gate in the wall of the service court, and then through another fine gateway beneath the clock tower into the Great Court. The house's plainer, and perhaps more elegant, south front contains another great portico topped with a 30-ton marble bust of Louis XIV. This was a spoil of war that the Duke had taken from Tournai in 1709.

SIR JOHN VANBRUGH

Vanbrugh was born in 1664 and served as a soldier, 1686–98. He was imprisoned in the Bastille in Paris as a spy. He came to eminence as a playwright in London, with *The Relapse* and *The Provok'd Wife*, and mixed with great men of the day in the Kit Cat Club, where he met Lord Carlisle, who commissioned him to design his first house, Castle Howard in Yorkshire. Vanbrugh worked with Nicholas Hawksmoor on Castle Howard, Blenheim Palace, and Kimbolton Castle. Working alone, he built Kings Weston House in Gloucestershire, Eastbury in Dorset and Seaton Delaval Hall in Northumberland – the last regarded as another great masterpiece. His final work was the north front of Grimsthorpe Castle, Lincolnshire (1722–6). Vanbrugh served as Comptroller of Royal Works under Anne and George I. Until his death in 1726, he worked for Carlisle at Castle Howard, where his Temple of the Four Winds was completed after his death.

Above: Sir John Vanbrugh, engraved by artist John Simon (c.1675–1751).

THE GREAT HALL

Blenheim's interior was designed on a correspondingly vast scale and decorated by the finest craftsmen. Behind the entrance portico stands the Great Hall – 67ft (20m) high, with vast Corinthian columns and tall arches, beneath a painted ceiling, by Sir James Thornhill, of Marlborough showing a map of Blenheim battlefield and being rewarded by Britannia with a laurel wreath. The hall leads into the Saloon, decorated with heroic murals and ceiling by Louis Laguerre and also featuring magnificent marble door frames by Hawksmoor. From the Saloon, a great room leads off on either side; these rooms were originally state apartments but were later turned into drawing rooms.

The last part of the house to be completed was the west wing. It contains the splendid Long Library, 180ft (55m) long, designed as a picture gallery but finished by Hawksmoor as a library, and the chapel, featuring a grand marble tomb designed by William Kent and carved by John Michael Rysbrack to hold the remains of the Duke and Duchess.

GARDEN AND PARKLAND

As at Castle Howard, Vanbrugh and Hawksmoor devoted as much attention to the setting of Blenheim as to its façades and interior. On the south side, a monumental parterre was laid out by Henry Wise, gardener at Hampton Court. A 134ft (41m) column of Victory, raised to celebrate the Duke's military triumphs, stands at the end of an avenue of elms planted to recall the arrangement of Marlborough's soldiers at the Battle of Blenheim. Vanbrugh channelled the River Glyme into three streams and built a vast bridge across them; the bridge was partly submerged when 'Capability' Brown landscaped the park in the 1760s and created a lake in place of the streams.

BAROQUE EMBODIMENT

The great house in its carefully orchestrated setting aims throughout for an impression of power, a celebration of great English victories and the military prowess of Marlborough himself: an embodiment that was, in Vanbrugh's words, a creation of 'beauty, magnificence and duration'. Such an achievement is not to everyone's taste, however. Even when it was newly finished, the great palace was not universally approved. At a time when the classical Palladian movement was gathering force, Blenheim appeared to many as heavy, indulgent and overblown. But others have seen it as the highest and fullest expression of the English Baroque, an achievement, according to Sir John Soane, architect of the Bank of England in 1788, that proves Vanbrugh (and perhaps, in truth, also Hawksmoor) to have been no less than 'the Shakespeare of architects'.

Above: An aerial view allows the eye to take in the complete composition, with 300ft (90m)-deep enclosure and colonnades linking to the east and west courts.

Right: In the Red Drawing Room hangs a portrait of the 9th Duke and his American heiress wife, Consuelo Vanderbilt.

MEREWORTH CASTLE
AND PALLADIAN HOUSES

The elegant Mereworth Castle in Kent, a domed rectangular block with a classical portico on each of its four sides, is a recreation of the mid-16th-century Villa Capra, or Rotonda, built by Andrea Palladio near Vicenza in Italy. Built by the Scottish architect Colen Campbell in 1720–3, Mereworth is one of the finest early examples of the Palladian movement in 18th-century English architecture (the first in England being Wilbury House in Wiltshire, built *c.*1710 by William Benson).

ROMAN STYLE

'Palladianism' takes its name from Andrea Palladio (1508–80), who, as well as being the architect and designer of elegant villas and churches, was an interpreter of classical building and, in particular, of the work of 1st-century BC Roman architect, Vitruvius. Palladio's illustrated volume, the *Four Books of Architecture*, first published in 1570, was reissued in a lavish English edition in London in 1715, at a time when – following the accession of King George I in 1714 – many of the wealthy elite of Georgian England, who had often travelled widely in Italy, were turning away from the prevailing taste for extravagantly ornate houses and developing an enthusiasm for more restrained, classical buildings.

The 'Palladians' looked back to the buildings of Inigo Jones, who, almost a century earlier, had tried to put the principles of Palladio into practice in the Queen's House, Greenwich, and the Banqueting House, Whitehall. Following Palladio, they believed buildings should be constructed 'rationally' in line with the principles of proportion, symmetry and harmony found in the natural world.

One of the leading Palladians was the architect of Mereworth Castle, Colen Campbell, who, also in 1715, published his *Vitruvius Britannicus* – a survey of classical buildings in England. In the introduction he praised 'great Palladio' and dismissed the Baroque artist, Bernini, as 'affected and licentious'.

PALLADIANISM AT MEREWORTH

Mereworth Castle is a triumph of elegant design. Its dome is encased in lead and contains 24 chimneys that pass through its shell to exit via a single opening at the top. Beneath the dome is a delightful circular hall, called the Saloon by Campbell, measuring 35ft (11m) in diameter and 80ft (24m) high, and lit from above by windows in the base of the dome. It has terracotta walls decorated with stucco in the form of foliage and graceful reclining figures. An extremely refined drawing room fills the whole length of the south front. A spiral staircase leads to a circular gallery at first-floor level that looks over the hall.

Above: Campbell built Stourhead House, Wiltshire, in the 1720s. Note the statues above the pedimented portico. The side pavilions were added in the 1790s.

Below: Palladio in England. This elevation of Mereworth Castle was published in Colen Campbell's Vitruvius Britannicus *(1724).*

Below: Stourhead gardens were designed by Henry Home II in 1741–80 and inspired by the landscapes of Poussin and Claude.

The villa stands on a mound in a broad valley and was, until the late 1800s, surrounded by a moat. The moat was a hangover from the original castle on the site, inherited and redeveloped by Campbell's patron John Fane, after 1736 the 7th Earl of Westmorland. The two graceful pavilions that flank the entrance front of Campbell's villa were added in the late 1730s, probably by James Stuart.

Above: The Palladian bridge at Prior Park was part of a landscape garden created by Bath entrepreneur Ralph Allen.

OTHER PALLADIAN HOUSES

Before he began work at Mereworth Castle in 1720, Campbell had already designed and started building (*c.*1714) a big influential Palladian villa at Wanstead House in Essex, as well as creating, in 1717, the first Palladian façade in London for Burlington House, Piccadilly, home of Richard Boyle, 3rd Earl of Burlington, himself a key figure in the Palladian movement. In addition, he built Stourhead House, in Wiltshire (*c.*1717–25), for banker Henry Hoare and later worked alongside James Gibbs at Houghton Hall, in Norfolk, from *c.*1722.

Several Palladian houses were built at this time. The 3rd Earl of Burlington, Campbell's patron for Burlington House, built his own Palladian villa, Chiswick House (now in west London), beginning in 1725. Burlington's protégé, the painter William Kent, turned architect in 1734 when he designed Holkham Hall in Norfolk with Lord Leicester, another influential figure in the Palladian revival. Finally, in 1735–48, John Wood the Elder built Prior Park, near Bath, with gardens created by Ralph Allen and advice from poet Alexander Pope and 'Capability' Brown.

Below: The 3rd Earl of Burlington's Chiswick House (now in west London) was based on the same Palladian villa at Vicenza that Campbell recreated at Mereworth Castle.

WANSTEAD HOUSE

Colen Campbell began work in 1715 on Wanstead House in Essex for banker, Sir Richard Child, later Earl Tylney. Now demolished, the house was a Palladian villa of significant size, measuring 260 x 70ft (79 x 21m), and was graced by a classical portico with a pediment 60ft (18m) wide and six Corinthian columns. It was built on the site of an earlier mansion Sir Richard inherited from his half-brother, Sir Josiah Child. Leading gardener George London developed the grounds.

Right: Wanstead House had a lavish ballroom, which is seen at its finest in this 'conversation piece' by William Hogarth.

HOLKHAM HALL
AND WILLIAM KENT

The stately Holkham Hall, near Wells in Norfolk, built after 1734 by William Kent and Matthew Brettingham, with copious advice from Lord Burlington and especially Thomas Coke, the Earl of Leicester, is celebrated as the most distinguished of all the great Palladian houses in England. Its coolly magnificent Marble Hall, which Kent and Leicester designed along the lines of a Roman basilica and which contains tall Ionic columns of alabaster, makes an unforgettable impression on all who see it.

The house consists of a rectangular central block containing the Marble Hall and staterooms, and four 'wings', one attached to each corner of the rectangle, containing visitors' apartments, family rooms, a chapel and kitchens. The wing containing the family rooms, which included the elegant Long Library, could be used as a self-contained house when Leicester was not entertaining in style and did not need the staterooms.

AUSTERE SOUTH FRONT

Holkham Hall's principal south, or garden, front is much discussed, for it takes Palladian restraint and distaste for ornament to the point of austere plainness. It is 344ft (105m) across, including the south-west and south-east wings at the sides. In the centre rises a portico with six tall columns; towers project at the corners of the main block, each containing an arched three-light Venetian window on the *piano nobile* (the first floor, containing the principal apartments). Above these – and above the four square windows that are aligned horizontally across the front – rises an expanse of plain yellow brickwork where the eye might normally expect to see further windows or architectural ornament.

Above: The wide south front at Holkham, with its six-column portico, looks across formal gardens (designed in the 1850s by Nesfield).

Beneath the *piano nobile* is a rusticated basement containing small, functional windows. The overall effect borders on the severe – a precise study in symmetry and proportion.

Below: Elegant proportions, beautiful symmetry. Kent and Leicester created a vast Palladian house at Holkham in windswept Norfolk.

ARCHITECT AS DESIGNER

The house's interior is comparatively lavish, but even its richest interiors are handled with a fine Palladian sense of restraint. The ravishingly elegant Marble Hall rises to a height of 50ft (15m) and contains a wide flight of marble steps. These climb to a peristyle forming a gallery, off which lead doorways to the state rooms. Classical influences abound: the gilded ceiling is taken from an Inigo Jones design that was copied from the Pantheon in Rome; the fluted columns of Derbyshire marble are derived from those in the Roman Temple of Fortuna Virilis.

The staterooms are grandly elegant and display paintings and statuary acquired by Coke during a famous and extended Grand Tour of 1712–18. Beyond the hall is the Saloon, with gilded ceiling and door surrounds and velvet-lined walls. The Statue Gallery, which leads across the house from south to north, houses Coke's fine classical statues in curved niches – including an ancient Greek bust of Athenian aristocrat and historian, Thucydides, dating to *c.*4BC. The rooms are furnished with velvet-covered chairs and sofas, as well as side tables, all designed by Kent (at Holkham, he pioneered a new role for the architect as designer of all aspects of the patron's living space). He also designed fine interiors for the family rooms in the south-west wing, especially in the Long Library.

HOLKHAM'S STYLE

Other men also had a significant input into the house's appearance. These were Thomas Coke himself and Kent's chief patron and the great promoter of the Palladian style, Lord Burlington, as well as the Norfolk architect Matthew Brettingham, who was Clerk of Works on the project and later a competent architect with a good practice.

Right: Badminton House, Gloucestershire, where Kent reworked an earlier house in the Palladian style. This view is by Canaletto.

WILLIAM KENT

William Kent excelled as an architect, and as an interior and garden designer. He began as a painter, and while studying painting in Rome in 1709–19 he met his great patrons Richard Boyle, 3rd Earl of Burlington, and Thomas Coke, later Earl of Leicester. In 1719, he formed a lifelong association with Burlington when he decorated Burlington House in Piccadilly, London. Burlington secured Kent the position of Master Carpenter in the Office of Works in 1725, and in this capacity he rebuilt the stable block of King's Mews, Charing Cross, in 1732. (Now demolished, it stood on the site of the National Gallery in Trafalgar Square.)

William Kent also designed the Treasury Buildings and built the Horse Guards Building, both in Whitehall. As well as designing Holkham Hall, he was also architect of Badminton House, Gloucestershire. He designed interiors for Ditchley Park, Oxfordshire, and furnishings for Hampton Court Palace. As a garden designer, his work at Rousham Park and Stowe House led a movement away from formal French-style gardens into informal 'natural' landscapes of the kind that would be further developed later in the century by 'Capability' Brown. He died in 1748.

Above: William Kent's ability as a garden designer and interior decorator probably outshone his skill as an architect.

Plans for the house may have first been conceived by Coke, Burlington and Kent when they met in Rome in 1715. Holkham Hall was not begun until 1734, however, largely because Coke lost a fortune in the collapse of the South Sea Company in 1720. Building work then carried on for 30 years until 1764, after the deaths of Kent (1748), Burlington (1753) and Leicester himself (1759). The house was dutifully completed by the Earl's widow – Lady Margaret, Baroness Clifford.

The park at Holkham, among the largest in England, contains an obelisk designed by Kent and erected before the house was built, in 1729. Formal avenues were created, but the park was landscaped by 'Capability' Brown later in the 18th century.

DITCHLEY PARK

AND JAMES GIBBS

The country house of Ditchley Park, near Oxford, is celebrated less for its exterior of weathered Burford stone and beautiful parkland setting, than for its elegant and well-preserved interiors designed by William Kent and Henry Flitcroft in the 1720s. It is also well known for its role in World War II, when it served as the weekend HQ for Winston Churchill and his War Cabinet in 1940–2, at a time when the Prime Minister's country residence at Chequers, in Buckinghamshire, was under threat of being bombed.

JAMES GIBBS: FAVOURED ARCHITECT OF TORY LORDS

Born in Aberdeenshire in 1682, James Gibbs studied in Rome and in his early career was an Italian Baroque architect. In this style he designed the Church of St Mary-le-Strand in London in 1714–17. But he was influenced by the prevailing enthusiasm for 'Palladianism' and began to mix classical and Baroque elements as in his celebrated Church of St-Martin-in-the-Fields, London (1722–6), which has both classical portico and towering steeple and was copied for churches throughout Britain and North America.

He was also a successful and influential country-house architect. He designed or contributed to at least 50 houses. While Vanbrugh was a favourite of the Whig nobility, Gibbs was the leading architect employed by Tories. His *Book of Architecture* (1728) was widely used as a pattern book. He was also a favourite at England's leading universities, designing the Senate House at Cambridge University (1722–30) and the Radcliffe Camera for Oxford University (1737–49).

Right: A Baroque Palladian? Gibbs's designs for both country houses and churches were highly influential.

INELEGANT ROOFLINE

The house was designed and built not by Kent but by James Gibbs in 1722. His patron was George Henry Lee, 2nd Earl of Lichfield and grandson of King Charles II, and his mistress Barbara Villiers, Duchess of Cleveland. It consists of a central block connected to two perfectly symmetrical wings by curved colonnades. The main block has a truncated appearance, for its two main floors, equipped with gracefully tall windows, are topped with a squat third level and an unsuccessful roofline with poorly positioned statues of Fortune and Fame and inelegant chimneys. Architectural historians point out that Gibbs' original designs proposed the use of either a pediment and cupolas or a columned portico, and speculate that the final design must have been the result of a sudden shortage of funds when building was underway. The two wings, however, are very attractive: each has ten windows in the façade, a hipped roof and a clock tower.

Below: Gibbs's design for Ditchley Park inspired that of Arundel Park, Sussex, in the 1950s, which in turn began a revival of Palladianism in the later 20th century.

ELEGANT INTERIORS

Ditchley Park's interiors are superb examples of early Georgian elegance. The entrance leads into a central hall two storeys high: its walls carry busts of leading philosophers and writers; carved embodiments of the Arts and the Sciences recline above the doorway into the Saloon, the splendid fireplace and the alcove opposite it; the hall ceiling was painted by Kent; and the Saloon contains a riot of Italian stucco work.

Above: A decidedly Eastern influence is evident in the design of this furnishing silk of 1738, which is hung at Ditchley Park.

Above: The entrance hall at Ditchley. Note the ceiling painting by Kent and the busts of thinkers and writers arrayed around the walls.

Furniture and works of art are of the highest quality: in the White Drawing Room are two very fine eagle tables designed by Kent, and portraits by Sir Peter Lely of Charles II and Barbara Villiers. The house's chimney-pieces – always the most expensive items in decorative schemes – are by Christopher Horsenail and Henry Cheere.

AMERICAN CONNECTIONS

The house passed from the 2nd Earl of Lichfield through many generations of Dillon-Lee descendants until 1932, when the 17th Viscount Dillon sold it. One branch of the Oxfordshire Lees settled in Virginia, where their most famous son was Confederate commander, Robert E. Lee.

In 1932, another American came to the rescue of Ditchley Park. He was Ronald Tree, a former managing editor of *Forum Magazine* in New York, who later became MP for Harborough, Leicestershire. With his wife, Nancy, also an American, he modernized the house and restored the garden. He came to know Churchill and agreed to the Prime Minister's request that leading Cabinet members might use Ditchley Park as a weekend HQ.

In the 1950s, David Wills bought the house and presented it to the Anglo-American Ditchley Foundation, which holds international conferences for invited academics, politicians, business people, industrialists and civil servants to further international understanding. The house is periodically open to the general public, subject to booking.

Left: Intricate beauty. This side table, elegantly designed by Kent, is part of the interior decor at Ditchley Park.

HOUGHTON HALL

AND SIR ROBERT WALPOLE

England's first prime minister, Robert Walpole, used Colen Campbell, James Gibbs and Thomas Ripley as architects and William Kent as interior designer in building the sumptuous Houghton Hall, near King's Lynn, Norfolk, in 1722–35. Walpole eschewed the Norfolk brick later used by his near-neighbour at Holkham Hall, and built his country house of fine Aislaby sandstone from Yorkshire, expensively transported by sea from Whitby to King's Lynn.

Robert Walpole had inherited a relatively small Jacobean manor house and estate at Houghton in 1700, at the age of 24, on the death of his father. In the same year he began his political life, when he was elected Member of Parliament for his father's seat of Castle Rising, Norfolk. After making an enormous fortune as Minister at War, Walpole began the building of a grand new house on the estate in 1722, by which time the politician had become Chancellor of the Exchequer and First Lord of the Admiralty.

Above: The entrance front, Houghton Hall. Note the standing statues above the portico, the double staircase and the side colonnades.

RESTRAINED EXTERIOR

The house has a coolly elegant Palladian exterior. The original design, by Colen Campbell, was reproduced in his *Vitruvius Britannicus* and called for a rectangular block with a tower at each corner, although the towers were replaced on James Gibbs' advice with four domes. The garden front has a grand double staircase and four-column portico beneath a carved pediment topped with three standing statues. Fine curving colonnades lead off at the sides to the wings, which contain a kitchen on one side and the one-time Picture Gallery on the other. On the entrance front, statues of Britannia and Neptune, carved by the great John Michael Rysbrack, rest above the central window.

Below: The rose garden at Houghton Hall contains 150 varieties of the species.

Below: Sir Robert Walpole. He was father of Horace Walpole, builder of Strawberry Hill.

Above: Colen Campbell's design for Houghton was improved by James Gibbs's addition of domes on the four corner towers.

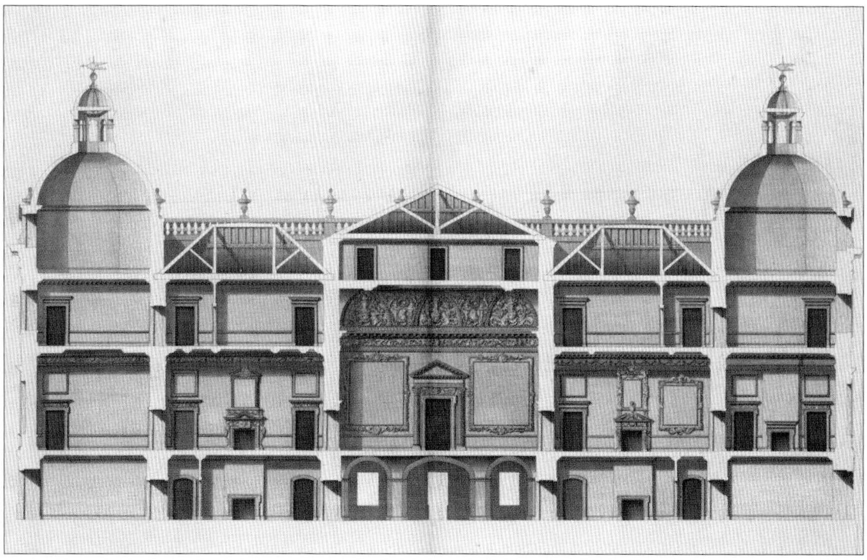

Above: A cross-section shows Campbell's design for the cube-shaped Stone Hall, with state rooms either side on the piano nobile.

SUMPTUOUS INTERIORS

The interiors are far more richly decorated than the restrained façades. Everywhere, especially in the Great Staircase, there is a profusion of mahogany, at that time only recently and expensively introduced to England. The staircase climbs stylishly to the staterooms on the *piano nobile*; the walls above the stairs are painted by Kent. Chief among the staterooms is the sumptuous Stone Hall: an elegant 40ft (12m) cube, lined with ashlar, it has a superb fireplace by Rysbrack and an extravagant stucco ceiling by Artari. The hall contains a marble bust of Sir Robert, again by Rysbrack, and a portrait of the great man by John Wootton. It also contains a bronze carving of the ancient Greek seer-priest, Laocoon, by the Frenchman François Girardon, which was given to Sir Robert by the Pope. The elegant chairs designed by William Kent are covered in their original velvet.

This is only one of many magnificent rooms in the house, for everywhere the immense wealth of Sir Robert is displayed. The Green Velvet Bedchamber contains an elaborate bed, designed by Kent, with a cockleshell headboard and green velvet hangings. The Marble Parlour, which was used as a dining room, has both a Rysbrack fireplace and serving alcoves carved from mauve and white marble, as well as portraits of Sir Robert by Jean van Loo and Sir Godfrey Kneller. The Saloon has walls lined with crimson velvet and a gold mosaic painting by Kent on its coved ceiling. It is extravagantly furnished with Kent's gilt furniture.

ARTWORKS FOR SALE

Above the chimney-piece in the Saloon hangs a portrait of Catherine the Great. In his long political career, Sir Robert amassed a magnificent collection of artworks: indeed, his group of paintings was of such size and quality that it later formed the basis of the collection of the State Hermitage Museum in St Petersburg, Russia. Sir Robert's grandson, the 3rd Earl of Orford, ran up such enormous debts that he was reduced to selling off the paintings in the late 1770s to Catherine the Great (Empress Catherine II of Russia).

The house stands in a 350-acre (142ha) park laid out by Charles Bridgeman, today occupied by a herd of white deer. The grounds contain a water tower built in 1731–3 to the designs of the 'Architect Earl', Henry Lord Herbert, subsequently 9th Earl of Pembroke. There is also a recently renovated 5 acre (2ha) walled garden with elaborate floral displays and a superb rose garden.

CHARLES BRIDGEMAN

Born in 1690, Charles Bridgeman first came to notice when working at Brompton Park Nursery in Kensington for Henry Wise. In 1726, Bridgeman was appointed joint Chief Gardener to George I with Wise, before filling the role alone on Wise's retirement the following year.

Bridgeman worked for the Prince of Wales and his mistress the Countess of Suffolk on the gardens at Marble Hill House, Twickenham. As well as laying out the grounds at Houghton Hall, he also worked on the gardens at Rousham Park, Stowe House, Chiswick House, Cliveden and Claremont.

In his capacity as royal gardener, he cared for and in places designed the royal gardens of Hampton Court, St James's Park, Windsor Castle, Richmond and Hyde Park, where he laid out the lake known as the Serpentine by damming the River Westbourne. Bridgeman also designed the elegant Round Pond in Kensington Gardens, near Kensington Palace. He died in 1738.

ROUSHAM PARK

'THE PRETTIEST PLACE'

The beautiful grounds at Rousham Park near Steeple Aston, Oxfordshire, were laid out by royal gardener, Charles Bridgeman, in the 1720s and developed by William Kent from 1738 onward. They are one of England's first landscape gardens, and the only one in the country to survive essentially unchanged to the present.

The first house at Rousham Park was built in the Jacobean style by Sir Robert Dormer in the 1630s. It has since been much altered, but the original hall remains at the centre of the house. Sir Robert, a proud Royalist who was imprisoned during the Civil War, died in 1649. His grandson, Robert Dormer, inherited the house in 1719 and hired Bridgeman to set out the grounds.

'THE PRETTIEST PLACE'

When poet Alexander Pope, a friend of Robert Dormer, visited in 1728, he was impressed with Charles Bridgeman's work, writing that: 'Rousham is the prettiest place for water-falls, jetts [sic], ponds inclosed with beautiful scenes of green and hanging wood, that ever I saw.'

Above: Nature orchestrated in a vision of Arcadia at Rousham Park. A circular pond is one of the attractions in 'Venus's Vale'.

Historians identify Charles Bridgeman as an early pioneer in the transition of the formal gardens of the later 17th and early 18th centuries into the 'landscape' gardens that were to be developed by William Kent and, subsequently, by 'Capability' Brown. It was Bridgeman who popularized the 'ha-ha', a concealed – usually sunken – boundary to garden or parkland that was used to make the country-house grounds appear to merge with the surrounding countryside.

THE PALLADIAN LANDSCAPE GARDEN

Palladian architects led a movement away from formal French- or Dutch-influenced gardens, with straight artificial plantings, to landscape gardens with meandering lines more like those found in nature. The landscape garden was no more natural than the formal parterres it replaced, but it was designed to look like nature – nature framed and perfected, like the vista reproduced (and perhaps slightly touched up) by a landscape artist such as Claude or Poussin. Kent and Burlington were the pioneers, creating at Chiswick House, in 1734 the first landscape garden, with wandering stream and pathways. For the Whig nobility, the straight lines of formal gardens symbolized the autocratic rule of the House of Stuart, from which England had been freed by the 'Glorious Revolution' of 1688, while the carefully produced natural appearance of the landscape garden was an image of freedom.

Left: A temple at Rousham. Roman temples and other romantic ruins appeared often in Palladian gardens.

Above: Kent designed the garden at Rousham so that a pedestrian on the winding paths would encounter a series of statues, ruins and other aesthetically pleasing 'classical' scenes.

KENT'S PICTURESQUE VISTA

Robert Dormer died in 1737 and was succeeded at Rousham by his ageing brother, James Dormer, who had served under the Duke of Marlborough and been wounded at the Battle of Blenheim in 1704. James Dormer called in William Kent in 1738 to develop the gardens further and to make alterations to the house. He set out to create visions of ancient Roman temples, statues and landscapes in the English countryside.

To the north of the house, Bridgeman's garden contained a bowling green and descending terraces that led down to the River Cherwell. Kent reworked the terraces as a smooth slope and set to work making the vista as picturesque as possible, incorporating an old mill beyond the Cherwell and a medieval bridge across the river and adding an eye-catching ruin of his own. In the woodland garden and Venus's Vale, he built temples in the style of ancient Rome, added statues and laid out circuitous paths and winding streams with ponds and artificial cascades. The whole was intended to have the appeal of a landscape painting by the then highly popular 17th-century artists, Nicolas Poussin and Claude Lorrain.

The circuitous stream Kent channelled through the Watery Walk has been claimed as the first 'serpentine' feature in garden design, the precursor of those so frequently employed in the landscaped designs of 'Capability' Brown. Kent was able to visit Rousham only infrequently, and much of the work was carried out under his direction by the estate's head gardener, John McClary, and Clerk of the Works, William White.

Kent's garden soon became an attraction for visitors. The architect-gardener had created a separate entrance for this purpose, allowing tourists to enter and view the landscape without going near the house.

PALLADIAN INTERIORS

Kent also set to work on the house, adding a battlement, cupola and very fine octagonal-paned windows (later sadly, replaced) in the entrance front. He added two wings to the house, each containing a typically elegant 'William Kent' interior: the Painted Parlour and the Library (partially altered as the Great Parlour in 1764).

In the Painted Parlour, Kent built an elaborate marble chimney-piece and over-mantel, together with wall brackets for the display of Dormer's bronzes. He also painted the mythological scene that decorates the ceiling, fitted a number of dummy doorways to provide the required symmetry and proportion, and designed the exquisite parcel-gilt chairs and gilt-wood tables. Only one element of his design is lacking: the original colour scheme, probably in gold and white, was later repainted, most recently in green *c.*1910.

In the Library, Kent constructed a ribbed and vaulted ceiling and Gothic-style cornice. The room was once lined with books, but these were removed in 1764 when Thomas Roberts transformed the Library into the Great Parlour for Jane, Lady Cottrell-Dormer, adding rococo plasterwork around portraits on the walls. In one of these frames hangs Lady Jane's portrait, by Benjamin West; that of Lt-Gen James Dormer, Kent's patron, is displayed nearby in a more restrained gilt-wood frame.

Below: The cupola was one of Kent's additions to Rousham Park. He also added the castellation to the roof, as well as building two substantial wings.

STOWE HOUSE AND GARDENS

AND THE ENGLISH PALLADIAN MOVEMENT

A colonnaded mansion set within a great park, Stowe House is a veritable English arcadia. House and gardens together form, perhaps, the finest embodiment of the English Palladian movement's vision.

MANY ARCHITECTS

The core of the mansion was built on the site of a medieval manor house in 1676–83 by Sir Richard Temple, 3rd baronet, employing Sir Christopher Wren's master joiner, William Cleare. Stowe House was then developed in the first half of the 18th century by architects including Sir John Vanbrugh, William Kent and James Gibbs. In the same period, Stowe's original formal gardens were gradually transformed into a landscape park by the leading architect-gardeners of the day – who included Charles Bridgeman, Kent and Lancelot 'Capability' Brown. More than 30 temples and picturesque 'classical ruins' were put up in the parkland.

RENOWNED PARKLAND

Initially, the house had a parterre garden, but this was replaced in 1711–26 by a Baroque parkland designed by Vanbrugh and Bridgeman. During this period, Vanbrugh also built several structures in the park, including the Temple of Bacchus (1719), the Doric Arch (1722) and the Egyptian Pyramid (1724–6), and he built the North Portico on the house.

Above: The Marble Saloon, beneath a dome 56ft (17m) high, was built after 1775.

Above: The Temple of Ancient Virtue is one of the classical buildings erected by Kent.

Kent, Gibbs and Giacomo Leoni, publisher of Palladio's *Four Books of Architecture* in English, worked at Stowe in the 1730s-40s. Kent built the two-tiered South Portico on the house *c.*1734 and the Temple of Venus (*c.*1731), the Temple of British Worthies (*c.*1735) and the Temple of Ancient Virtue (*c.*1736); he laid out the 'Elysian Fields' and applied the 'natural' landscaping techniques developed at Rousham to the parkland.

Lancelot 'Capability' Brown was head gardener in 1741–50 and laid out the 'Grecian Valley', building the Grecian Temple (later called the Temple of Concord and Victory) in 1747. He reworked Charles Bridgeman's more formal 'Eleven-Acre Lake' and 'Octagonal Pond' in an irregular shape. The very fine 'Palladian Bridge' is one of three near-identical bridges built at around the same period; the other two bridges are at Prior Park near Bath (see page 179) and Wilton House near Salisbury (see pages 144-5).

The parkland became renowned throughout the country and attracted many noble visitors. Brown's first employment at Stowe involved showing visitors around, and in this way probably made many valuable connections that later paid off in the form of commissions to improve the grounds of country houses. Stowe is said to be the first house and grounds for which a guide book was published. The house is, today, home to an English public (fee-paying) school, while the grounds are open to the public through the National Trust.

Left: The building of Stowe House's north front was completed by the 1780s.

PETWORTH HOUSE
AND 'CAPABILITY' BROWN

Lancelot 'Capability' Brown was one of England's leading garden designers when, in 1751, the 2nd Earl of Egremont hired him to redesign the grounds at his 17th-century mansion of Petworth House, West Sussex. Brown created a vast serpentine lake filled via a one-mile (1.6km)- long brick conduit. To do this he moved 47,000 tons of earth and lined the lake with 17,000 tons of clay. He did away with the formal gardens near the house and, by means of skilful plantings of trees, including limes, beeches, sycamores, oaks and horse chestnuts, created the impression that the Earl's parkland led away naturally into the surrounding countryside.

Today, the 700 acre (280 ha) park at Petworth House is celebrated as the finest surviving example of Brown's work. A great herd of fallow deer – the largest and oldest herd in England – graze the park, and come right up to the windows of the house.

Above: More 'natural' than nature. At Petworth House, by moving trees and digging a great lake, 'Capability' Brown created an ideal piece of countryside.

'CAPABILITY' BROWN

Born in 1716, Lancelot Brown began life as a gardener's boy in his native Northumberland. His first big break came when he found employment in the gardens at Stowe House in Buckinghamshire. There he contributed to the creation of one of the country's best-known informal landscape parks, initially working for William Kent but later working as head gardener in his own right.

Following Kent's death in 1748, he set to work independently as a garden designer. He got his nickname of 'Capability' because he was renowned for declaring that places always had 'capabilities of improvement'. In contrast to Kent, he seldom used statuary or classical buildings in his landscaped grounds, preferring to create natural-looking forms using – as at Petworth House – areas of grass, irregularly shaped lakes, the rising and falling of the terrain and trees planted singly and in groups.

Among 'Capability' Brown's many other commissions was his reworking of the park at Blenheim Palace, where he created the splendid lakes that partly submerged John Vanbrugh's majestic bridge. At Chatsworth House, he did away with formal parterres and planted the park, while rerouting the River Derwent in a serpentine course more pleasing to the eye. He also worked on the gardens and parks of a great many other prominent country houses, including Audley End, Burghley, Longleat and Syon House.

Left: 'Capability' Brown. He learned from the architect and garden designer William Kent.

Below: A neoclassical Doric temple stands in the gardens of Petworth House.

CHAPTER TEN

LATE GEORGIAN AND REGENCY HOUSES

*c.*1760–1830

In 1811, King George III began rebuilding the state apartments at Windsor Castle in the Gothic style, to the designs of James Wyatt. His reign had seen the rise of Robert Adam and the spread of his 'Adam style' in architecture and interior decoration, which brought a lighter touch, an increased knowledge of 'antique' decoration and a breadth of knowledge of French and Italian influences to the pure Palladianism of the early 18th century.

The Gothic transformation of Windsor Castle was completed by James Wyatt's nephew, Jeffry Wyatville, for George IV. This gradually developing taste for a revival of indigenous English styles in architecture, which can also be seen at Penrhyn Castle in Wales and Dalmeny House in Lothian, Scotland, was partly a reaction to the French Revolution of 1789, forming a desire to set aside continental influences, to emphasize the continuity of British-English traditions and to celebrate great British victories, from Trafalgar to Waterloo. At around the same time, more exotic influences also made an appearance, as Chinese and 'Hindoo' (Indian-Turkish) styles were enthusiastically employed at Carlton House in London and the Royal Pavilion in Brighton. Then, as the 19th century advanced, these Gothic and Tudor Revivals were balanced by a renewed enthusiasm for classicism in the Greek Revival movement, which was seen in the design of country houses such as Meldon Park, Belsay Hall and The Grange.

Left: In the Great Hall at Syon House, London, the use of recesses and the effect of the black-and-white floor exemplify the 'movement' that was a key element of the 'Adam style'.

STRAWBERRY HILL
AND THE GOTHIC REVIVAL

Writer and connoisseur Horace Walpole, youngest son of Prime Minister Robert Walpole, inspired an architectural movement with his villa at Twickenham, then a country village but now part of south-west London. Over 45 years, beginning in 1747, he added medieval-style towers, battlements, arches, fireplaces, stained-glass windows and other features to transform his villa, Strawberry Hill, beside the River Thames into a 'Gothick Castle'.

The Gothic Revival movement was born in the Georgian era among imitators of Walpole's light-hearted experiments. It then became a more serious and scholarly movement in the 19th century, when it gave rise to buildings such as Sir Charles Barry and A.W.N. Pugin's rebuilt Houses of Parliament at Westminster. The Victorian Gothic Revival continued as a popular style for churches and university buildings well into the 20th century.

Above: In creating a 'little Gothick Castle' at Strawberry Hill, Walpole indulged his taste for 'charming irregularities' in architecture.

'COMMITTEE OF TASTE'

Walpole used medieval architectural elements for decorative effect and – because of their romantic associations with little concern for architectural integrity – for reproducing features in the way they would have been used in their original setting. He worked alongside his friends, some of whom he appointed to a 'Committee of Taste', instructed to adapt Gothic architectural details (seen in other buildings or in books of reproductions) for his use at Strawberry Hill. Friends who served on this committee included illustrator Richard Bentley, John Chute, owner of The Vyne in Hampshire, and poet Thomas Gray.

GOTHIC *SHARAWAGGI*

Walpole chose the Gothic because he was attracted to its lack of symmetry. He was doubtless reacting against the Palladian orthodoxy in England, which called for ordered, harmonious and symmetrical design, and perhaps also

Below: The Long Gallery's delicate ceiling at Strawberry Hill was based on that of the Henry VII Chapel in Westminster Abbey.

Above: Walpole wrote the first history of art in English, as well as the first Gothic novel.

against the first appearance around him of Neoclassical designs inspired by the temples of ancient Greece. In a letter to his friend Sir Horace Mann, Walpole declared that the trouble with classical-inspired buildings was that they lacked variety and 'charming irregularities'; he was instead attracted, he wrote, to *sharawaggi* or 'want of symmetry'.

Walpole began by 'Gothicizing' the outside of the villa, adding battlements, quatrefoil (four-leaf) windows and Tudor-style chimneys. Subsequently, he built an extension containing a Long Gallery, with a fan-vaulted ceiling based on that of Henry VII's Chapel in Westminster Abbey, and erected two towers – the Beauclerc Tower and the Round Tower.

Strawberry Hill was extended in the mid-19th century by Frances, Countess Waldegrave, who added a new wing. Today the house belongs to St Mary's College, part of the University of Surrey.

Besides building Strawberry Hill and leaving a vast collection of letters that provide a wonderful picture of 18th-century aristocratic life, Walpole's other claim to fame is that he was the author of the first 'Gothic novel'. His *The Castle of Otranto* was first published anonymously in 1765, supposedly as a translation of an Italian book of 1529. Earlier in 1757, he had established a private press at Strawberry Hill, in which he published several of his own books and Thomas Gray's *Odes*.

Above: Walpole's reinvention of the Gothic has had a wide influence. Strawberry Hill does not look as unusual today as it did when new.

THE VYNE

In 1754, Walpole's friend John Chute inherited The Vyne in Hampshire – a Tudor mansion later given the first classical portico on an English country house. A member of Walpole's 'Committee of Taste' – which often met in The Vyne – Chute shared his friend's passion for the 'Gothic'; Walpole referred to him as 'my oracle in taste … the genius that presided over poor Strawberry!' Chute intended to Gothicize the entire interior of The Vyne (indeed, he had his portrait painted while holding a plan for a Gothicized interior at the house) but, in the event, applied the new style only to one room, the Antechapel. Elsewhere, he used a serene classical style to build a staircase and galleries in place of the Tudor Great Hall.

ARBURY HALL, WARWICKSHIRE

Sir Roger Newdigate, for 30 years from 1750 MP for Oxford University, was a pioneer of the Georgian Gothic Revival in his house at Arbury, Warwickshire. His exuberant and light-hearted alterations of an old house of monastic origins were, like those at Strawberry Hill, chiefly for decorative effect, having no structural function. In the Drawing Room (designed in 1762), he installed a fireplace inspired by the tomb of Aymer de Valence in Westminster Abbey. The Dining Room (designed by Henry Keene *c.*1772) has an elaborate fan vault and another extraordinary chimney-piece. The Saloon (designed by Henry Couchman and Sir Roger in 1776–96) is probably the house's finest room and features delicate plaster tracery above its large bow window. The novelist, George Eliot, grew up on the estate and represented Sir Roger and his house in her *Scenes of Clerical Life* (1858). Sir Roger is also remembered as the founder of the Newdigate Poetry Prize for Oxford University students, won by poets such as Matthew Arnold and Andrew Motion.

Right: An extravaganza of delicate and beautifully finished plasterwork rises above the bow window in the Arbury Hall Saloon.

KEW PALACE
AND QUEEN CHARLOTTE'S COTTAGE

Above: Palace and formal garden. After a major restoration by Historic Royal Palaces, Kew Palace opened to the public in April 2006.

On the banks of the Thames in south-west London, Kew Palace, originally known as 'the Dutch House', was a significant royal residence between 1728 and 1818. Apart from Queen Charlotte's Cottage, the orangery and pagoda, the palace is the only surviving royal building of many that once stood at Kew.

Kew Palace is a fairly modest four-storey brick manor house, built in 1631 by Dutch merchant, Samuel Fortrey: his initials, those of his wife, and the date can be seen on a carved brick set above the south door. It is a villa, with symmetrical south and north façades featuring pediments and pilasters. Its chief room is the King's Dining Room, measuring 31 x 21ft (9.3 x 6.3m), with ceiling decoration featuring a Tudor rose.

The house was leased by Queen Caroline in 1728; William Kent added new stairs and sash windows at this time. It was principally used as a residence for the princesses Anne, Amelia and Caroline. Then, in the 1750s, Frederick, Prince of Wales, was living in the adjacent White House and used the Dutch House as a school for his eldest sons, George, Prince of Wales (the future George III), and Prince Edward. The house was again a princely school in the 1770s, this time for George III's sons George, Prince of Wales, and Frederick, Duke of York.

King George bought the house outright in 1781. In 1801–6, he lived there occasionally with Queen Charlotte; by this stage the King's health was poor following recurrent attacks of porphyria. He subsequently lived mainly at Windsor. Then Queen Charlotte, herself seriously ill, lived in Kew Palace for the last few months of her life in 1818 – during which three royal weddings took place in the building. These were the marriages of Prince Adolphus to Princess Augusta of Hesse-Cassel, of William, Duke of Clarence (the future William IV), to Princess Adelaide of Saxe-Meiningen and of Edward, Duke of Kent, to Princess Victoire of Saxe-Coburg (the parents of Queen Victoria).

Below: This engraving shows Kew Palace as it was c.1815–20, around the time when Queen Charlotte lived there briefly.

THE WHITE HOUSE, KEW

Kew Palace originally stood alongside a much larger royal residence: Kew House. This was used by George III's parents, Frederick, Prince of Wales, and his wife, Princess Augusta, from the 1730s onward. It was rebuilt by William Kent, who gave it a coolly elegant white stucco façade that earned the building its new name of 'the White House'. Kent also designed the lavish interiors.

Frederick died in 1751 and Augusta lived on in the White House as Dowager Princess of Wales. Several buildings and features in the gardens were built for her by Sir William Chambers, including an orangery and pagoda. The house was demolished in the early 19th century.

Right: White Lodge, Richmond Park. George II's queen, Caroline, loved this Palladian villa. The future Edward VIII was born here on 23 June 1894.

RICHMOND LODGE

Another riverside residence with delightful gardens was Richmond Lodge in Richmond Old Deer Park. It stood on the site of a ruined ancient royal palace, in a position where Charles II had considered building a new residence to designs by Sir Christopher Wren; William III subsequently built a hunting lodge on the ancient ruins. The future George II and Queen Caroline used William III's lodge as Prince and Princess of Wales from 1718 and, after coming to the throne, made it Queen Caroline's dower house. In the 1730s, Charles Bridgeman and William Kent redesigned the gardens, adding a temple, a dairy and even a 'Merlin's Cave'. (These grounds and those surrounding the Dutch House and the White House were joined together during George III's reign and became the Royal Botanic Gardens of Kew in 1841.)

George III and Queen Charlotte used Richmond Lodge as a country house for over a decade after 1761, but in 1772 they moved into the White House, following the death of his mother, and the lodge was demolished.

THE QUEEN'S COTTAGE

Queen Charlotte's Cottage stands in a nature conservation area amid a wild bluebell wood in Kew Gardens. The cottage was given to Queen Charlotte, in September 1761, on her marriage to George III. The royals used the building as a summerhouse. In 1818 it was the venue for the tea, following the double wedding of her sons William, Duke of Clarence, and Edward, Duke of Kent.

Below: Queen Charlotte's Cottage was opened to visitors in 1959.

THE 'NEW PALACE'

King George III had grand plans for a new palace in the Old Deer Park, Richmond. Sir William Chambers drew up three sets of plans, the first of which was for a Palladian-style palace with a Corinthian portico like that of Holkham Hall, but these all came to nothing. Then, in 1800, James Wyatt designed a Gothic-style castle-palace with a square central keep and four cylindrical towers. Building began in 1801 on the site of the demolished White House and continued for a decade at a cost of £500,000. But work was halted in 1811 because of the King's illness, at a stage when the castle was just a shell. George IV hated the new palace and had it destroyed with explosives in 1827.

THE WHITE LODGE

The New Park Lodge (or White Lodge) in Richmond Park was a hunting lodge in the form of a Palladian villa, designed by Roger Morris for George I in 1727. This building stands in the park we know today as Richmond Park, which was originally called the New Park. (The New Park is on the other side of Richmond from the older royal hunting grounds of the Old Deer Park.) George died before the lodge was finished and George II completed it for Queen Caroline. Today it is the junior section of the Royal Ballet School.

Below: William Chambers drew inspiration from a youthful visit to China when he designed the 163ft (50m)-tall Great Pagoda for the Dowager Princess Augusta in 1761.

SYON HOUSE
AND ROBERT ADAM

Sir Hugh and Lady Betty Smithson, later Duke and Duchess of Northumberland, commissioned the rising architect-designer Robert Adam to remodel and redecorate the interior of Syon House, Middlesex, in 1762. The house, built in the mid-16th century by Edward Seymour, Duke of Somerset and Lord Protector of the Kingdom, already had a long and colourful history (see pages 110–11).

Adam was forced to work with the structure he inherited, for Sir Hugh and Lady Betty did not want him to rebuild the Tudor mansion and turned down his request to build a circular domed room in the central courtyard. Instead, he created a suite of five rooms running around the west, south and east sides of the courtyard house.

THE 'ADAM STYLE'

Adam's five rooms – the Great Hall, the Ante-room, the Dining Room, the Red Drawing Room and the Long Gallery – lead one into another. They are celebrated as the first fully realized statement of the 'Adam style', which deployed ancient Roman architectural elements with a new freedom and lightness of touch. The key element of the 'Adam style' is 'movement', which Robert and James defined in the Preface to *The Works in Architecture of Robert and James Adam* (two volumes, 1773 and 1779) as 'the rise and fall, the advance and recess, with other diversity of form, in the different parts of a building'.

Below: The Red Drawing Room. The finest Spitalfields silk hangs on its walls.

Adam's use of recesses and steps in the cool black-and-white Great Hall at Syon House exemplifies this movement. In the gorgeously grand Ante-room he brought Rome to London in the form of a dozen green antique marble columns found on the bed of the River Tiber. The floor of muted yellow, red and blue makes a harmonious composition with the gold of the statues on top of the columns and the gilt stucco panels in the walls.

'GREAT VARIETY'

The Dining Room, a triple cube 63ft long by 21ft wide and high (19 x 6 x 6m), contains gilt and ivory decoration. The Red Drawing Room has sumptuous red silk wall coverings, an elegant coved ceiling beautifully painted by Angelica Kauffman and a fine carpet designed by Adam and woven by Thomas Moore in 1769. After this series of triumphs, Adam achieved perhaps his finest effect in redecorating the Jacobean-era Long Gallery. This room, 136ft long by 14ft wide and high (41 x 4 x 4m), was decorated and furnished in a colour scheme of pale green and gilt, with bookshelves and furniture of his own design. He achieved, in his own words, 'a style to afford great variety and amusement'.

Right: These designs, including folding doors, are from one of Adam's pattern books.

Above: Grandly transformed within, thanks to its Adam decorations, on the outside Syon House is a rather plain Tudor block.

AMERICAN CONNECTION

Robert Adam's patron at Syon House, Sir Hugh Smithson, had an illegitimate son named James Smithson, born in France to his mistress, Elizabeth Kate Hungerford Macie. James was a chemist and geologist, and on his death in 1829 he left $508,318 to found 'an establishment for the increase and diffusion of knowledge among men': the result was the Smithsonian Institution, established in Washington, D.C., in 1846.

HAREWOOD HOUSE
AND THE 'ADAM STYLE'

The stately Palladian mansion of Harewood House, near Leeds, was built in 1759–72 for the immensely wealthy Edwin Lascelles, 1st Lord Harewood. John Carr of York designed the main block, while Robert Adam was responsible for the side wings and interiors.

CHIPPENDALE AND ADAM

The 16 staterooms on the principal floor of the house are exquisitely decorated and furnished in the 'Adam style', with elegant chairs and other furniture by the leading 18th-century cabinetmaker Thomas Chippendale. Adam's grand Entrance Hall has Doric half-columns painted to imitate red marble; they make a telling contrast with the elegant grey-blue walls. The room now called the China Room was originally the Study in Adam's plan; it contains a collection of superb Sèvres porcelain with pieces once owned by Louis XV and XVI and Queen Marie Antoinette.

The State Bedroom was intended for visiting members of the royal family: it contains magnificent Chippendale pieces including a spectacular state bed, fine wall mirrors and a satinwood commode and secretaire that many identify as Chippendale's finest work. The less grand East Bedroom was used by 1st Lord Harewood: it retains its Adam frieze and sunflower ceiling decoration.

Above: Originally, Harewood House's south front gave on to the park, but a formal terrace garden was added in the mid-19th century.

The sumptuous Long Gallery is 77ft long, 24ft wide and 21ft high (23 x 7 x 6m). The ceiling was designed by Adam and painted by Biagio Rebecca. Of all the staterooms, the Music Room remains closest to Adam's original design: the colourful Adam carpet contains lyres and reflects the ceiling roundels painted by Angelica Kauffman; trumpets, lyres and pipes are carved in the marble chimney-piece; the chairs and sofas, and even the frame for the portrait of the 1st Earl's sister-in-law are by Chippendale.

LATER ALTERATIONS

In 1772, Lancelot 'Capability' Brown began to redesign the park. In the 19th century, Sir Charles Barry removed Carr's classical portico on the south front, added a third storey to the house and swept away part of Brown's landscape to create a terrace garden. For part of the 20th century, Harewood House was home to George V's daughter, Mary, the Princess Royal, who married the 6th Earl of Harewood in 1922. The house, today, belongs to her grandson David, the 8th Earl.

ROBERT ADAM

The architect and designer Robert Adam was born in 1728 in Fife, son of the leading Scottish architect of his day, William Adam, who served as Master Mason to the North British Board of Ordnance. On his father's death in 1748, Robert and his brother James were appointed to the position and in 1748–54 undertook many architectural and decorating commissions, including Fort George, near Inverness, and Dumfries House in Ayrshire. After travelling in continental Europe in 1754–7, Robert settled in London and soon made his name with his 'Adam style'.

By 1761 he was already receiving major commissions to redecorate the interiors of grand houses both in London and in the country, such as Alnwick Castle (Northumberland), Kedleston Hall (Derbyshire) and Osterley Park (Middlesex – now the London Borough of Hounslow). In the same year he was appointed Architect to the King's Works. Both before and after his work on the interior at Syon House in 1762, Adam was architect on a number of houses, designing the south front at Kedleston Hall in 1757–9, then building Mersham-le-Hatch (Kent) in 1762–72 and Luton Hoo (Bedfordshire) in 1766–74; he remodelled Kenwood House in 1767–8. In later life he designed a number of Gothic Revival castles including Culzean in Ayrshire; he is particularly remembered in Scotland for his design of Edinburgh University and of Edinburgh's Charlotte Square. He died in 1792 and was buried in Westminster Abbey.

Left: Robert Adam closely studied the architecture of ancient Greece and Rome to create the 'Adam style'.

KEDLESTON HALL

AND KENWOOD HOUSE

Robert Adam was initially commissioned at Kedleston Hall *c.*1758 to design classical temples and rustic buildings in the park, while Sir Nathaniel Curzon, subsequently 1st Baron Scarsdale, was rebuilding his family mansion. But Adam impressed Sir Nathaniel sufficiently to be granted control over the design of the house, ousting architects Matthew Brettingham and James Paine.

DRAMATIC FAÇADE

Adam's south front contains a four-column triumphal arch – based on the Arch of Constantine in Rome – beneath a domed roof and above a beautiful curving double staircase, which leads up to a large glass entrance door. To right and left of this central block are identical wings of three floors. The façade combines great drama with wonderful delicacy, and – perfectly embodying the Adam concept of 'movement' – is considered both a quintessential Robert Adam design and an architectural masterpiece.

Above: The north front at Kedleston was largely as designed by Brettingham, but Adam emphasised the six-column portico.

Kedleston was the first building to make use of a triumphal arch in an English stately house.

The impressive north, or entrance, front, 350ft (107m) across, was beg un by Brettingham. It consists of two substantial end pavilions linked to the main block by curving corridors. The east pavilion contains rooms for the use of Sir Nathaniel and family, the main block houses the staterooms and the west pavilion the service quarters. The main building has an imposing six-column portico; it was begun by Paine and completed by Adam in more dramatic style than originally planned.

Below: The Marble Hall at Kedleston, with its 20 pink alabaster columns, lies directly behind the vast portico on the north front.

MARBLE AND ALABASTER

The portico entrance leads into the grandly classical Great Hall, probably designed by Brettingham like a Roman basilica, along the lines of the equally magnificent Marble Hall he built with William Kent and Lord Leicester at Holkham Hall, Norfolk.

The Great Hall at Kedleston has an Italian marble floor and contains 20 fluted alabaster columns set before alcoves containing classical statues; the walls and doors are decorated with classical scenes; the hall fills the entire height of the house and the only sources of light are the skylights in the roof. The hall leads into the circular Saloon, which stands behind the arch of the south front and is lit from above through glass in the dome 62ft (19m) above. The room was designed as a sculpture gallery; it contains four sets of double doors, with surrounds of green *scagliola*.

KEDLESTON AND INDIA

Kedleston Hall was the model for the residence of the Governor-General of India, the Raj Bhavan in Calcutta, which was built in 1799–1803, complete with Palladian columns and dome. The Raj Bhavan was later occupied by Lord Curzon, Viceroy of India in 1898–1905, who must have enjoyed the familiarity of the surroundings because, as a descendant of Sir Nathaniel Curzon, he had been born at Kedleston Hall in 1859. Kedleston Hall has an 'Indian museum' containing artefacts and furniture brought back to Derbyshire by Lord Curzon; the former Viceroy's tomb stands in the tiny 13th-century church in the grounds at Kedleston – the only remnant of the medieval village that was moved during the creation of the 18th-century landscape park.

The other staterooms include the Great Apartment – a formal bedroom with gilded chairs and a superb state bed – and the Drawing Room, which boasts a chimney-piece of the Derbyshire stone bluejohn and doorcases and window surrounds made from local alabaster. The other main rooms are the Dining Room, the Library and the Music Room. A magnificent staircase leads down from the principal rooms on the *piano nobile* to Caesar's Hall on the ground floor.

ADAM'S LANDSCAPED PARK

At Kedleston Hall, Adam also landscaped the 820-acre (332-ha) park with the help of the landscape gardener, William Emes. He created five serpentine lakes in the style of 'Capability' Brown from canals and ponds that had been laid out earlier by Charles Bridgeman. Adam also built a beautifully judged bridge, fishing house and boat house, as well as a number of classical buildings, such as the North Lodge – which was another triumphal arch.

KENWOOD HOUSE

In 1764–79, Robert Adam remodelled the early 17th-century Kenwood House in Hampstead for the Scottish-born politician and judge, William Murray, 1st Earl of Mansfield. Adam built an Ionic portico on the north, or entrance, front and created a celebrated library on the east side of the south front. The Library's widely admired interior has a curved ceiling with flat oval and rectangular panels for decoration, its shape described by Adam as 'much more perfect than that which is commonly called the cove ceiling'. The house originally stood close to the road from Hampstead to Highgate, but in the 1790s the 2nd Earl of Mansfield moved the road; the house now stands in a secluded position on Hampstead Heath, in gardens designed by Humphry Repton. The 1999 film *Notting Hill* was partly filmed at Kenwood House.

IVEAGH BEQUEST

In 1928, Kenwood House and a substantial collection of fine art was bequeathed to the nation by Edward Cecil Guinness, the 1st Earl of Iveagh, head of the Guinness brewing family from Ireland and the man responsible for the lavish rebuilding of Elveden Hall in Suffolk. Lord Iveagh built up the art collection in the late 19th century. It included some very important paintings, including a self-portrait of *c.*1665 by Rembrandt, the delicate *Guitar Player* by Vermeer and several fine works by Turner, Lawrence and Reynolds. Further paintings have been added to The Iveagh Bequest over the years. They are on display in the beautiful surroundings of Kenwood House.

Above: The highly colourful Library at Kenwood House is thought to be one of the finest of all Robert Adam interiors.

Below: A modern touch at Kedleston Hall. In the recesses of the Saloon, the pedestals beneath the urns are actually stoves.

HEVENINGHAM HALL
AND JAMES WYATT

When James Wyatt returned to London from six years' study in Italy in 1768, he quickly won national renown for his theatre, The Pantheon, in Regent Street. The extraordinary domed building, which opened in 1772 but was later demolished, was based on the design of the Hagia Sophia ('Church of Sacred Wisdom') in Istanbul. Horace Walpole called it 'the most beautiful edifice in England'.

Wyatt began to work as a country-house architect in the Neoclassical style at Heaton Hall in Lancashire (1772); at Heveningham Hall, Suffolk, the Dutch merchant Sir Gerard Vanneck commissioned him in 1788 to complete the grand 25-bay remodelling (begun by Sir Robert Taylor) of an earlier house.

Wyatt was principally responsible for Heveningham Hall's interiors, which include the beautiful Vaulted Hall. The rooms are considered to be among Wyatt's finest work and have recently been restored and renovated.

Below: Inner beauty. Heveningham Hall – detail of James Wyatt's library.

Above: The great expanse of Heveningham Hall. Between them, Wyatt and Taylor created a most impressive house.

Heveningham Hall still stands in extensive parkland, which was originally set out by Lancelot 'Capability' Brown. This includes a stable block in the shape of a horseshoe, a temple and an ice-house. The recent restoration includes the addition of further Neoclassical buildings, including a bridge across the lake, a new temple, an orangery and a boat house.

JAMES WYATT

Born in 1746 in Staffordshire, James Wyatt was still in his twenties when he set out as a country-house architect with his work at Heaton Hall. He became Robert Adam's great rival in the Neoclassical style, but could work with equal success in the Gothic Revival mode. Wyatt enjoyed a long career that stretched into the second decade of the 19th century; from 1796 he served as Surveyor General to the Board of Works and was involved in the restoration of many great English cathedrals, including Durham, Salisbury and Hereford. His ventures into the Gothic were dismissed by more serious followers of the Gothic Revival in the mid-19th century. Wyatt built a number of Gothic Revival country houses, including Lee Priory in Kent (1783–90) and Ashridge in Hertfordshire (1808 onward). But he is remembered, above all, as the designer of the extravagant and extraordinary Gothic country house of Fonthill Abbey in Wiltshire (now ruined), built in 1796–1807 for William Beckford, author of *Vathek* (1786).

Below: The design for Fonthill Abbey. Its steepled tower collapsed three times.

CASTLE COOLE
AND THE NEOCLASSICAL REVIVAL

James Wyatt was the leading architect of his day when he designed Castle Coole for the 1st Earl of Belmore in 1790–8. The palatial building, alongside the river that links the lower and upper lakes of Lough Erne in Co Fermanagh, Ulster, is celebrated as one of Northern Ireland's finest country houses.

The two-storey central block is nine bays in width. On the entrance front, a towering pedimented portico containing four plain Ionic columns 27ft (8m) tall stands in the centre of the main block; on either side, two wings each fronted by a colonnade of six Doric columns lead to an end pavilion. On the garden front, the central bow is curved on account of the Oval Saloon within. Wyatt used pale Portland stone brought at great expense from Dorset. The stone was taken by ship to Ballyshannon (Co Donegal), carried overland to Lough Erne, then shipped by barge across the water as far as Enniskillen, before being brought the final 2 miles (3km) by cart.

Above: The main front at Castle Coole. Note the elegant symmetry of the two Doric colonnades leading to twin end pavilions.

TOP-LIT LOBBY

Behind the entrance portico, the restrained Great Hall is of one storey only and contains a line of Doric columns, two plain chimney-pieces and a Doric frieze. The hall gives on to the Staircase Hall, which contains a double-return stone staircase up to a first-floor landing with four Doric columns of brown and yellow *scagliola*. The lobby, also on the first floor, is lit from above, in line with Irish country-house tradition, by glass domes hidden on the entrance front behind pediment and balustrade. The lobby contains an attic-level gallery, from which rooms lead off, with a graceful colonnade said to be copied from the interiors of the temple of the sea god Poseidon at Paestum and the Parthenon in Athens.

Behind the curved centre of the garden front is the elegant Oval Saloon, which runs out to the Drawing Room and Dining Room on either side, with plasterwork to Wyatt's designs by Joseph Rose of London and *scagliola* work by Dominic Bartoli.

Below: The entrance hall, Castle Coole. The door leads to the Oval Saloon.

THE GREEK REVIVAL

In his use of more austere, less ornamented ancient Greek rather than Roman architectural elements, for example the baseless column used in the colonnades on the entrance front, Wyatt followed the fashion for Hellenism in Neoclassical architecture at the close of the century. Under the influence of James Stuart and Nicholas Revett's *The Antiquities of Athens* (published in three parts in 1762, 1789 and 1795), a growing interest in archaeology and the discovery of Greek antiquities, Neoclassicists held that ancient Greek architecture was purer and more rational than ancient Roman building. This enthusiasm fed into the Greek Revival movement of the 19th century.

ALTHORP

THE SPENCERS AND THE ROYALS

In *c.*1790 Henry Holland handsomely refaced the Spencer family's country house at Althorp, Northamptonshire, also adding pediments to the south and north fronts and corridors along the forecourt wings. By this date the Spencers were already well established at Althorp, having lived there since 1508, when Sir John Spencer bought the original moated medieval manor house, built of a local orange stone, with grounds of 300 acres (120ha). Today, Althorp is one of the most visited country houses in England, for its estate contains the burial place of Diana, Princess of Wales, whose father was the 8th Earl Spencer.

Above: Classical good taste. Althorp is an Elizabethan house in 18th-century dress.

PRINCESS DIANA AND ALTHORP

Lady Diana Spencer was born at Park House on the Sandringham estate. Her parents divorced in 1969, when she was eight, and her father was awarded custody of the children. He inherited Althorp in 1975 when she was 13, and she spent her teenage years there, when she was not at boarding school or staying at her mother's home in London. Indeed, she first met her future husband, Prince Charles, at Althorp when he visited to shoot in November 1977.

Below: The summerhouse at Althorp, now a memorial to Diana, once stood in the grounds of Admiralty House, London.

Following her death in Paris in 1997, her body was brought in a cortege from the funeral at Westminster Abbey to Althorp, where she was interred on an island in the lake known as the Round Oval. An urn on the island, designed by Edward Bulmer and made by Dick Reid, celebrates her memory, which is also honoured by an exhibition of her life and work in Althorp's Italianate stables, built by Roger Morris *c.*1733. The summerhouse by the lake is set aside in her memory.

Below: Princess Diana in May 1997. As Lady Diana Spencer, she spent part of her childhood at Althorp.

THE GROWTH OF ALTHORP

The first Sir John Spencer or his grandson, another Sir John, rebuilt the medieval house at Althorp to make a more substantial redbrick dwelling with an internal courtyard. Then, in 1575, the younger Sir John added two wings on the south side to create the entrance forecourt. In 1660–2, Dorothy, widow of Henry Spencer, 1st Earl of Sunderland, covered the internal courtyard and built the Grand Staircase. Her son, Robert Spencer, 2nd Earl of Sunderland, created a classical façade with columns and balustrade, and internally transformed the Great Hall on the upper floor of the west wing into a Long Gallery, while on the north side creating staterooms including the Saloon. He had formal gardens laid out to designs by the Frenchman André Le Nôtre, landscaper of the royal Palace of Versailles. The house in this era greatly impressed diarist John Evelyn, who called the house a 'palace...a noble pile', and declared its rooms and furnishings to be 'such as may become a great prince', also noting that its gardens were both 'exquisitely planted and kept'.

The next stage of work was in the 18th century. First, Charles Spencer, the 5th Earl of Sunderland, refashioned the Entrance Hall following Palladian designs by Colen Campbell that were actually implemented by Roger Morris after Campbell's death (1729); Morris also built the stone stables with two classical porticoes, and artist John Wootton painted a series of Spencer hunting scenes. Then, George Spencer, the 2nd Earl Spencer, commissioned the fashionable architect Henry Holland – who was simultaneously working for the Prince of Wales on the Marine Pavilion in Brighton (later rebuilt as Brighton Pavilion) and redesigning Carlton House in London – literally to give the essentially Elizabethan house an 18th-century facelift.

Above: At Althorp, Earl Spencer stands before a 1994 portrait of Diana that once hung in her home, Kensington Palace.

A 'MATHEMATICAL' FAÇADE

Holland refaced the red brick with white brick rebate tiles, which were called 'mathematical tiles' by contemporaries because they fitted together so exactly. The view then current was that brick was not a suitable material for a grand house, despite the great and enduring beauty of Tudor brick houses such as Compton Wynyates; rebate tiles were popularized by Holland, who used them to face his own London house, Sloane Place.

In addition to adding pediments to the garden and entrance fronts, Holland filled in the medieval moat, and within the house moved the main reception rooms to the ground floor of the west wing, creating a fine progression of rooms through the Long Library, the Yellow Drawing Room and the Dining Room. Althorp has changed little over the 200-odd years since Holland's alterations were carried out: although a medieval and Elizabethan house at its core, its classical 18th-century facing dominates its appearance and gives it its essential character.

THE SPENCER 'FAMILY SILVER'

Althorp is also celebrated for the Spencer family's superb collection of sculpture, ceramics, furniture and paintings, including fine works by Rubens, van Dyck, Lely, Reynolds and Gainsborough. In addition, it contains widely admired doors, chimney-pieces and other fittings designed by John Vardy and James 'Athenian' Stuart for the family's London mansion, Spencer House, in the 18th century. The fittings were removed to Althorp when Spencer House was leased in 1924.

Left: Althorp is full of the finest furniture, paintings and other fittings – much of it brought there from Spencer House, London.

BRIGHTON PAVILION
AND THE PRINCE REGENT

The exotic domes and minarets of the Royal Pavilion in Brighton were built in 1815–23 by architect John Nash for George, the former Prince of Wales, who was Prince Regent in 1811–20 due to the illness of his father, George III, and King in 1820–30. Nash used the briefly fashionable 'Hindoo' style, derived mainly from that of Islamic temple architecture in India and a strain of the taste for the exotic that flowered in the Regency period, partly in reaction to the uncluttered, 'rational' designs of Palladian and Neoclassical architects. Nash built on and around the Prince's earlier house, the Marine Pavilion, which had itself been constructed on the site of a humble farmhouse by Henry Holland from 1787 onward.

Above: Oriental romance by the Sussex sea – the domes and minarets of the Pavilion suggest a temple more than a palace.

GEORGE'S FIRST PAVILION

George, Prince of Wales, was very taken with Brighton – then a village called Brighthelmstone – when he first visited in 1783 to stay with his uncle, the Duke of Cumberland. George returned in 1784 and leased a farmhouse on the Steine, an area of grassy land to the east of the village, later setting up home there with his Roman Catholic wife, Maria Fitzherbert, whom he had secretly married in 1785. The house built on this site by Henry Holland was Neoclassical, with a domed saloon and wings extending to south and north.

In 1802–3, the Prince began to redevelop his Pavilion in an oriental style. Initially, the look was Chinese rather than 'Hindoo': he redecorated the interior of the house with bamboo panelling and with Chinese chimney-pieces, wallpaper, porcelain, statuary and furniture, and commissioned William Porden to refashion the exterior as a Chinese pagoda. But then the Prince's taste turned to Indian- and Turkish-inspired architecture, and in 1804–8 he had Porden build a splendid domed stable block and riding school in a 'Saracenic' style that most closely resembles a Turkish mosque.

NASH REPLACES REPTON

The prominent landscape gardener, Humphry Repton, was known to the Prince because he had worked on the gardens at Carlton House in London. He was invited to Brighton, where he acclaimed Porden's domed stable block as 'stupendous and magnificent…distinct from either Grecian or Gothic' and drew up a detailed plan to rebuild the entire Pavilion in a 'Hindoo' style. The Prince declared himself delighted and indicated that he would 'have every part

Left: The Court at Brighton à la *Chinese. Cruikshank's cartoon satirizes George's lavishly indulged taste for the Oriental.*

Above: It cost more than £500,000 to furnish the Banqueting Room, a setting for exotic dinners, in such brilliant luxury.

JOHN NASH

After training under Sir Robert Taylor, Nash began his career as a speculative builder in London. Declared bankrupt in 1783, he moved into country-house architecture to rebuild his reputation and worked with landscape gardener Humphry Repton. Nash returned to London in the 1790s and from 1798 was employed by the Prince of Wales, later working on redesigning the Brighton Pavilion and the rebuilding of Buckingham House in London, as well as developing Regent's Park and Regent's Street. Nash's own house, East Cowes Castle on the Isle of Wight, was an influence on the early 19th-century phase of the Gothic Revival. His country houses include the 'picturesque' Italianate Cronkhill in Shropshire (1802) and Sandridge Park in Devon (*c.*1805), and also the Gothic Revival-style Caerhays Castle in Cornwall (1808). He also built four Gothic castles in Ireland, including Killymoon Castle in County Tyrone (1803).

of it carried into immediate execution'. Due to financial difficulties, however, he did not actually begin the work until 1815, and then, to Repton's dismay, it was carried out to designs by John Nash.

Using a cast-iron framework over Holland's original house, Nash added the distinctive onion-shaped domes, minarets, cupolas and pinnacles that give the Pavilion such a distinctive look today. The interior was lavish, decorated and furnished with great Regency wit and an extravagant sense of the exotic. First, Nash built a new pink and green Entrance Hall and light green Long Gallery, decorated in the Chinese style with dragon panels. Then he planned the kitchen with four remarkable iron columns, made to look like palm trees with bronze leaves, to support the lantern roof, and equipped it with all the latest gadgets to enable the staff to get food to the Prince Regent's table piping hot.

PUBLIC ROOMS

Next, in 1812–20, he built new end wings containing the Pavilion's main apartments, the Music Room and the Banqueting Room, each measuring 40 x 60ft (12 x 18m). In the Banqueting Room, the 45ft (13.5m)- high domed ceiling was painted to resemble an eastern sky with a silver dragon holding a vast chandelier, lit by gas rather than candles, and almost a ton in weight and 30ft (9m) high. The Music Room also had a domed ceiling and gas chandelier; here, the Prince entertained his guests with music performed by an orchestra dressed in Turkish costumes, sometimes himself singing as a baritone. On one occasion, he received the Italian composer Gioacchino Rossini there. In his private apartments, George had a bath 6ft deep, 10ft wide and 16ft long (1.2 x 3 x 4.8m), which was filled with salt water pumped directly from the sea.

AN ABANDONED PALACE

George apparently grew bored of all this splendour: after 1827 he did not return to the Pavilion, preferring Windsor Castle and Buckingham Palace. As Brighton grew, so the Pavilion was gradually surrounded by housing and the King felt the need for greater privacy. According to some accounts, he finally abandoned his Brighton house because his new mistress, Lady Conyngham, declared that she disliked it. Among his successors, William IV used the Pavilion, but Queen Victoria loathed it and was considering having it knocked down before she and Albert settled at Osborne. The building, owned by the Brighton local authority, has recently been restored.

Below: This contemporary aquatint indicates that the Pavilion may simply have been too grand for comfortable living.

PENRHYN CASTLE
AND THE NORMAN REVIVAL

The favoured royal architect, Thomas Hopper, built the Norman-style Penrhyn Castle near Bangor *c.*1825. This romantic building, complete with turrets and battlements, was one of a series of early 19th-century houses in the shape of Norman and Tudor castles – in what came to be known as the Norman and Tudor Revival styles.

Before building Penrhyn Castle, Hopper served the Prince of Wales by designing a glass-and-iron 'Gothick' conservatory at the Prince's lavish town-house, Carlton House, in 1807. In 1819 he began Gosford Castle in Co Armagh, Northern Ireland, for Archibald Acheson, 2nd Earl of Gosford, who later served as Governor of Canada. Built of pale local Bessbrook granite with an angular keep, circular towers and bastions, Gosford was Ireland's largest country house when built.

Hopper's patrons at Penrhyn were the relations of a Liverpool merchant, Richard Pennant, who had built up a great fortune from Jamaican sugar and, after 1785, developed the local Penrhyn Quarry for mining slate. The castle at Penrhyn incorporates a medieval hall dating to the time of Llywelyn ap Iorwerth ('Llywelyn the Great') and a later 'mock castle'. Hopper designed the castle interior and fittings using fine wallpapers, 'Norman' furniture, stained glass and delicate carvings. The building and fitting took 25 years (1820–45).

Penrhyn Castle also contains a splendid Grand Staircase, a bed made of local slate weighing one ton for a visit by Queen Victoria, and a magnificent art collection put together by the Pennant family. Its kitchens and servant quarters have been restored to their condition in 1894, when they were prepared for a banquet in honour of a visit by the Prince of Wales (the future Edward VII). With magnificent views of Snowdonia and the Menai Straits, the castle stands in impressive grounds, which include a sheltered walled garden with many tropical plants such as palm trees and Chinese gooseberries.

Above: Penrhyn Castle stands in 45 acres (18ha) of park. In spring, the daffodils and snowdrops are a glorious sight, with distant views of Snowdonia to further stir the spirit.

Below: 'Prodigy house' revisited. Anthony Salvin's extravagant Harlaxton Hall used a hybrid Elizabethan-Jacobean Revival style.

REVIVAL STYLES

At the close of the 18th century and in the early 19th century, architectural styles for country houses became increasingly diverse. The general adherence to Palladian and Neoclassical designs was submerged in a return to a number of earlier styles, including the Gothic, Tudor (sometimes called Elizabethan), Jacobean and Greek Revivals.

THREE REVIVAL CASTLES

A precursor of the Norman Revival was the castellated Norris Castle on the Isle of Wight, built on the site of a 16th-century fortress by James Wyatt for Lord Henry Seymour in the 1790s. (Happy memories of childhood visits here led Queen Victoria to buy Osborne nearby.)

In 1810–20, Sir Robert Smirke then used the Norman Revival style at Eastnor Castle in the Malvern Hills for John Somers Cocks, the 1st Earl Somers. Within the castle, Sir George Gilbert Scott built a Great Hall measuring 55ft high, 30ft wide and 60ft long (17 x 9 x 18m) and A.M.W. Pugin used the Gothic Revival style in the Drawing Room.

In Northern Ireland, Edward Blore employed the Tudor Revival style – sometimes called 'Tudor-Gothic' or 'Elizabethan Revival' – at Narrow Water Castle in Co Down in the 1830s. His patron was Roger Hall, High Sheriff of Co Down. The elegant Revival house stands alongside a long house built in a loose Wren style in the 17th century and close to the original 13th-century Norman castle on the site. Blore's castle has a beautiful interior with exquisite panelling, plasterwork, wooden over-mantel and furniture.

Above: Robert Smirke's Staircase Hall at Eastnor Castle has cast-iron bannisters, plus a wooden chandelier, dragon benches and hall chairs, all dating from the 17th century.

OTHER REVIVAL BUILDINGS

A similar Tudor Revival style was used by the architect William Wilkins in 1815 for Dalmeny House in Lothian, Scotland, and the following year for his reworking of Tregothnan, near Truro, in Cornwall. Both have the elaborate profile of an Elizabethan 'prodigy house'. Jeffry Wyatville used Tudor Revival elements at Lilleshall Hall in Shropshire in the 1820s–30s for George Granville Leveson-Gower, Marquis of Stafford and later 1st Duke of Sutherland. Around the same time William Burn built an Elizabethan Revival mansion, Carstairs House, Strathclyde, for Henry Montieth.

The extraordinary Harlaxton Hall at Harlaxton in Lincolnshire was slightly later, built in a Jacobethan style and combining elements of Elizabethan and Jacobean architecture and extraordinary internal features in German Baroque. It was constructed in 1837–45 by Anthony Salvin, later a master of Norman Revival castle-building in the mid-19th century. Today the house, known as Harlaxton College, is the British campus of the University of Evansville, Indiana, USA.

BUCKINGHAM PALACE
AND ST JAMES'S PALACE

Buckingham Palace was originally a town house, built for the Duke of Buckingham in 1702 by William Talman and a gentleman architect by the name of William Winde, on the site of an earlier pre-Civil War residence named Arlington House. George III bought Buckingham House in 1762 as a family residence to which he and Queen Charlotte could escape from court life at St James's Palace. Renaming it the Queen's House, he built a large library. Fourteen of George and Charlotte's 15 children were born in the Queen's House – all except George IV, who was born in St James's Palace.

After his accession in 1820, George IV initially wanted to modernize Buckingham House and to continue using it as a private dwelling. However, in 1826 he decided to convert it into a palace, using designs by John Nash, who had recently completed work on the Royal Pavilion in Brighton.

Above: This view dates to c.1820, before George IV and John Nash set to work to transform Buckingham House into a palace.

THE MARBLE ARCH

Nash enlarged the main house, building a new set of rooms on the garden, or west, side and replacing the existing north and south wings, thus creating a U-shaped house enclosing an east-facing courtyard on three sides. He designed the façades of Bath stone in a French Neoclassical style favoured by the King. To use the courtyard, iron railings and a grand Marble Arch, inspired by the Arch of Constantine in Rome, were constructed. The arch was intended partly as a war memorial to Britons killed at the battles of Trafalgar and Waterloo; it was also a tribute to the King and was intended to support a statue of George IV by Sir Francis Chantrey. However, George died before the work was complete and the statue was finally erected in Trafalgar Square. The arch itself was built in 1827 and formed the eastern entrance to the palace forecourt for almost a quarter of a century, until it was moved in 1851 to its present position, at the north-east corner of Hyde Park.

Below: A view of Buckingham Palace and Marble Arch from St James's Park, c.1835. The arch was moved to Hyde Park in 1851.

THE NEW STATEROOMS

Internally, Nash laid out a splendid set of staterooms in Buckingham Palace. From the Grand Hall, the marble Grand Staircase rose to the Picture Gallery in the centre of the block and beyond it to new staterooms on the garden front, with its elegant bow: the Blue Drawing Room, the White Drawing Room and, in the domed bow, the Music Room.

ST JAMES'S PALACE

A stone's throw from Buckingham Palace, St James's Palace is today ranked as the 'senior palace of the sovereign' and is still officially a royal residence. It was largely constructed in red brick by Henry VIII in 1531–6 on the site of the Hospital of St James. Several parts of the original palace survive, including the Chapel Royal and the great Gate House, now at the southern end of St James's Street. For three centuries it was one of the principal royal residences in London, birthplace of Charles II, James II, Mary II, Queen Anne and George IV. After most of Whitehall Palace burned down in 1698, all monarchs spent part of the year at St James's Palace. It was badly damaged by fire in 1809, and George IV undertook a grand refurbishment of its staterooms in the 1820s. William IV was the last monarch to live at St James's; from the reign of Victoria, the ruling monarch has resided in Buckingham Palace when he or she is in London.

Right: The gatehouse of St James's Palace.

Above: Carlton House's Grand Staircase rose majestically beneath a great chandelier.

Below: The lavish surroundings of the Throne Room at Buckingham Palace. Queen Victoria would use it as a second ballroom.

On the east front, facing into the open courtyard, the apartments included the Throne Room and Green Drawing Room. Many of the fittings in these rooms had been salvaged from Carlton House when it was demolished in 1827.

PUBLIC OUTCRY

The designs, amid a clamour for parliamentary reform, were not popular. There was considerable public disquiet over the cost and Nash's perceived extravagance: George IV initially asked for £500,000, but his prime minister agreed to only £150,000 – a sum later increased to £200,000. But when George IV died in 1830, it emerged that the still unfinished work had cost £501,530. The dome on the garden side was ridiculed as 'a wretched inverted egg-cup'.

Following a government investigation, amid concerns that some of the work was not structurally sound, Nash was dismissed, having been judged to be guilty of 'inexcusable irregularity and great negligence'. George's successor, William IV, commissioned the more modest Edward Blore to complete the palace; the well-known east front facing the Mall, which contains the balcony, was added in 1850, then redesigned and refaced in Portland Stone in 1913 by Sir Aston Webb.

THE GRANGE AT NORTHINGTON
AND THE GREEK REVIVAL

The Greek Revival arose following the circulation in the late 18th and early 19th centuries of illustrations of Greek art and architecture and the arrival, in London in 1803, of the 'Elgin Marbles' – fragments of ancient Greek sculpture brought to London by Thomas Bruce, 7th Earl of Elgin, who had been British ambassador to the Ottoman Empire. The British upper classes became convinced of the superiority of ancient Greek sculpture and buildings in comparison with those of other ancient or more modern cultures. The Revival was principally an urban phenomenon – evidenced in town halls, courts of justice, hospitals, colleges, theatres and other buildings decorated with Greek columns and loosely made to look like Greek temples. The Revival, which swept through Europe, was also particularly popular in the United States, where it became known as the 'National style'.

Above: This engraving shows The Grange in 1830, within a quarter-century of its building by William Wilkins in 1804–9.

Above: The original house looks out between columns at The Grange. Pevsner declared the Doric portico to have 'tremendous pathos'.

AN ARCADIAN VISION

A striking early example of Greek Revival style in country-house building was The Grange at Northington, near Winchester in Hampshire. In 1804–9, William Wilkins refashioned an existing 17th-century house in the image of a Greek temple, specifically in the likeness

Below: The Grange's great portico of Doric columns faces east; note also the central block of four square piers and pilasters between the bays on the south side.

of the Theseum in Athens. On the east side, overlooking a lake, Wilkins raised a portico consisting of two lines of six great Doric columns. On the north and south sides, each composed of nine bays, he added a central block containing four square piers.

The archaeologist and architect C.R. Cockerell had boundless admiration, writing of The Grange in the early 19th century: 'Nothing can be finer (or) more classical... there is nothing like it on this side of Arcadia.' Today, the house is partly ruined, but the extraordinary portico can still be seen.

Above: Doric columns surround the front door at Arlington Court in Devon. Visitors may try out one of the National Trust's large collection of horse-drawn carriages there.

JOHN DOBSON

The country house of Meldon Park in Northumberland was built in 1832 by the well-known Newcastle architect John Dobson for Isaac Cookson. Its Ionic entrance porch and clean lines make it a good example of the Greek Revival style.

Dobson was an accomplished town architect, and like Nash in London, the builder of delightful Regency-style town-houses. In Newcastle he built Grainger, Market and Grey Streets and, after completing Meldon Park, constructed the city's acclaimed railway station. At Meldon he produced a studiedly plain exterior that is decorated only by the columns of the entrance porch; all its essential drain-pipes and guttering are hidden from view.

BELSAY HALL, NORTHUMBERLAND

At Belsay Hall, in 1807–15, Sir Charles Monck built an austere square limestone house with a vast Doric portico and a Doric frieze running around the building. Sir Charles had returned in 1806 from a two-year trip to Greece, in which he was greatly impressed by ancient Greek temple architecture. With the help of John Dobson, designer of Meldon Park, Sir Charles set out to create a Greek Revival house for his recently inherited estate. Internally, he laid out the rooms around a central space lit from above, in the style of a Greek or Roman dwelling. The Belsay Hall estate also contains a 14th-century tower house (called 'the Castle') and the ruins of one wing of a 17th-century house. There are magnificent gardens, partly laid out by Sir Charles himself, including one in the quarry from which his workmen cut out the limestone to build the Hall.

Below: The imposing Doric columns on the main front at Belsay Hall. Note also the Doric frieze running around the building.

MORE REVIVAL HOUSES

Other early examples of the Greek Revival country house include Longford Hall in Shropshire, designed in 1789 by Joseph Bonomi: its portico has four columns and its Great Hall a fine Grecian frieze. In 1803, at Stratton Park in Hampshire, George Dance the Younger built a two-storey portico with vast Doric columns; the house has been demolished but the portico remains as part of a 1960s mansion.

In 1808, Joseph Gandy, the highly talented assistant of Sir John Soane, who so imaginatively illustrated Soane's architectural schemes, built a fine Greek Revival house at Storrs Hall on the shores of Lake Windermere: it has a splendid Doric colonnade on its entrance front. Arlington Court near Barnstaple in Devon was designed with a Doric-columned entranceway and Doric entablature by local architect Thomas Lee for Colonel John Chichester in 1820.

RESTORATION AT WINDSOR

UNDER GEORGE IV

In the 1820s, George IV and his architect Jeffry Wyatville carried out a major restoration of the royal buildings at Windsor, which, combined with earlier work by James Wyatt in 1800–11, created the 'picturesque' Gothic castle we see today. Within the palace, George and Wyatville swept away many of the superb interiors created by Charles II (see page 153), but they were also responsible for a magnificent series of royal apartments and the creation of the remarkable Waterloo Chamber to house portraits of the military heroes who had defeated Napoleon at the Battle of Waterloo.

Above: The Green Drawing Room is one of the splendid set of new rooms that was created by Wyatville in the castle's east front.

GEORGE III AT WINDSOR

In 1778–82, George III and Sir William Chambers rebuilt Queen Anne's Lodge, which stood to the south of the castle's upper ward. Renamed the Queen's Lodge, the building was George and Queen Charlotte's favoured residence at Windsor (it was demolished by George IV in 1823). Within the castle in the 1780s and 90s, he restored St George's Chapel (see also page 82) and made improvements to the staterooms, including the addition of historical paintings of scenes from the life of Edward III by the American artist, Benjamin West.

WYATT'S ADDITIONS

James Wyatt began work for the royal family at Windsor with the rebuilding of Queen Charlotte's House at Frogmore, adjoining Windsor Great Park. George III bought the Frogmore estate for the Queen in 1790 and Wyatt impressed both with his work there in the 1790s. In 1800–11, he was commissioned to rebuild the state apartments in the castle's upper ward in the Gothic style. He put in pointed Gothic windows to replace those inserted by Hugh May in the 17th century, constructed a cloister in Horn Court and raised a splendid entrance from the quadrangle. He also installed a Grand Staircase to replace the former 'King's Stair' and created a suite of private rooms on the ground floor of the north block. In these rooms, George III was confined in his final illness.

WINDSOR TRANSFORMED

The Prince Regent used John Nash to rebuild the Lower Lodge, situated about 3 miles (4.5km) south-east of the castle in the Great Park, as the Royal Lodge.

Left: The State Dining Room. Both this and the Green Drawing Room were restored after the damage caused by fire in 1992.

The Prince lived there while at Windsor, but following his father's death in 1820 he moved into the castle, and began a new round of rebuilding. Jeffry Wyatt, nephew of James Wyatt, won a competition in 1823, whose details had been drafted by Sir Charles Long, to take on the work. (Although now referred to as Jeffry Wyatville, the architect was known by his original name until 1824, when he changed his name to Wyatville in line with the taste for the Gothic; he was knighted in 1828.)

In the upper ward, Wyatville added a battlemented upper storey to the south-east and north sides of the quadrangle. He moved the private apartments from the north to the south and east sections. The north-side rooms were set aside for state occasions.

In the east front, he created a superb set of royal rooms, including the Dining Room and the White and Crimson Drawing Rooms, which are as grand as any of the interiors lost for posterity when Carlton House in London was demolished. Indeed, these rooms at Windsor, like the apartments in Buckingham Palace, contain several fittings and pieces of furniture salvaged from Carlton House. Along the inner and south front of the quadrangle, he created the splendid Grand Corridor, more than 500ft (150m) in length. He raised the height of the Round Tower by around 30ft (9m), and remodelled the outer walls of the upper ward's south wing, creating a distinctive symmetrical façade for the castle.

Above: Windsor Castle from the Great Park. The 19th-century work at Windsor created a skyline in the Picturesque Gothic.

LONGLEAT HOUSE

Jeffry Wyatville is also remembered for his work at Longleat House – the 16th-century 'prodigy house' in Wiltshire built by the Elizabethan courtier Sir John Thynne. In 1806–14, Wyatville reconstructed the north front, built a magnificent Grand Staircase to connect the two inner courtyards and redecorated several rooms. Among other houses on which he worked were Chatsworth House, where he built an extension to the north wing in 1820–41, and Fort Belvedere in Windsor Great Park, famously the home of Edward, Prince of Wales, briefly Edward VIII and later Duke of Windsor, where he added extensions in 1827–30.

WATERLOO CHAMBER

Wyatville created the Waterloo Chamber by roofing in the former Horn Court. Here, he placed some Grinling Gibbons' carving removed from the Charles II-era Royal Chapel, and hung specially commissioned portraits by Sir Thomas Lawrence of royal and military figures associated with Wellington's triumph at Waterloo – including Georges III and IV, the Duke of Wellington and Field Marshall von Blücher.

LONGER WALK

As part of Wyatville's rebuilding, the Long Walk created by King Charles II to link the castle to Windsor Great Park was lengthened in 1823 to run right up to a new entranceway, the George IV Gateway. This entailed knocking down King George III's Queen's Lodge. (See also page 224.)

Below: This 19th-century aquatint shows the castle's sweeping Grand Staircase shortly after its completion.

CHAPTER ELEVEN

VICTORIAN STYLE AND REVIVALS

*c.*1830–1901

On 27 August 1839, the 13th Earl of Eglington held a medieval tournament complete with jousting in the lists at Eglington Castle in Ayrshire. A great crowd of spectators in medieval costume saw Lady Eglington – styled the 'Queen of Beauty' – receive the chivalrous offerings of mounted knights. Unfortunately, after these preliminaries, Scottish rain sweeping in from the west was the winner, for the competition was washed away by a great noon downpour that obscured visibility and reduced the lists to a mud bath. But the tournament at Eglington was a remarkable reflection of an aristocratic interest in the cult of chivalry and medieval life that resulted in the rebuilding of many country homes in the style of castles.

At Cardiff Castle and Castell Coch in Wales, John Crichton Stuart, the 3rd Marquess of Bute, and his architect William Burges produced exquisite romantic recreations of the medieval castle. Likewise, at Arundel in Sussex and at Alnwick in Northumberland, the dukes of Norfolk and Northumberland and their architects 'improved' the ruins of their ancient strongholds and castles to create picturesque turreted skylines and sumptuous interiors. Certainly not least among these ambitious essays in the revival castle was the rebuilding by Queen Victoria's husband, Prince Albert, at Balmoral, in which he turned a modest country house on the River Dee in Scotland into a turreted fairy-tale fortress in the Scottish Baronial style.

Left: Arundel Castle ranks below only Windsor and Alnwick as a supreme example of the Romantic recreation of the Middle Ages by Georgian and Victorian architects.

BUCKINGHAM PALACE

THE OFFICIAL LONDON RESIDENCE OF QUEEN VICTORIA

In July 1837, three weeks after her accession, Queen Victoria moved into Buckingham Palace from her childhood home at Kensington. She made the palace the monarch's official London residence. Shortly after moving in, she put in train a number of improvements to make her quarters more private; as part of these works Nash's unpopular dome (previously derided as 'a wretched inverted egg-cup') was removed (see pages 208–9).

Above: The palace Ballroom as it looked on completion in c.1855. It has since been redecorated in white with gold details.

A NEW EAST WING

On Victoria's marriage in 1840 to Prince Albert of Saxe-Coburg-Gotha, it became clear that the lack of nursery accommodation in the palace would be a problem; in addition, the state apartments of George IV were found to be too small to hold a court ball. In 1847–50, the famous London builder, Thomas Cubitt, constructed a new wing along the east side of the palace courtyard, facing the Mall. It was designed by Edward Blore, with nurseries on the top floor and apartments for prominent visitors on the first floor. The building work was partly funded by the sale of Brighton Pavilion, and the interiors of the new wing also made use of furnishings and fittings from the Pavilion, notably in the Chinese decorations of the Luncheon Room and the East Room. To make room for the new wing, the Marble Arch was moved to its present position at the north-east corner of Hyde Park, formerly the site of the Tyburn gallows. Blore used a soft French stone that proved vulnerable to the weather and London atmosphere, and the east wing of the palace was refaced with Portland stone just before World War I by Sir Aston Webb (see page 232).

THE ROYAL MEWS

The Royal Mews in Buckingham Palace Road, which house the Queen's carriages, horses and motor vehicles, were built in 1824–5 by John Nash, with two Doric arches and two sets of stables as well as grand coach-houses.

The Mews had been established in this location in 1760 by George III: Sir William Chambers built an indoor riding school there in 1763–6. In 1855, Victoria added a school on the site for the children of Royal Mews staff, and in 1859 constructed further accommodation there. Visitors to the Mews can see the gold state coach built for George III to designs by Sir William Chambers in 1762 and used for all coronations since.

Left: The gold state coach of George III, used for coronations and state occasions.

A LAVISH BALLROOM

The required Ballroom was added, together with a State Supper Room and new galleries, on the west front of the palace. This work was designed by James Pennethorne, a pupil of the disgraced John Nash, and built in 1852–5 by Cubitt. The impressive Ballroom measured 123 x 60ft (37 x 18m). The interior was lavishly decorated, under the guidance of Prince Albert, as advised by his artistic designer, Professor Ludwig Grüner, with murals by Niccola Consoni and sculptures by William Theed.

BALMORAL
AND THE SCOTTISH BARONIAL STYLE

Queen Victoria and Prince Albert bought the estate and modest manor house of Balmoral on the River Dee in the Grampian region of Scotland in 1852. Albert and architect William Smith at once demolished the existing house and in 1853–5 built a turreted castle in the Scottish Baronial style.

The Queen and her husband had fallen in love with Scotland during holidays at Taymouth and Blair Atholl in the early 1840s. They leased Balmoral and stayed there for the first time in the autumn of 1848. Their initial visit was a great success, although the original house – called 'a pretty little castle in the old Scotch style' by Victoria – was too small for their needs: members of the royal household had to stay in nearby cottages and wait each morning for their breakfast to be delivered by wheelbarrow from the main house.

Below: Balmoral has been a favoured royal retreat since Prince Albert designed it and Victoria described it as 'this dear paradise'.

A COUNTRY HOUSE

Albert set out to design a holiday retreat rather than a grand royal residence, in his words a building 'not like a palace but like a country gentleman's house'. In contrast to Osborne House, Balmoral has no Audience Chamber or Council Room in which the Queen may receive ministers and other officials; there are only general-purpose rooms for significant visitors on the south side of the main block's ground floor. Otherwise, the main block contains the Dining Room, Drawing Room, Billiard Room and Library, with private rooms for the Queen and Prince on the floor above. Throughout, as at Osborne House, the most modern conveniences were provided, with hot-air heating, four bathrooms for the royal family and 14 water-closets – at the time, a record for a British country house. There was also a servants' wing, stables and offices.

Victoria and Albert moved into the main house in September 1855, and returned each autumn until Albert's death in 1861. After that dark event, Victoria often visited twice a year: in June and from August to November. The place had special significance because of its association with her husband: it was, she wrote, 'Albert's own creation, own work, own building, own laying out', and she added 'my dearest Albert's ... great taste and the impress of his dear hand have been stamped everywhere'.

BELFAST CASTLE

Above: The 19th-century Scots Baronial house stands on the site of a Norman fortification and a 17th-century castle.

Prince Albert's work at Balmoral set a fashion for the Scottish Baronial architectural style. In the light of this and as a way of underlining Ulster's connection to Scotland, the architect W.H. Lynn used the same romantic blend of gables and turrets for Belfast Castle, built in a beautiful position overlooking the city, for the 3rd Marquess of Donegall and his wealthy son-in-law, Lord Ashley, in 1867–70.

OSBORNE HOUSE
VICTORIA'S FAVOURITE HOUSE

Queen Victoria's favourite royal residence was the palatial seaside villa of Osborne House on the Isle of Wight. At Osborne – designed and built by her beloved husband, Prince Albert, in collaboration with Thomas Cubitt – she spent many of her happiest hours of family life and here, at the end of a long and highly productive reign, she died on 22 January 1901 surrounded by her children and grandchildren.

Victoria wanted a seaside retreat but intensely disliked the Royal Pavilion in Brighton, with its associations with the extravagant and colourful private life of George IV and which had been engulfed by the growth of the resort and therefore lacked privacy. She decided to sell the Pavilion and to buy a house and estate on the Isle of Wight, which she knew from happy childhood visits to Norris Castle in 1831 and 1833.

With the help of her then prime minister, Sir Robert Peel, Victoria and Albert found Osborne House, overlooking the Solent on the north side of the Isle of Wight, and, after a successful stay in 1843, the royal couple purchased the 1,000 acre (405 ha)-estate – which came with its own private beach as well as a substantial Georgian house – from Lady Isabella Blanchford in 1845. Victoria wrote of her pleasure at having 'a place of one's own, quiet and retired'.

Above: Palazzo style. The view from the Lower Terrace, with the Andromeda Fountain, back up to the Clock Tower.

AN ITALIANATE VILLA

The Queen and Prince Albert demolished the existing house, and, with Cubitt, who had made his reputation developing Highbury and Belgravia in London, Albert built a splendid Italianate villa in 1845–51. Osborne's design, with two *campanile* towers, was a tribute to the Italian Renaissance *palazzo* (palace) and influenced by a pair of villas built by Sir Charles Barry: Mount Felix at Walton-on-Thames, Surrey (1836), and Trentham Hall in north Staffordshire (1842). Its façades mixed Roman, Florentine and Palladian elements to charming effect. When he visited Osborne, the twice prime minister, Benjamin Disraeli, was enraptured, describing it as 'a Sicilian Palazzo with garden terraces, statues and vases shining in the sun, than which nothing can be conceived more captivating'.

The house was laid out, with the privacy of the royal family in mind, in two main parts: a rectangular Family Pavilion for the Queen, Albert and children

BRODSWORTH HALL

The Italianate *palazzo* style used by Prince Albert at Osborne House was widely influential. A particularly fine example is Brodsworth Hall in South Yorkshire, designed for Charles Thellusson by an unknown Italian architect, Chevalier Casentini, in 1861–3. Casentini replaced the original 18th-century hall with an elegant but very substantial villa containing more than 30 rooms.

The house has been maintained carefully since it was taken over from its last owner, a Thellusson descendant, by English Heritage in 1990 and is one of the least altered of all Victorian country houses. The estate has fine gardens with an Italian-style fountain and statue walks, summerhouse, woodland, ornamental flowerbeds and a quarry area – all restored since 1990 to their 1860s' condition and plan.

Above: Casentini did not visit Yorkshire. His design for Brodsworth was implemented by English architect, Philip Wilkinson.

Above: At Osborne, where she had often retreated following the loss of Albert, Victoria lay in state after her own death.

linked by the grand Marble Corridor to a substantial and asymetrical east wing, intended for visitors and members of the royal household.

The Family Pavilion was built in 1845 and splendidly fitted out in 1846, and the royal family moved in during September of that year. On their first night of residence, Prince Albert led prayers seeking God's blessing on the house and recited sections of a Lutheran hymn.

The German art professor, Ludwig Grüner, acting as Prince Albert's artistic designer from 1845, was in charge of decorating the interior of the Family Pavilion. Its most splendid section was without doubt the Marble Corridor, which featured floor tiles designed by Prince Albert and polychrome stencilling on the walls in blue, umber, black and red. Along the walls were displayed Albert's collection of contemporary sculptures by artists including R.J. Wyatt and John Gibson.

Prince Albert believed that English country houses were generally too gloomy, so he designed the three main rooms on the ground floor of the Family Pavilion with large plate-glass windows. These rooms are the Dining Room, the Drawing Room and the Billiard Room, the last two divided only by Corinthian columns in yellow marble, together essentially forming one sizeable L-shaped room. The Drawing Room contains a bow window giving fine views over the terraced gardens to the Solent.

On the first floor was a private suite designed for the Queen and Prince Albert, consisting of two bathrooms, two dressing rooms, a bedroom and a sitting room. Above that, on the second floor, were the nursery rooms. Albert and Cubitt also co-operated in the design of formal terraced gardens at Osborne in 1847. The grounds included a Swiss Cottage – a miniature dwelling designed as a playhouse for the royal children.

INDIAN HALL

Towards the end of Queen Victoria's reign, after she had become Empress of India in 1877 and was taking a significant interest in Indian affairs, a new wing was added at Osborne House in 1890–1. Its ground floor consisted of a large Reception Hall decorated in Indian style by imported craftsmen and designed by Bhai Ram Singh, an expert on Indian architecture, with advice from Rudyard Kipling's father, John Lockwood Kipling, who was director of Lahore Central Museum. Called the Durbar Hall, the new building featured elaborate Moghul-style plasterwork. Above the Reception Hall, on the second floor of the wing, were apartments for Victoria's youngest daughter, Princess Beatrice, and her family.

A MODERN HOUSE

Throughout Osborne House, Cubitt used the most up-to-date materials, providing the very latest plumbing and central-heating systems. Also in 1890, electric lights were fitted throughout Osborne House.

Victoria's son and successor Edward VII disliked Osborne House and donated it to the nation. Her apartments have been open to the public since 1954.

Right: Italian towers and terraces look down on formal gardens at Osborne House and have beautiful views of the Solent.

ALNWICK, HICHCLERE AND ARUNDEL

GREAT VICTORIAN CASTLE REVIVALS

In the 1850s, the architect Anthony Salvin and Algernon Percy, 4th Duke of Northumberland, substantially rebuilt the great Percy stronghold of Alnwick Castle in Northumberland, adding both the imposing Prudhoe Tower and the North Terrace. Salvin's very impressive rebuilding, which swept away much of the Georgian Gothic remodelling carried out at Alnwick in the 18th century by Robert Adam, was one of the greatest of a swathe of Victorian castle revivals undertaken in the mid-19th century.

ALNWICK'S HISTORY

The first castle on the site was built in 1096 by Yves de Vescy, Baron of Alnwick. Strongly fortified in the next century, it twice repelled sieges by William I 'the Lion' of Scots; on the second occasion, in 1174, 'the Lion' was

Below: In the 1860s, Anthony Salvin converted the courtyard at Muncaster Castle into the barrel-vaulted Drawing Room.

taken prisoner in fog outside the castle and thrown into jail. The first Percy ancestor at Alnwick, Henry, 1st Lord Percy, bought the castle in 1309 and began its restoration.

Of this work, one semicircular tower survives today (of the seven that initially comprised the keep), as does much of the curtain wall, several other towers and the gateway that stands between the two baileys. Later Percys were to suffer for their Roman Catholic faith: Thomas Percy, 7th Earl of Northumberland, lost his head for his part in the 'Rising of the North' against Queen Elizabeth I.

In the 17th century, the castle fell into decay, but it was rebuilt and modernized by Sir Hugh Smithson and Percy heiress, Lady Betty Seymour, later the 1st Duke and Duchess of Northumberland, in the mid-18th century. At the same time they commissioned Robert Adam to redecorate Syon House in Middlesex. At Alnwick, they employed Adam alongside James Paine to work in the

Above: For all the rebuilding and restoration work, Alnwick Castle retains its original plan – of a motte and two baileys.

Georgian Gothic Revival style, remnants of which include the life-size stone figures on the battlements.

THE 4TH DUKE'S ADDITIONS

In 1847, and at the age of 55, Algernon Percy succeeded his brother Hugh as 4th Duke of Northumberland towards the end of a very busy and fruitful life in which he had served in the navy during the Napoleonic Wars and had, subsequently, been one of the first Englishmen to excavate the tombs of ancient Egypt. He displayed several of his archaeological finds in the Castle Museum at Alnwick, established in the Postern Tower and opened to the public as early as 1826.

In their rebuilding of Alnwick, Salvin and the 4th Duke constructed a new chapel, the Guest Hall, the Falconer's Tower and a riding school with stables, in addition to the great Prudhoe Tower. The Duke combined the castle's rugged Gothic Revival exterior with the most luxurious Italian Renaissance-style interiors, including widely admired coffered ceilings and superb scarlet damask and gold hangings in the Drawing Room. Within the Prudhoe Tower, he installed a fine Library and, in the place of the medieval Great Hall, created a Dining Hall with a wonderful carved, unpainted pine and cedar ceiling.

ANTHONY SALVIN

Salvin, architect of the extraordinary 'Jacobethan-Baroque' Harlaxton Manor in Lincolnshire in 1837–45, ably extended and rebuilt a large number of castles for Victorian patrons. These included Muncaster Castle, overlooking the River Esk near Ravenglass in Cumbria, where he worked for Gamel Augustus Pennington, 4th Lord Muncaster, from 1862 onward. Salvin converted the courtyard into the fine Drawing Room with barrel ceiling, built a north-west tower to match the 14th-century pele tower at the south-west of the site and added battlements and transomed and mullioned windows.

Another of Salvin's notable commissions was Peckforton Castle in Tarporley, west Cheshire. Peckforton was a new country house built in the style of a medieval castle for MP John Tollemache (subsequently Lord Tollemache) in 1844–51. Its centrepiece was the Great Hall, with stone vaulted ceiling, minstrels' gallery and intricately carved screen; the main reception rooms gave on to a splendid pentagonal stairwell.

HIGHCLERE CASTLE

Home to the Carnavon family since the late 1600s, Highclere was originally a square, classical mansion. It was remodelled by Sir Charles Barry in 1842–49 who was also working on the construction of the Houses of Parliament during the same period. Indeed, there is a great deal of similarity in the silhouettes of both buildings.

Barry was a great exponent of the Renaissance revival and described the style of Highclere as 'Anglo-Italian'. Working mainly in the Jacobethan style, Barry added some motifs to the building based on the Italianate style.

Below: Social unrest persuaded John Tollemache that Peckforton Castle should be fit to withstand a siege.

Above: Highclere Castle was the main setting for the British television period drama Downton Abbey.

The park surrounding Highclere was laid out in 1774–1777, according to a design by Capability Brown, commissioned by the 1st Earl of Carnavon.

ARUNDEL CASTLE

Arundel Castle in West Sussex stands on a Norman motte (of 1068), and contains a medieval gatehouse and barbican, but it is primarily a Victorian recreation of the Middle Ages. This magnificent achievement is in small part the work of Charles Howard, the 11th Duke of Norfolk, and architect Francis Hiorne in 1791-1815, and in large part the creation of Henry Fitzalan-Howard, the 15th Duke, and architect CA Buckler in 1870-1900. The superb Gothic library, with its vaulted roof of mahogany, was built by Jonathan Ritson in 1802. Buckler's chapel is celebrated as one of the best Victorian Gothic interiors. The 15th Duke also equipped the castle with 'mod cons' – Arundel was one of the pioneers of fitting electricity and central heating in English country houses.

Above: Purists may dismiss many Victorian 'improvements' of England's medieval legacy, but it is impossible not to admire the Gothic chapel at Arundel.

CARDIFF CASTLE AND CASTELL COCH

WILLIAM BURGES AND CONJECTURAL RESTORATION

John Crichton Stuart, 3rd Marquess of Bute, was said to be the richest man in the world in the 1860s. He had inherited a vast fortune, derived partly from the export of Welsh coal from Cardiff, as an infant in 1848. In 1866, aged only 19, he commissioned architect William Burges to rebuild Cardiff Castle in an opulent Victorian Gothic style.

ROMAN AND NORMAN REMAINS

The castle stands in the centre of Cardiff, on the site of a Roman fort and a Norman stronghold. Remains from both these periods are incorporated into the building: approaching the main entrance, for example, Roman stonework is visible at the base of Norman walls, while within the enclosure the Norman shell keep still stands proudly on its motte. For centuries, the castle was an important fortress, passing from one powerful lord to another: the de Clare family in the 12–13th centuries; Hugh le Despenser in the reign of Edward II; Richard Neville, Earl of Warwick ('the Kingmaker'), and Richard, Duke of Gloucester (later Richard III), in the 15th century; and the Herbert lords in the 16th century. It was finally passed by marriage into the hands of the Bute family in 1766.

Below: The Gothic towers and crenellations of Bute and Burges combine with Roman and Norman stonework at Cardiff Castle.

Above: Kaleidoscope of colours – a detail of the fantastically elaborate decoration in the Arabian Room, Cardiff Castle.

THEMED ROOMS

Bute and Burges raised Gothic towers and created elaborate interiors with stained glass, murals, wood and stone carving and marble fireplaces. A number of the rooms were elaborately themed: the Winter Smoking Room, for example, has the theme of passing time, being decorated with images of the seasons and days of the week.

THREE GREAT TOWERS

The work on Cardiff Castle was complemented by Bute and Burges' equally lavish restoration of the Marquess's country retreat near Cardiff – the 13th-century castle of Castell Coch. Beginning in 1875, Burges built almost from scratch, for the original fortress had been reduced to ruins in the 15th century. He raised three great towers with conical roofs: the Keep Tower, next to the gatehouse, was linked to the Kitchen Tower by the Banqueting Hall; the curtain wall then followed an irregular circle around to the Well Tower.

The castle was compact, its three towers grouped around a courtyard only 55ft (17m) across. It stood within a dry moat and, with great attention to medieval detail, was fitted with a portcullis and a drawbridge, as well as murder-holes for pouring boiling water or oil on to intruders.

Below: Eastern promise. Beautiful blue-black floor tiles combine with delicate carving in this lavish interior at Cardiff Castle.

Left: The reddish sandstone used at Castell Coch, near Cardiff, gives the building its popular name of the 'Red Castle'.

LAVISH DECORATION

As at Cardiff Castle, the interiors were lavishly finished; many were, in fact, not decorated under the architect's supervision, for he died in 1881, but were overseen by William Frame working from Burges' detailed plans for the decor. The Keep Tower contains a two-storey Drawing Room, decorated with scenes from Aesop's Fables: delicate painted panels depicting plants, mouldings of animals and birds and, above the splendid tiled fireplace, exquisitely carved figures of the Three Fates from ancient Greek mythology. A raised balcony runs around the second-storey level and a beautiful azure and gold vaulted ceiling painted with stars and birds rises above.

On the third and fourth floors of the tower, beneath a double dome ceiling, is the Lady's Bedroom, decorated with gilt and mirrors and containing a remarkable 'Moorish' bed fitted with eight crystal balls and derived from the interiors of the Alhambra in Granada, Spain. Other rooms include the more austere Banqueting Hall, the Lord's Bedroom, the Servants' Hall and kitchen. All the work at Castell Coch was meticulously researched by Burges in the British Museum for historical accuracy, and he wrote extensive justifications of this 'conjectural restoration'.

Below: The two-storey Drawing Room at Castell Coch. Note the Three Fates above the fireplace, the painted panels and the balcony beneath the domed azure ceiling.

CARLTON TOWERS

Carlton Towers at Goole in North Yorkshire was twice 'Gothicized' in the Victorian era, creating one of the most celebrated of Victorian Gothic country houses. The original Jacobean house of 1614 was initially remodelled in 1840 by Miles, the 8th Lord Beaumont, before it was reworked more substantially, in 1873–6, by E.W. Pugin (son of Augustus Welby Pugin) for Henry, 9th Lord Beaumont. Then, after Lord Beaumont quarrelled with his architect, he commissioned John Francis Bentley, the Roman Catholic architect of Westminster Cathedral, to decorate the interior. The result was a superb suite of staterooms that incorporated the Armoury, Venetian Drawing Room, Card Room and Picture Gallery.

WINDSOR CASTLE AND FROGMORE

VICTORIA AND ALBERT

Queen Victoria and Prince Albert are particularly associated with Osborne House and Balmoral, but in fact they spent the majority of each year at Windsor, where Albert was a Ranger of the Great Park and carried out a number of improvements on the estate. He worked in the Home Park, encompassing the Frogmore estate and Shaw Farm to the north of the castle, as well as in the Great Park. He rebuilt the Home Farm in 1852 in a Tudor Revival style and in 1858 reconstructed George III's dairy building with an admired interior featuring Minton tiles and sculpture by John Thomas. See also pages 82, 153 and 212.

PRIVATE BURIAL

Victoria broke with royal tradition in being buried in a mausoleum on private ground rather than in a cathedral or major church. The idea of a mausoleum had come from her Uncle Leopold, who built one at Claremont for his wife, Princess Charlotte – which in turn inspired Prince Albert to raise one at Coburgh for his father and Victoria to construct one for her mother, the Duchess of Kent, also at Frogmore. After Victoria's death, the former Edward VIII was buried at Frogmore following his death in 1972 and his wife, Wallis, the woman for whom he gave up the throne, was buried alongside him in 1986.

Above: Windsor's Albert Memorial. On her death in 1901, Victoria joined her late husband in the Frogmore Mausoleum.

ALBERT MEMORIALS

However, the most significant building work at Windsor Castle during Victoria's reign was carried out in memory of Albert, who died of typhoid fever there on 14 December 1861. Victoria insisted that Albert's rooms were kept exactly as they had been on the day of his death, and rebuilt the chapel that stood above the Tomb House (behind St George's Chapel) as the magnificent Albert Memorial Chapel. This work was carried out in 1863–73, principally by George Gilbert Scott, who installed fine stained-glass windows and marble reliefs by Jules Destréez on the walls.

At Frogmore, Victoria built a mausoleum for her husband and herself. Designed by Ludwig Grüner and built by A.J. Humbert in 1862–71, the mausoleum has a granite and Portland stone exterior with gunmetal doors; the interior features frescoes by Italian and German painters in the style of Italian Renaissance master Raphael, whom Albert had considered the finest of all artists. The sarcophagus is of marble, granite and bronze and bears effigies of Albert and Victoria, both carved in the 1860s, although Victoria's was, of course, not put in place until her death in 1901.

Below: An aerial view of Windsor Castle shows the upper ward to the right and the lower ward to the left of the Round Tower.

CHATSWORTH
AND JOSEPH PAXTON

William, 6th Duke of Devonshire, began a 19-year programme of alterations at Chatsworth House, Derbyshire, in 1818 (see also pages 154-5). Sir Jeffry Wyatville began by remaking the Long Gallery as a Library, then added a new north wing to the house (in 1820–7), containing the Theatre, Sculpture Gallery, Dining Room and offices. He redecorated the staterooms in 1832–42 and proceeded to work on the Duke's private apartments in the west front. In October 1832, the first stage of Wyatville's redecoration was inspected by the future Queen Victoria, who, aged 13, was entertained to dinner in the new, lavish gold and white Dining Room with her mother, the Duchess of Kent.

Above: The Emperor Fountain, installed by Paxton in 1844, can send its waters twice as high as the house behind.

GARDENS TRANSFORMED

The Duke appointed the 23-year-old Joseph Paxton – future designer of the Crystal Palace – as Head Gardener at Chatsworth House in 1826. He had met Paxton in Chiswick, where the Horticultural Society gardens the young man managed abutted the grounds of Chiswick House, which the Duke had inherited, along with the other Devonshire estates, in 1811. Paxton transformed the gardens at Chatsworth, creating a vast rock garden, planting rare species from around the world and experimenting with glasshouses and heating apparatus to help them flourish in Derbyshire. His extraordinary Great Conservatory, built in 1840 (and demolished in 1920), was the forerunner of the Crystal Palace. Paxton also designed and installed the Emperor Fountain, capable of launching a water jet to a height of 298ft (90m), and so called because its installation was intended to mark a visit to Chatsworth by Tsar Nicolas I of Russia, though in the event the visit did not take place.

The 6th Duke spent lavishly at Chatsworth and by his death in 1858 owed a massive £1,000,000. Yet debt did not detract from the great pleasure he received from the house and gardens: 'What happiness I have in Chatsworth, adorable Chatsworth, happiness beyond words.' He entertained continuously on a grand scale: notable visitors included Queen Victoria and Prince Albert.

Below: Chatsworth's Long Gallery, remade by Wyatville as a Long Library, offers exercise for both the body and the mind.

Below: In addition to building glasshouses, Paxton dug a coal tunnel in the gardens, which has recently been excavated.

KNEBWORTH HOUSE
AND HUGHENDEN MANOR

Above: Edward Bulwer Lytton's study at Knebworth House. He was a highly popular and influential writer in his day.

Left: Disraeli followed the fashion for rebuilding an old house in Gothic style.

Edward Bulwer Lytton, author of best-selling historical novels and former Member of Parliament, inherited Knebworth House on the death of his mother, Elizabeth, in 1843. The original house was a quadrangular brick manor built by a distant ancestor, Sir Robert Lytton, in 1492; this had been reduced to a single wing rebuilt in the Regency Gothic style and covered in stucco by Mrs Bulwer Lytton in 1811–16. Employing the architect H.E. Kendall Junior and the decorator John G. Crace, Edward added pinnacles, towers, gargoyles and heraldic decorations. In the State Presence Room (now known as the State Drawing Room), Crace designed a Victorian Gothic chimney-piece and over-mantel, installed Tudor rose panelling and fine stained glass with a portrait of Henry VII, and fitted 44 coats of arms into the ceiling. This room survives and is, as Crace designed it to be, 'very Gothic'. The Tudor connection arose because some ancestral research revealed that one of Bulwer Lytton's ancestors on his mother's side was an aunt of Henry VII.

HUGHENDEN MANOR

The country house of Hughenden Manor, in Buckinghamshire, was the home from 1848 to his death in 1881 of Benjamin Disraeli, a favourite of Queen Victoria and twice Conservative prime minister (1868 and 1874–80). Queen Victoria visited Hughenden Manor in 1877 – the year after Disraeli had secured her the title she longed for, that of 'Empress of India' – and again in 1881, following his death, to lay a wreath on the vault containing his body in the local church. She later erected a memorial to Disraeli in the church.

Hughenden's main interest lies in its association with 'Dizzy'. The house, bought by the rising politician in 1848 for £35,000, was originally a modest farmhouse but was rebuilt in the Gothic style by John Norris in the 1840s. In 1862, the architect Edward Buckton Lamb made a number of alterations, in particular adding pinnacles to relieve the stark outline of the main façade. The gardens were laid out by Disraeli's beloved wife, Mary Anne, now carefully restored to their Victorian prime by the National Trust.

Within, the house is kept as a museum of Disraeli's life and times. It contains a wealth of mementoes of his career as statesman, including a fan signed by all the representatives at the Berlin Congress of 1878, and in the hall – which he called his 'Gallery of Friendship' – hang portraits of several leading political figures of the 19th century. His study remains substantially as he left it.

Below: The main façade of Knebworth House, showing the towers and crenellation added by Edward Bulwer Lytton.

SANDRINGHAM
AND YORK COTTAGE

Albert Edward, Prince of Wales and the future Edward VII, bought the house and estate at Sandringham, in Norfolk, in 1862 for £220,000. The next spring he settled there with his new wife, Princess Alexandra of Denmark.

The idea of a country home for Albert Edward had begun with his father, Prince Albert, who thought that time spent in outdoor pursuits, such as shooting, would be a healthy change for the Prince of Wales, and that country life would help him keep away from the temptations of city delights, such as courtesans and gambling. However, following Prince Albert's death in December 1861, it was left to his son to complete the search for a house. He chose Sandringham on 3 February 1862.

Above: Sandringham sits in 60 acres of gardens. After a bomb from a German zeppelin made a crater in 1915, King George VI had it turned into a duck pond.

HUMBERT'S NEW HOUSE

After making do with minor amendments for a few years, the Prince of Wales decided in 1870 to knock down the existing house and start from scratch. He used one of his late father's favoured architects, A.J. Humbert, who, employing red brick with stone dressings, built a large and entirely uninspiring house in a Jacobean Revival style with gables, mullion windows and turrets.

Below: Jacobean style at Sandringham. Houses such as Blickling Hall were the model for A.J. Humbert's design here.

YORK COTTAGE

A second architect, R.W. Edis, made additions, including a bowling alley and the Ballroom in 1883 and in the next decade added a new top storey to the house following a fire that broke out during the Prince of Wales's 50th birthday party in 1891. Edis also built a villa, later called York Cottage, in the grounds.

Edward VII's second son, Prince George, Duke of York and the future King George V, moved into York Cottage in 1893 following his marriage to Princess Mary of Teck. It was George's favourite house, reputedly because its modest rooms reminded him of cabins aboard ship and recalled the enjoyable years he had spent in the Royal Navy. Indeed, after his accession he always stayed in York Cottage when visiting, and left the big house to his widowed mother until she died in 1925. George V died at Sandringham in 1936.

Born at York Cottage, George VI felt particularly at home on the estate. He wrote to his mother, Queen Mary, 'I have always been so happy here, and I love the place'. He too died at Sandringham House, on 6 February 1952. Elizabeth II made many visits to Sandringham during her childhood and continues to enjoy her Norfolk estate as a welcome country retreat.

CHRISTMAS AT SANDRINGHAM

By the 1930s, Sandringham had become established as the royals' Christmas and New Year retreat. George V made his first Christmas broadcast live by radio on Christmas Day 1932, while, 25 years later, Elizabeth II delivered the first televised Christmas message from the Library.

Below: In November 1902, a royal shooting party gathered at Sandringham during the visit of Germany's Kaiser Wilhelm II.

DROGO NOMEN ET VIRTUS ARMA DEDIT

CHAPTER TWELVE

THE COUNTRY HOUSE REVIVAL

1901–TODAY

On his death in 1940, Philip Henry Kerr, 11th Marquess of Lothian, bequeathed his handsome Jacobean mansion of Blickling Hall, Norfolk, to the National Trust. It was the first house to be passed to the Trust under the Country House Scheme of 1937, which Lothian had helped establish, and which enabled owners to leave their property to the Trust in lieu of death duties.

In the 20th century, although country houses continued to be built and lavishly remodelled, and although King Edward VII and his descendants continued to rework Buckingham Palace and other royal residences, many landed families struggled to maintain their houses and estates. Taxes mounted, depression in agriculture ran almost continuously from 1875 to the outbreak of World War II and rental income from land declined. As a result, art collections were broken up and rare library collections sold off to pay for repairs and meet demands for taxes and death duties. Eventually, in the interwar years, some people began to focus on ways to preserve the more historic houses and their collections. By the end of the 20th century, the National Trust carefully maintained and preserved around 350 stately homes, buildings and gardens.

Among new country houses built in these years, the fashion was predominantly neo-Georgian. Buildings such as Castle Drogo and Eaton Hall proved the exception, while neo-Palladian designs, such as Arundel Park, were generally considered more appropriate for a house expected to take its place at the heart of a country estate.

Left: Julius Charles Drewe, immensely wealthy founder of a chain of grocery shops, sought immortality in stone with Castle Drogo, Devon, built by Edwin Lutyens in 1912–30.

ELVEDEN HALL, POLESDEN LACEY
AND THE ROTHSCHILD MANSIONS

In the first years of the 20th century, the great Irish philanthropist and businessman, the 1st Earl of Iveagh, immensely wealthy head of the Guinness brewing dynasty of Dublin, lavishly rebuilt his recently acquired country house, Elveden Hall in Suffolk. It contained, in the Indian Hall (1900–3), perhaps the grandest of several great marble halls created in the Edwardian era. It was sufficiently magnificent for Edward VII to agree to spend every other New Year week there – in alternation with Chatsworth.

Lord Iveagh bought Elveden Hall in 1894 following the death of its previous owner, the former Indian maharajah, Prince Duleep Singh. Removed by the British from his throne following the annexation of the Punjab in 1849, the Prince had been granted a substantial government pension and settled in Suffolk, where he lived in great style and, after buying the original Elveden Hall in 1863, redeveloped it in Indian style. Lord Iveagh built a new wing in the same shape and style as the Prince's house and connected the two with a great copper-domed central block.

ROTHSCHILD MANSIONS

In the late 19th and early 20th centuries, leading members of the Rothschild banking dynasty entertained lavishly in magnificent English country houses. Among these was Exbury in Hampshire, where Lionel de Rothschild built a Neoclassical house in the 1920s and created a superb 200 acre (80 ha)- woodland garden. Other Rothschild houses are Waddesdon Manor, Buckinghamshire, built in the style of a French chateau for Baron Ferdinand de Rothschild by the French architect, Gabriel Hippolyte Destailleur, in 1874–89, and Mentmore Towers, also in Buckinghamshire, built in a neo-Elizabethan style for Baron Meyer Amschel de Rothschild by Sir Joseph Paxton (former Chatsworth head gardener and designer of the Crystal Palace). Another was Ascott House, 3 miles (4.5km) from Mentmore Towers, built by Leopold de Rothschild in the 1870s.

Right: Baron Ferdinand de Rothschild filled Waddesdon Manor with artworks.

THE INDIAN HALL

Within the domed block was the Indian Hall, built on the basis of Indian durbar halls to designs by William Young with the advice of Sir Caspar Purdon Clarke, who was in charge of the Indian collection at the Victoria and Albert Museum in South Kensington, London. Lord Iveagh spent £70,000 on the marble for this vast, dazzlingly white and intricately carved hall, which fills the full height of the domed section of the house. A special branch railway line was created from the nearest station, at Barnham, to bring the marble, stone, sand and other materials to the site.

Left: Imperial grandeur – the superb Marble Hall at Elveden. In creating it, Lord Iveagh doubled the size of the existing hall.

Below: At Elveden Hall, Lord Iveagh hosted the grandest guests. King George V arrives for a shooting party in 1910.

Above: Entrance front at Polesden Lacey. In summer, vegetables and fruit grown on the 1,000 acre (400 ha) estate were sent to Mrs Greville's London home each day.

Grandeur, however, was clearly more important than comfort: the hall had only two fireplaces and, despite underfloor central heating, was described by Elizabeth, Countess of Fingall, as 'England's coldest room'.

ROYAL SHOOTING PARTIES

Elvedon was especially renowned for its shooting; indeed, Lord Iveagh was first attracted to the estate because Prince Duleep Singh had developed it for game. Before Lord Iveagh's time, Edward VII, while still Prince of Wales, enjoyed shooting at Elveden in the company of Prince Duleep Singh; Lord Iveagh then hosted not only Edward VII but also George V and the future George VI for shooting parties on the estate.

POLESDEN LACEY

Another ostentatious Edwardian country house supported by brewing money was Polesden Lacey in Surrey: its owner, Margaret Greville, was the daughter of the Edinburgh brewer, Sir William McEwan. She entered English high society when, in 1901, she married Captain Ronald Greville, who through his friends the Keppels had access to Edward VII. Margaret Greville became one of the leading hostesses of the day, welcoming politicians, ambassadors, foreign heads of state and the King himself to her lavish weekend parties.

The house at Polesden Lacey had once belonged to dramatist Richard Brinsley Sheridan in the 18th century, but became so dilapidated that it was entirely rebuilt by the great London builder Thomas Cubitt for Joseph Bonsor *c.*1835. The house was restructured and redecorated in 1902–5 by Ambrose Poynter for Sir Clinton Dawkins before it was bought by Sir William McEwan in 1906.

Employing the celebrated architects Charles Mewès and Arthur Davis (designers of the Ritz Hotel in London), Mrs Greville transformed the interior. Some of her rooms would have seemed overdone and even distasteful to a Victorian guest, but they were appreciated by the racy, sophisticated, 'modern' members of Edward VII's set. For example, she installed the reredos of a demolished Sir Christopher Wren church – St Matthew's, Friday Street, London – above the fireplace in her darkly panelled Hall; in her Drawing Room she fitted gilded panelling from an Italian palace and lines of tall mirrors. A second Drawing Room was provided for playing bridge.

A gentlemen's wing at Polesden Lacy included a Smoking Room, Billiard Room and Gun Room. There was also a Library and a fine Dining Room. The finest food was a necessary attraction when the gourmand Edward VII was among the guests, and Mrs Greville was famed for the quality of her 'table'and her French chef.

Below: The Drawing Room at Polesden Lacey had five pairs of French windows – when they were unshuttered, the room was a blaze of light on chandelier and gilding.

BUCKINGHAM PALACE

AND CLARENCE HOUSE: ROYAL REFURBISHMENT

Standing proudly at the end of The Mall in central London, Buckingham Palace is the Queen's official London residence and probably the most recognizable and celebrated royal building in Britain (see also page 216). Its balcony facing The Mall has been the setting for many iconic royal moments, such as the celebration of victory in 1945 by George VI and the royal family, including a teenage Princess Elizabeth (the future Queen Elizabeth II). However, before the start of the 20th century the palace was little used by the country's royals.

It was Queen Victoria who established Buckingham Palace, rather than St James's Palace nearby, as the monarch's official London residence. But she did not spend much time there, living with Prince Albert mainly at Windsor Castle when they were not in the country, and, after Albert's death, spending prolonged periods at Balmoral and Osborne House while dust sheets covered the fine furniture and lavishly decorated rooms at Buckingham Palace.

Above: The base of the Victoria Memorial, which is at the east front of Buckingham Palace, contains 23,000 tons of marble.

GLITTER AND GLAMOUR

Edward VII, however, had different ideas. He moved into the palace on his accession in 1901 from his previous London base, Marlborough House. He redecorated and refurnished the palace in the year of his coronation, 1902, and restored glitter and glamour to court life. Unfortunately, his redecoration of the palace swept away many of the splendid Regency and early Victorian interiors, which were replaced by a rather uninspiring white and gold decorative scheme designed by C.H. Bessant.

IN MEMORY OF VICTORIA

The forecourt in front of the palace's east front was laid out at the beginning of George V's reign, in 1911. At the same time, the Victoria Memorial statue by Thomas Brock was set up before the palace on a great base of white marble, designed by Sir Aston Webb. The statue of Victoria faces towards The Mall, while

Left: While Edward VII certainly breathed new life into Buckingham Palace, historians regret that his redecoration (here of the King's private Sitting Room) was uninspiring.

on the other three sides are figures of the Angels of Justice and Truth and a personification of Charity. The golden figure on the pinnacle represents Victory.

The Admiralty Arch at the other end of The Mall, separating it from Trafalgar Square, was designed by Sir Aston Webb as part of the Victoria Memorial scheme and erected in 1910, a year earlier than the statue itself.

NEW EAST FRONT

In 1913, Sir Aston undertook the refacing of the east front of Buckingham Palace. When building the east front in 1847–50, Edward Blore had used a soft Caen stone, which had not weathered well in soot-laden London and so needed replacing; Sir Aston used a fine, grey Portland stone. His dignified east façade faces on to a gravelled forecourt enclosed by splendid ironwork gates and railings, providing a suitably grand public face for the palace. Webb created new gateposts but reused a number of older stone piers between the lengths of railing: among these are some, with floral swags and regal lions' heads, made in 1800 by Edward Wyatt for George III. The forecourt is the setting for the Changing of the Guard ceremony.

'GEORGIAN' REFURBISHMENT

In George V's reign, Queen Mary carried out a substantial refurbishment at the palace. She used what was then considered a 'Georgian' colour scheme of Chinese yellow, buff and celadon green. In 1914, the Picture Gallery was remodelled, and a new glazed ceiling installed to replace the work of Nash. Charles Allom decorated it using Chinese wallpapers and silk hangings that had been found in storage (and were probably originally intended by George IV for the Brighton Pavilion) to redecorate the Yellow Drawing Room and the Centre Room. Allom's work was much acclaimed and rewarded with a knighthood.

Above: A bedroom in the royal suite at Buckingham Palace in the time of Edward VII, who redecorated the palace interior.

CLARENCE HOUSE

An elegant stuccoed building in Stable Yard Road, beside St James's Palace, Clarence House is the London residence of the Prince of Wales and Duchess of Cornwall. It was built by John Nash in 1825–7 for William, Duke of Clarence (the future William IV), who continued to live there while reigning as King in 1830–7.

The house has had a varied history within the royal family, having been the London home of William IV's unmarried sister, Princess Augusta, in 1837–40, then of Victoria's mother, the Duchess of Kent, in 1840–61. Subsequently it served as the official residence of Prince Alfred, Duke of Edinburgh, in 1866–1900: during these years, a Russian Orthodox chapel was installed on the first floor for use by Alfred's wife, Marie Alexandrovna, Duchess of Edinburgh, who was the daughter of Tsar Alexander II of Russia. In 1900–42, Arthur, the Duke of Connaught and third son of Queen Victoria, lived in the house. For the last three years of World War II, Clarence House was the headquarters of the Red Cross and the St John's Ambulance Brigade.

Clarence House became the London home of Princess Elizabeth (the future Elizabeth II) and the Duke of Edinburgh on their marriage in 1947. Following Elizabeth's accession, Clarence House was the London residence of Queen Elizabeth, the Queen Mother, from 1953 to 2002.

Above: The Drawing Room at Clarence House in 1981, when it was the London residence of Elizabeth, the Queen Mother.

MANDERSTON AND SENNOWE PARK
THE EDWARDIAN COUNTRY HOUSE

The 18th-century country house of Manderston at Duns, in Berwickshire, was lavishly rebuilt in 1901–5 by the architect John Kinross for Sir James Miller. A wealthy trader's son, Sir James had entered the top drawer of the British aristocracy in 1893 by marrying the Honourable Eveline Curzon, daughter of Lord Scarsdale. Lady Miller had grown up amid the splendour of the Robert Adam interiors at Kedleston Hall in Derbyshire, and Sir James wanted to keep his bride in the style to which she was accustomed. He told Kinross that money was no object in the redevelopment of Manderston. In the event, the house combined the elegance of Kedleston Hall with the convenience of the latest 20th-century inventions.

Above: The garden front at Manderston. The house combined elegance and tradition with all the latest modern conveniences.

TRIBUTE TO KEDLESTON HALL

Kinross enlarged the main house, rebuilding the attic, as well as adding a basement, a service court and a new west wing of gentlemen's rooms, including a gun room and bachelor bedrooms. He completely rebuilt the entrance front.

Much of the interior was a tribute to Kedleston Hall: in the Entrance Hall, the stuccoed fireplace and rounded patterning of inlaid floor marble are copies of those in the Marble Hall at Kedleston, while the Ballroom ceiling is derived from that of the Kedleston Dining Room. The lavish interior also features a Louis XVI-style staircase with a silvered balustrade, based on that of the Petit Trianon palace at Versailles. Kinross also took account of the requirements of modern comfort and style, including electric lighting and a 'motor house' containing a basement engineer's area.

Below: The Drawing Room at Manderston. The Millers' designers, Mellier and Co., used an opulent, French-influenced style.

SENNOWE PARK

Sennowe Park, at Guist in Norfolk, was designed by the Norwich architect, George Skipper, for Thomas Cook, grandson of the founder of the travel firm of that name, beginning in 1905. Skipper created a flamboyant mansion with a curved bay on the entrance front topped with standing figures. Within, the highly decorated staircase beneath an oval cupola and the vast fireplace with Grinling Gibbons-style carving in the grand 50ft (15m)- long Saloon added to the highly individual mix of styles. Elaborate stone carving throughout was done by Italian masons.

CASTLE DROGO

SIR EDWIN LUTYEN'S 20TH-CENTURY CASTLE

Above: Like a castle of old, Lutyens' building occupies the high ground, overlooking steep banks and a river far below.

Celebrated as the last castle built in Britain, this imposing granite pile occupies a crag overlooking the River Teign gorge in Devon, with breathtaking views of Dartmoor. It was built in 1912–30 by Edwin Lutyens for Julius Charles Drew, who had made a great fortune importing Indian tea and establishing a chain of grocer shops.

Armed with a genealogy that suggested he was descended from a Norman knight named Drogo via the Drewe family of Drewsteignton, in Devon, Drew was determined to create a stone memorial to his wealth and his family's descent. He added an 'e' to his surname by deed poll and bought an estate in Drewsteignton. He then engaged the leading architect, Edwin Lutyens.

Drewe demanded a genuine stronghold, not a pastiche castle. The site was chosen in 1910. Over the next two decades, architect and client had many disagreements. Lutyens was often away setting out the new Indian capital of Delhi, and work proceeded under the supervision of Devon masons, Cleeve and Dewdney, and Clerk of Works, John Walker.

Below: Above the doorway is the Drewe lion and beneath it the family motto Drogo Nomen et Virtus Arma Dedit *('Drewe is the name and Valour gave it Arms').*

Below: As well as laying out Delhi and building many country houses, Lutyens designed the Cenotaph (London) and the British Embassy in Washington, D.C.

A FORMIDABLE CASTLE

In the end, Lutyens and Walker created a formidable structure, with solid granite walls in places 6ft (1.8m) thick, austere façades, a turreted entrance with genuine portcullis, and a medieval-style interior with great expanses of granite and oak. Above the entrance door is a bas-relief of the Drewe lion by Herbert Palliser.

Drewe died in 1931, only a year after Drogo was completed; his grandson gave the castle to the National Trust in 1974.

ATTENTION TO DETAIL

The house combines a principal two-storey wing containing staterooms with a three-storey wing housing rooms for family and servants, both connected by a grand staircase. The Drawing Room and Dining Room are wood-panelled; the first contains large mullion windows and the second has an elaborate plasterwork ceiling. There is Edwardian luxury in the bathrooms. Lutyens attended to every feature of the design, down to the billiard table in the Billiard Room.

ELTHAM PALACE

THE COURTAULDS' ART DECO FANTASY

In 1931–6, Stephen and Virgina Courtauld built a splendid Art Deco house adjoining the historic remains of Eltham Palace in south-east London. At the same time, they undertook the restoration of the 15th-century Great Hall, built by Edward IV, and other parts of the palace, which was a boyhood haunt and great favourite of Henry VIII.

ART DECO STYLE

The Courtaulds commissioned John Seely and Paul Paget to build the new house and Peter Malacrida to decorate it. The sleek, elegant Art Deco style they used swept Europe and the United States in the wake of the 1925 Exposition Internationale des Arts Décoratifs et Industriels Modernes in Paris, from which it took its name. It used 'modern-looking', streamlined shapes often decorated with stylized or geometric ornament.

Below: The elegant Entrance Hall. After taking control of the house in the 1990s, English Heritage used period photos to restore the furnishings to their 1930s look.

Above: In the 1930s, Stephen and Virginia Courtauld remodelled the Tudor remains of Eltham Palace into an Art Deco house.

The Courtaulds' new house was built with all the most modern conveniences, such as underfloor heating and a sound system in all rooms. The interior was lavish: onyx and gold plate in the bathroom, an aluminium-foil ceiling in the Dining Room, veneered walls and elegant fitted furniture. The Entrance Hall was lit through a glazed concrete dome.

OLD-FASHIONED CLEANING

One way in which the new Eltham Palace was less than up-to-date was its use of a centralized vacuum cleaning system, which had been the latest thing at around the turn of the century, rather than the newest mobile vacuum cleaners. These centralized pumps had been used since *c.*1905, when one was fitted at Minterne Magna in Dorset.

NEW OWNERSHIP

The Courtaulds also redesigned the gardens at Eltham Palace, which contain the original moat and bridge. They lived at Eltham until 1944, when they moved to Scotland, and the Royal Army Education Corps took on the lease. In 1995, the palace and Art Deco house passed into the care of English Heritage, who carried out a painstaking restoration.

Below: The bathroom is lined with gold mosaic. A statue of the goddess Psyche looks down on the bath and its gold-plated taps.

PLAS NEWYDD AND PORT LYMPNE

REX WHISTLER AND THE MODERN COUNTRY HOUSE

The handsome late 18th-century country house of Plas Newydd on Anglesey, North Wales, is notable for its architecture and situation as well as for its interior decoration. The house was built in 1793-9 by James Wyatt, architect of Heveningham Hall, Suffolk, and Fonthill Abbey, Wiltshire. It combines the Classical style with the Gothic for which Wyatt was celebrated. Situated overlooking the Menai Straits, the house has breathtaking views of Snowdonia.

Above: Herbert Baker drew on his experience building Cecil Rhodes's South African home in designing Port Lympne.

REX WHISTLER

Whistler had made his name aged 22 in 1927, when still a student at the Slade School of Art in London, by creating a highly imaginative mural entitled *The Expedition in Pursuit of Rare Meats* in the Tea Rooms at the Tate Gallery. As well as painting society portraits and working in book illustration, theatre design and advertising, he continued throughout his short career to paint large-scale murals at country homes such as Plas Newydd, which is particularly celebrated for his 58ft (18m) mural of a romantic Italianate coastal landscape in the Dining Room, painted in 1936-7. It was commissioned by Plas Newydd's owner, Charles Paget, 6th Marquess of Anglesey, and while staying there Whistler fell in love with his daughter, Caroline, and made a number of rather whimsical references to his passion in the painting. In one part of the image, Lady Caroline (as Juliet) stands on a balcony while beneath stands the pining figure of Romeo (a self-portrait). Although apparently a mural, the painting is in fact a vast canvas.

Below: Whistler's extraordinary mural in the Dining Room at Plas Newydd is the largest of the artist's many wall paintings.

Whistler's work inspired a vogue for ambitious country-house murals that lasted throughout the 20th century, but his career was cut short when he was killed, aged 39, during active service in World War II in July 1944. Earlier, at Mottisfont Abbey, a former priory turned country house in Hampshire, he painted, in 1938–9, an extraordinary *trompe l'oeil* Gothic Drawing Room that mimics intricate plasterwork in paint.

PORT LYMPNE

This handsome house in Kent was built for Sir Philip Sassoon, just before World War I, by the fashionable architect, Sir Herbert Baker, in the 'Dutch Colonial Style' used in South Africa. It was very highly regarded at the time, being described as 'the most remarkable modern house in England'. Here, Whistler created a widely admired 'tent room'.

THE 'GOLDEN TRIANGLE'

GATCOMBE, HIGHGROVE AND NETHER LYPIATT

Gloucestershire claims the name of 'the royal county' because there were once three country houses owned by members of the Queen's family in the area. The three houses – Gatcombe Park near Minchinhampton, Highgrove House near Tetbury, and Nether Lypiatt Manor near Stroud – were known together as the royals' 'Golden Triangle'.

GATCOMBE PARK

The Queen bought Gatcombe Park, near Minchinhampton, for Princess Anne and her first husband, Captain Mark Phillips, as a belated wedding present in 1976.

Both keen riders, Princess Anne and Captain Phillips held the annual Gatcombe Park horse trials on the estate each August. After their marriage was dissolved in 1992, Princess Anne married Commander Timothy Laurence and the Princess and her family continued to hold the annual event.

Above: Gatcombe Park was built in the 1740s of Bath stone. The estate, venue for the horse trials, is of 730 acres (295ha).

Gatcombe Park was built in the 1740s by a local master mason, Francis Franklin, for Edward Sheppard; wings were added in the early 19th century by George Basevi, cousin of Disraeli and pupil of the architect, Sir John Soane. Later work included the addition of a conservatory in 1829. Its owners have included Samuel Courtauld and the Conservative minister 'RAB' Butler.

HIGHGROVE HOUSE

Purchased by the Duchy of Cornwall in 1980, Highgrove House was home to Prince Charles and Diana, Princess of Wales, during the early years of their marriage. The three-storey five-bay Georgian building is rectangular with an originally columned portico (now glazed and enclosed) on the entrance front; within, there are four reception rooms. It was built in 1796–8 for a locally prominent Huguenot family named Paul. It originally stood in 350 acres (140ha), but the estate has been greatly enlarged by the Prince, who practises organic farming on the land. The Prince has also developed a fine walled garden on the Highgrove estate.

NETHER LYPIATT MANOR

Prince and Princess Michael of Kent bought Nether Lypiatt Manor in 1981. The house was built in 1698 by Judge Cox. It is said to be haunted by the ghost of the judge's son, who committed suicide in one of the rooms. Most of the main rooms are fitted with elegant beech, chestnut or oak panelling; there is a splendid original staircase. The house is faced in Cotswold stone.

Below: Highgrove House. The Prince of Wales's sheep graze on the lawn before the Georgian building. In the 1980s, the Prince added an open balustrade to the house.

Below: Nether Lypiatt. Apart from the fact that it had royal owners, the house is most celebrated for its 17th-century staircase.

BIRKHALL, MEY AND GLAMIS
SCOTLAND'S ROYAL RESIDENCES

The modern period has seen the restoration of several ancient buildings by members of the British royal family.

BIRKHALL
The relatively modest royal house of Birkhall stands on the edge of the Balmoral estate in Aberdeenshire, overlooking the River Muick. It is the Deeside residence of the Prince of Wales, where he spent a two-week honeymoon in 2005, following his marriage to the Duchess of Cornwall.

Birkhall was built in 1715. The house was bought by Queen Victoria and Prince Albert in 1849, the year after their first stay at Balmoral. It has been popular with many generations of their descendants, including the Duke and Duchess of York (the future George VI and Queen Elizabeth) in the 1930s; and by Princess Elizabeth (the future Queen Elizabeth II) and Prince Philip, the Duke of Edinburgh, in 1947–52; as well as Prince Charles. Queen Elizabeth, the Queen Mother, made it her Deeside residence in 1952–2002; she built a new wing containing six bedrooms in the 1950s and visited every spring. Prince Charles and the Duchess of Cornwall used the interior designer Robert Kine to redecorate the house.

Below: The Castle of Mey stands just 1,200ft (370m) from the sea, with views of Pentland Firth and the Orkney Islands.

Above: The Sitting Room used by Queen Elizabeth, the Queen Mother, at Glamis Castle. With two bedrooms, it is part of a suite set aside for royal visitors at Glamis.

THE CASTLE OF MEY
This castle in Caithness was restored by Queen Elizabeth, the Queen Mother, after she purchased it in 1952. The castle, a stone tower house built on a Z-plan by George, 4th Earl of Caithness, in 1566–72, was seriously dilapidated when the Queen saw and fell instantly in love with it in 1952, when she was mourning the death of her husband, King George VI. In a romantic position on the rugged Caithness coast, just 6 miles (9.5km) from John O'Groats and overlooking the Pentland Firth, it is Britain's most northerly castle. Its 2,000 acre (800 ha)- estate includes celebrated gardens. When purchased by the Queen in 1952, it was known as Barrogill Castle, but has since reverted to its ancient name, the Castle of Mey.

GLAMIS CASTLE
Queen Elizabeth, the Queen Mother, always had a strong emotional attachment to Scotland, having spent many childhood summers at her family's ancestral home, Glamis Castle in Tayside. The castle, famous above all as the setting for William Shakespeare's play *Macbeth*, was originally a royal hunting lodge. It was transformed into a castle with an L-shaped keep in the early 15th century by the Queen Mother's ancestor, Sir John Lyon. In the Victorian era, the castle was modernized, with the introduction of gas and electricity; the east wing, in the Scottish Baronial style, was added in 1891. In 1930, the future Queen Mother gave birth to Princess Margaret there.

Below: In the words of the late Queen Elizabeth, the Queen Mother, Birkhall is 'a small big house, or a big small house'.

EILEAN DONAN AND CLANDON PARK

MAGNIFICENT RESTORATION

Beneath vast skies, on its own small island at the head of Loch Duich and looking towards Skye, Eilean Donan castle is perhaps the most spectacularly situated building in Britain. A castle has stood here since *c.*1220, but the building we see today is the product of a painstaking 20th-century rebuilding. For 20 years, beginning in 1912, Lt-Col. John MacRae-Gilstrap rebuilt the ruined castle that had been guarded by his MacRae ancestors in the 16th century.

Above: Strategic position. Eilean Donan Castle commands the waters of Loch Duich. On clear days, the Isle of Skye is plainly visible in the distance.

EARLY BEGINNINGS

The original castle had a long and romantic history. Its name refers to Abbot Donan, an Irish missionary to Scotland from Iona who reputedly built his hermitage on this spot during the early 600s. The first castle was built around 600 years later, in the reign of Alexander II, to defend this strategically important location against Danish and Norse incursions. Alexander III gave the fortress to Colin Fitzgerald, ancestor of clan MacKenzie, in 1263, as a reward for service at the Battle of Largs, in which the defeat of Norway won Scotland control of the Western Isles. Then, in 1306, Robert the Bruce was given refuge in the castle.

THE MACRAE PROTECTORS

In *c.*1360, the MacRaes entered the service of the MacKenzie clan as bodyguards, proving so effective that they became known as 'MacKenzies' Mail Shirt'. The MacRaes were appointed hereditary constables of Eilean Donan Castle in 1509, a position that brought with it significant rights of control and enforcement over the surrounding hotly contested region. They often came under attack – famously in 1539, when Donald MacRae and his garrison kept at bay an army of 400 under Donald Gorm, Lord of the Isles, and MacRae is said to have killed Gorm with his very last arrow.

NAVAL ONSLAUGHT

The castle was reduced to ruins by the might of the English Navy in 1719. William MacKenzie, 5th Earl of

HIDDEN GLORIES: RESTORING CLANDON PARK AND UPPARK

The National Trust has carried out a series of painstaking restorations of castles and country houses. Pride of place should, perhaps, go to its first major restoration project: Clandon Park, near Guildford in Surrey. The Palladian mansion – designed *c.*1730 by Italian architect Giacomo Leoni and set in 'Capability' Brown parkland – was given to the Trust in 1956. Over two years, the Trust spent around £200,000 restoring the house to its 18th-century prime.

Its magnificent Marble Hall features stucco work by the celebrated Italian craftsmen Arturi and Bagutti, which was skilfully finished to look like marble. Restorers discovered this delicate work beneath thick layers of whitewash.

The Trust's inspired and painstaking restoration of the 17th-century country house of Uppark, West Sussex, in the 1990s, combined the latest scientific techniques with a revival of a number of historic crafts. The project was made necessary by a devastating fire that struck on 30 August 1989. The Trust's craftsmen and -women restored Uppark – which, prior to the fire, was celebrated as one of England's best-preserved houses – to quite superb condition.

Left: Clandon Park was given the kind of meticulous restoration appropriate for one of England's finest Palladian mansions.

Above: Eilean Donan Castle's colourful past and beautiful situation – and the romance associated with its restoration – explain its great appeal as a subject for photographs.

Seaforth, was a supporter of the Jacobite cause (the movement to restore the House of Stuart to the throne) and garrisoned Eilean Donan with a small group of Spanish troops sent to lead an uprising. Three English warships bombarded the fortress until it was a mere ruin. Meanwhile, because a Spanish support fleet failed to arrive, the 1719 uprising petered out in a low-key defeat of a small force of Spaniards and highlanders at Glenshiel by a royalist army from Inverness.

RETURN TO GLORY

Eilean Donan remained an evocative ruin for almost two centuries until a 20th-century MacRae set out to honour his ancestors' memory by restoring the castle to its former glory. Even the restoration has a romantic tale attached to it. Because the castle was so badly ruined, the restorers could not be sure what it had looked like, but a clan descendant named Farquhar MacRae had a vision in a dream of the castle as it once was, and worked with the castle's new owner to make the vision a reality. Then, when restoration was nearing completion, plans of the castle dated to 1714 were found in Edinburgh; curiously, they matched the details of the vision in remarkable detail.

THE CASTLE TODAY

A stone causeway leads from the mainland across the loch to the island. A portcullis guards the entrance in the outer walls; above the entrance is a Gaelic inscription that translates: 'If a MacRae is inside, there will never be a Fraser outside.' This refers to an alliance between the clans that dates back to the 14th century, when the MacRaes fostered a young heiress who later married into the Frasers. On the gate of Beaufort Castle, she raised a similar inscription, in Gaelic: 'If a Fraser resides within, no MacRaes will be left without.'

Within, across a walled courtyard, stands the three-storey main tower of the castle. In its barrel-vaulted basement, which has walls 14ft (4m) thick, is the Billeting Room, hung with pictures of the MacRaes in battle, at Sheriffmuir in 1715 and Glenshiel in 1719. Above is the Banqueting Hall, with an oak-timbered ceiling, a circular wrought-iron chandelier and splendid chimney-piece. The hall also contains a portrait of Lt-Col. John MacRae-Gilstrap, the castle's rebuilder, and a broadsword connected to his ancestor John MacRae, dubbed 'the Bard of Kintail', who fought at the Battle of Culloden in 1746 and then in the American War of Independence. On the floors above are sleeping chambers, accessed via a staircase turret. From the battlements stretch magnificent views of three lochs: Alsh, Long and Duich.

Below: A stone roadway connects the castle on the 'Isle of Donan' to the mainland. It was added as part of the restoration work.

NEO-PALLADIAN COUNTRY HOUSES

ARUNDEL PARK, KINGS WALDEN BURY, WAVERTON AND NEWFIELD

Waverton House in Gloucestershire and Newfield in North Yorkshire are fine examples of the Neo-Palladian country house that has been widely popular since the mid-20th century. Both houses were designed by architect Quinlan Terry, the first in 1977 for Jocelyn Hambro of the Hambro banking family, and the second in 1980 for carpet magnate Michael Abrahams. Although some country house patrons have chosen to build in the Modern style (see below), most have chosen neo-Palladian or neo-Georgian architecture for its emphasis on continuity and tradition – and perhaps also from a desire to celebrate England's heritage.

ARUNDEL PARK

The revival of Palladian designs began at Arundel Park, Sussex, in the 1950s. The Duchess of Norfolk became unhappy with the lack of privacy resulting from the opening of Arundel Castle to the public, and persuaded her husband to build a new house in a more secluded spot in the grounds. Architect Claud Phillimore built the house in 1958–62 on Neo-Palladian lines, with a central block linked to two side pavilions. (This design was in fact the Duchess's own idea; she is said to have been inspired by a visit to Ditchley Park in Oxfordshire.)

Arundel Park's handsome main block contains a Dining Room and Drawing Room along the garden front and a grand, top-lit Staircase Hall filling the whole height of the house beneath a vaulted ceiling. The interior harmonizes with the 18th-century elegance of the exterior: Phillimore designed double doors that are a copy of those in the Double Cube Room at Wilton

THE MODERN STYLE IN COUNTRY HOUSES

Eaton Hall in Cheshire was once the most notable modern country house. It was built in 1971–3 for Robert Grosvenor, 5th Duke of Westminster, to designs by John Dennys on the site of an imposing but largely demolished Victorian house at Eaton. Dennys's angular design caused a major controversy and was likened by the Duke of Bedford to a factory office block on a bypass. But in 1989 work began to encase it in a more traditional facing believed to blend more happily with the countryside.

Stratton Park in Hampshire is among the most prominent of the country houses built in the later 20th century in the Modern style. Constructed in 1963–5 by Stephen Gardiner and Christopher Knight, it stands alongside a vast Doric portico – all that remains of a 19th-century Greek Revival mansion built by George Dance the Younger. The L-shaped house contains the main family rooms in a wing (the long arm of the L) running parallel with the portico, while at right angles a conservatory and pond link to the evocative classical remains of the portico. Another substantial Modern country house is Witley Park, Surrey, built by Patrick Gwynne in 1961–2. Its two wings are hexagonal, its interior filled with gadgetry.

Above: The white block of Eaton Hall stood a little incongruously at the centre of a very grand estate – with formal gardens on one side and an avenue on the other.

Left: John Dennys's angular design for Eaton Hall was the subject of controversy and the building was refaced in 1989.

House and imported antique marble chimney-pieces. Interior decorator, John Fowler, supervised the colours and decorative details.

KINGS WALDEN BURY

Arundel Park's three-part neo-Palladian design was highly influential, as was a house in a similar style – built by Quinlan Terry with his then partner, Raymond Erith, at Kings Walden Bury in Hertfordshire, in 1967–71. The patron, Sir Thomas Milburne-Swinnerton-Pilkington, wanted to replace the 1890s house on the site with a new and elegant mansion.

Erith and Terry, outspoken critics of the Modern movement in architecture and ardent promoters of Classicism, produced a handsome and substantial house in Italian-Palladian style, with a columned and pedimented entrance front with 'Venetian windows', leading into a large hall with a stone floor and a barrel-vaulted staircase. The four principal rooms are the Drawing Room, Sitting Room, Dining Room and Kitchen.

Below: Quinlan Terry used classic Palladian proportions at Waverton House. The doorcase on the entrance front has Ionic supports.

Above: Newfield was designed as a working house at the centre of a farm. A substantial forecourt extends before it, just as in Palladio's villas in the Veneto.

WAVERTON HOUSE

Kings Walden Bury proved to be a prototype for country houses in the last decades of the 20th century. At Waverton, Gloucestershire, Terry again used the design of a central block and side pavilions. The large, seven-bedroom main house has a grand Staircase Hall, featuring a central staircase lit from above. The Drawing Room, Kitchen, Study and Dining Room are on the ground floor. Staff quarters and service rooms are in the long side wings. Terry made good use of local materials (on the insistence of the local planners): the roof has flags of Cotswold stone, while the walls are faced in stone from demolished local barns.

NEWFIELD

At Newfield in North Yorkshire, Quinlan Terry reworked the designs of his patron, Michael Abrahams – who had himself studied Palladio. The house they produced between them consists of a handsome central block, containing the Drawing Room, Hall and Dining Room with kitchen, with small side wings for staff and necessary service spaces. As at Waverton House, it is built of local stone.

A CLASSICAL FUTURE?

The preference for Neo-Palladian and other English classical styles in country house architecture has remained strong in the early years of the 21st century. In 2001–3, Quinlan Terry worked with his son, Francis, in the creation of the country house of Ferne Park, Dorset: its entrance is adorned with four large columns and a pediment and leads into a square hall with Doric columns. It is built in Portland and Chilmark stone.

Another design by Quinlan Terry, at Juniper Hill in Buckinghamshire in 1999-2002, features a large Ionic portico on its main entrance that strongly recalls the first English Palladian houses, such as Colen Campbell's Stourhead House, Wiltshire.

GLOSSARY

architrave Part of the entablature (upper part) of a classical order. The architrave is the lintel (horizontal beam) directly above the top of the column and beneath the frieze. Also the moulded pane of a window or door.

bailey Area enclosed by the walls of a castle; also called 'ward'. Compare motte, the mound on which the keep was built. The most common early Norman castles consisted of a motte (with an, initially, wooden and, later, stone tower) and a bailey enclosed by an earthwork wall topped with a palisade.

barbican Heavily fortified defensive structure, often a double tower, usually built out from the castle gateway.

Baronial Style of Scottish architecture, employed only rarely in England, in vogue from the early 1800s until *c.*1920. The Baronial style used towers with small turrets, stepped gables and crenellations to create the appearance of a 'fairytale castle', such as Balmoral Castle.

Baroque Sensuous and dramatic style in art and architecture, originating in Rome around 1600, that found expression in highly ornamented, monumental buildings set in grand, landscaped parks. English Baroque buildings in *c.*1700–30 are characterized by their dramatic use of space and movement, surface ornamentation and dynamic interaction with their setting. Great examples include Castle Howard and Blenheim Palace.

basilica In ancient Roman buildings, a big public hall.

bastide Walled town built alongside a castle. Originally, a French term, but applied to castle-town developments, such as Conwy in Wales.

bastion Projecting fortification on the curtain wall of a castle.

battlements Low defensive wall or parapet on the top of a castle's curtain wall or its towers, with indented sections (*embrasures* or *crenelles*) and raised parts (*merlons* or *cops*). Battlements were later used for decoration to give homes the appearance of a castle.

Above: Buckingham Palace.

bay Section of a house's outer wall, defined by vertical features, such as windows, columns and pilasters.

belvedere Raised building or room that commands a fine view.

burgh Anglo-Saxon fortified town.

chinoiserie Originally, French term for interior decoration that mimicked Chinese arts and colour schemes. Starting in the 17th century, chinoiserie remained in vogue until the 19th century.

classical Style in English architecture pioneered by Inigo Jones in the 17th century, inspired by buildings of ancient Greece and Rome and Italian Renaissance interpretations of them. Fine examples of Jones's classical architecture in England are the Queen's House, Greenwich, and the Banqueting Hall, Whitehall. *See also* Palladian.

corbel Projecting bracket in a wall supporting a vault or beam.

cornice Part of the entablature (upper part) of a classical order, consisting of a moulded decoration set horizontally above the frieze. Also (more generally) the moulding between wall and ceiling.

course Continuous line or layer of stones or bricks in a wall.

cupola Dome.

curtain wall A castle's outer wall, linking its towers.

drawbridge Movable bridge across the castle moat. Drawbridges could be moved horizontally or lifted vertically.

dressed stone Trimmed, smoothed and neatly cut stone.

eave Part of a sloping roof that projects over the top of the wall.

English bond In brickwork, the alternating use along a course of the brick ends ('headers') and the brick sides ('stretchers'). *See also* Flemish bond.

entablature The part of the classical order that is above a wall or column. Includes the architrave, the frieze and the cornice.

façade One of the main exteriors of a building, usually containing an entrance.

facing Layer of one material laid over another.

Flemish bond In brickwork, the use of the brick ends ('headers') throughout one course and then the brick sides ('stretchers') throughout the next. *See also* English bond.

fluting Vertical series of grooves cut on classical columns etc. *See also* orders.

frieze Part of the entablature of a classical order, found above the architrave and consisting of decorative sculpted or painted decoration. Also used more generally for a continuous strip of decoration around the upper walls of a room.

gable Triangular profile at the end of a gable-roof (one with two sloping sides). Sometimes, also, a triangular extension above a doorway.

garderobe In castles and medieval houses, a privy or toilet. Alternatively, a walk-in wardrobe.

Gothic Series of styles in medieval architecture *c.*1150–*c.*1500. In England, it applied principally to ecclesiastical architecture: there were no castles or fortified manor houses built in the Gothic style.

Great Hall Main room in the castle or medieval house, used up to Tudor times for dining and social occasions.

ha-ha Sunken ditch creating a hidden boundary between gardens and parkland in a country estate. Invented in the 18th century, it was invisible from the house and was reputedly named after the expression of surprise ('Ha! Ha!') uttered when a visitor chanced upon it. It kept grazing parkland animals out of the gardens.
hammer-beam roof One in which the roof arch is supported by short beams set into the wall at the base of the roof.
keep Most strongly fortified part of a castle, usually containing the lord's apartments and often called the *donjon* (French for 'lordship'). It functioned as a stronghold within the castle to which defenders could retreat if the outer bailey were captured by besiegers. The keep was usually a stone tower standing on the motte, when there was one.
linen-fold panelling Tudor decorative carving of wood, which was made to look like folded linen. An example is the linen-fold panelling screen in the Great Hall at Compton Wynyates.
Long Gallery Feature of Tudor and especially Elizabethan-Jacobean houses, a long room was used as a promenade in bad weather and to display portraits and sculptures. There are fine examples at Hardwick Hall and Montacute.
machicolation Section projecting from the outer face of a castle's curtain wall, with holes in the floor through which the defenders dropped missiles. Strictly, the machicolations were the actual holes.
mathematical tiles Tiles that resemble brick or stone. Used, for example, by Henry Holland to reface Althorp *c.*1790. Brick taxes around this time boosted the popularity of tiles as an alternative to bricks.

moat Man-made ditch surrounding a castle or town walls, usually full of water.
motte Mound on which the keep of a castle was built. *See also* bailey.
mullion Vertical divider in a window containing more than one pane of glass (light). *See also* transom.
obelisk Tall square column tapering to a pyramidal tip. Obelisks were often raised among temples and other garden buildings in the carefully planned parklands of Baroque and Palladian houses.
orders Column types in ancient Greek and Roman architecture, used in classical, Palladian and Greek Revival English buildings. There are five types: the plain and unornamented Tuscan; Doric, which has triglyphs (channelled blocks) along the frieze; Ionic, which has decoration like a scroll of parchment in the capital (the head of the column); Corinthian, which has decoration representing acanthus leaves on the capital; and Composite, which combines scroll and leaf decoration.
oriel window Projecting window supported by stone brackets or corbels.
Palladian 18th-century development of the classical style in architecture, named after and inspired by the works of the great Italian Renaissance architect Andrea Palladio (1508–80). Holkham Hall and Mereworth Castle are good examples of Palladian country houses.
pediment Raised triangular feature above a portico, door or window. It derived from the triangular gable ends of Greek temples with pitched roofs.
piano nobile Derived from the Italian *palazzo*, the first-floor level containing the main rooms in a classical building.
pilaster Flattened column used for decorative effect on a façade. A pilaster follows the rules of the classical orders. It has no structural function.
portcullis Grill of wood or iron lowered for added defensive strength over a castle gateway.
portico Porch with roof and often pediment supported by columns.

Left: Conwy Castle.

Above: Balmoral Castle.

postern Small, secondary gate (often concealed) in castle or town walls. Members of the garrison could use the postern to make inconspicuous exits and entries or to launch a surprise attack on a besieging force.
revetment Retaining wall of masonry etc supporting the face of an earthen rampart or ditch.
Revival Use by patrons and architects of elements from an earlier architectural style. Examples include the late 18th-century/early 19th-century Greek Revival, and the several allied Victorian movements, such as the Norman, Tudor, Elizabethan and 'Jacobethan' Revivals.
rusticated Stone blocks that have been dressed roughly to suggest strength.
scroll Decorative moulding in the shape of an S.
shingles Wood pieces used in place of tiles.
solar Private chamber, usually on the first floor of a medieval–Tudor house, to which the lord's family could retreat from the public space of the Great Hall. The solar was so called because it was fitted with large windows to allow in as much sunlight as possible.
spandrel Triangular space between an arch and a wall or between two arches.
squints (hidden openings) in a wall.
strapwork Late 16th- and early 17th-century style in ornament, making use of interlaced leather-like bands.
transom Horizontal divider in a window containing more than one pane of glass (light). *See also* mullion.

PROPERTY LISTINGS

All information was accurate at the time of going to press.

Alnwick Castle
Alnwick, Northumberland
NE66 1NQ
01665 511100
www.alnwickcastle.com

Althorp
Althorp, Northampton NN7 4HQ
01604 770107
www.spencerofalthorp.com

Antony House
Torpoint, Cornwall PL11 2QA
01752 812191
www.nationaltrust.org.uk

Arbury Hall
Nuneaton, Warwickshire CV10 7PZ
01676 540529
www.arburyestate.co.uk

Arundel Castle
Arundel, West Sussex BN18 9LH
01903 882462 www.arundelcastle.org.uk

Audley End House
Saffron Walden, Essex CB11 4JF
0370 333 1181
www.english-heritage.org.uk

Balmoral Castle
Balmoral, Ballater, Aberdeenshire
AB35 5TB
013397 42534
www.balmoralcastle.com

Bamburgh Castle
Bamburgh, Northumberland NE69 7DF
01668 214208 www.bamburghcastle.com

Banqueting House, The
Whitehall, London SW1A 2ER
0203 1666327
www.hrp.org.uk/BanquetingHouse

Beaulieu
Brockenhurst, Hampshire SO42 7ZN
01590 612345
www.beaulieu.co.uk

Beaumaris Castle
Beaumaris, Anglesey LL58 8AP
01248 8103921
www.beaumaris.com

Belsay Hall
Belsay, near Ponteland, Northumberland
NE20 0DX 0370 333 1181
www.english-heritage.org.uk

Belton House
Grantham, Lincolnshire NG32 2LW
01476 566116 www.nationaltrust.org.uk

Belvoir Castle
Grantham, Leicestershire NG32 1PE
01476 871001 www.belvoircastle.com

Berkeley Castle
Gloucestershire GL13 9BQ
01453 810303
www.berkeley-castle.com

Berkhamsted Castle
Berkhamsted, St Albans, Hertfordshire
0370 333 1181
www.english-heritage.org.uk

Bignor Roman Villa
Bignor, Pulborough, West Sussex
RH20 1PH 01798 869259
www.bigromanvilla.co.uk

Left: Marlborough House.

Blenheim Palace
Woodstock Oxfordshire OX20 1UL
01993 810530
www.blenheimpalace.com

Blickling Hall
Blickling, Norwich, Norfolk NR11 6NF
01263 738030 www.nationaltrust.org.uk

Bodiam Castle
Bodiam, near Robertsbridge, East Sussex
TN32 5UA 01580 830196
www.nationaltrust.org.uk

Bolsover Castle
Castle Street, Bolsover, Chesterfield,
Derbyshire S44 6PR 0370 333 1181
www.english-heritage.org.uk

Boughton House
Kettering, Northamptonshire NN14 1BJ
01536 515731
www.boughtonhouse.co.uk

Broch of Gurness
Aikerness, Orkney KW17 2NH
01856 751414
www.historicenvironment.scot

Brodsworth Hall
Brodsworth, near Doncaster, South
Yorkshire DN5 7XJ 01302 722598
www.english-heritage.org.uk

Broughton Castle
Broughton, near Banbury, Oxfordshire
OX15 5EB 01295 276070
www.broughtoncastle.com

Buckingham Palace
London SW1A 1AA
0303 123 7300
www.royalcollection.org.uk

Burghley House
Stamford, Lincolnshire PE9 3JY
01780 752451
www.burghley.co.uk

Caerlaverock Castle
Glencaple, Dumfries DG1 4RU
01387 770244
www.historicenvironment.scot

Caerleon Roman Fort
High Street, Caerleon, Gwent NP18 1AE
01633 422518
www.cadw.gov.wales

Caernarfon Castle
Castle Ditch, Caernarfon LL55 2AY
01286 677617 www.caernarfon.co.uk

Caerphilly Castle
Caerphilly CF3 1JD 029 2088 3143
www.visitcaerphilly.com

Caister Castle
Caister-on-Sea, Great Yarmouth,
Norfolk NR30 5SN 01664 567707
www.caistercastle.co.uk

Camber Castle
Camber, near Rye, East Sussex
TN31 7TD 0370 333 1181
www.english-heritage.org.uk

Cardiff Castle
Castle Street, Cardiff CF10 3RB
029 2087 8100
www.cardiffcastle.com

Carisbrooke Castle
Newport, Isle of Wight PO30 1XY
0370 333 1181
www.english-heritage.org.uk

Castell Coch
Tongwynlais, Cardiff CF15 7JS
029 2081 0101
www.cadw.gov.wales

Castle Coole
Enniskillen, Co Fermanagh BT74 6JY
028 6632 2690 www.nationaltrust.org.uk

Castle Drogo
Drewsteignton, Exeter EX6 6PB
01647 433306
www.nationaltrust.org.uk

Castle Fraser
Sauchen, Inverurie AB51 7LD
0131 458 0200 www.nts.org.uk

Castle Howard
York, North Yorkshire YO60 7DA
01653 648333
www.castlehoward.co.uk

Castle of Mey
Thurso, Caithness KW14 8XH
01847 851473
www.castleofmey.org.uk

Cawdor Castle
Nairn IV12 5RD 01667 404401
www.cawdorcastle.com

Chatsworth
Bakewell, Derbyshire DE45 1PP
01246 565300
www.chatsworth.org

Chepstow Castle
Chepstow, Gwent NP16 5EY
01291 624065
www.cadw.gov.wales

Chesters Roman Fort
Chollerford, near Hexham,
Northumberland NE46 4EU
0370 333 1181
www.english-heritage.org.uk

Chiswick House
Burlington Lane, London W4 2RP
07468 524874
www.chiswickhouseandgardens.org.uk

Clandon Park
West Clandon, Guildford,
Surrey GU4 7RQ 01483 222482
www.nationaltrust.org.uk

Cliveden
Taplow, Maidenhead, Buckinghamshire
SL1 8NS 01628 605069
www.nationaltrust.org.uk

Conwy Castle
Conwy LL32 8AY
01492 592398. www.cadw.gov.wales

Above: Hampton Court Palace.

Crathes Castle
Banchory AB31 5QJ 01330 844525
www.nts.org.uk

Culzean Castle
Maybole KA19 8LE 01655 884455
www.nts.org.uk

Deal Castle
Victoria Road, Deal, Kent CT14 7BA
0370 333 1181
www.english-heritage.org.uk

Ditchley Park
Enstone, Oxfordshire OX7 4ER
01608 677346
www.ditchley.com

Dover Castle
Dover, Kent CT16 1HU
0370 333 1181
www.english-heritage.org.uk

Dunfermline Abbey and Palace
Dunfermline, Fife KY12 7PE
01383 739026
www.historicenvironment.scot

Eastnor Castle
near Ledbury, Herefordshire HR8 1RL
01531 633160
www.eastnorcastle.com

Edinburgh Castle
Castlehill, Edinburgh EH1 2NG
0131 225 9846
www.edinburghcastle.scot

Eilean Donan Castle
Dornie, Kyle of Localsh, Wester Ross
IV40 8DX
01599 555202
www.eileandonancastle.com

Eltham Palace
Court Yard, Eltham, London SE9 5QE
0370 333 1181
www.english-heritage.org.uk

Falkland Palace
Falkland KY15 7BU
01337 857397
www.nts.org.uk

Felbrigg Hall
Felbrigg, Norwich, Norfolk NR11 8PR
01263 837444
www.nationaltrust.org.uk

Fishbourne Roman Palace
Salthill Road, Fishbourne, Chichester, West Sussex PO19 3QR
01243 785859
www.sussexpast.co.uk

Framlingham Castle
Framlingham, Suffolk IP13 9BP
0370 333 1181
www.english-heritage.org.uk

Glamis Castle
Glamis by Forfar, Angus DD8 1RJ
01307 840393
www.glamis-castle.co.uk

Goodrich Castle
Ross-on-Wye, Herefordshire
HR9 6HY
0370 333 1181
www.english-heritage.org.uk

Goodwood House
Goodwood, Chichester, West Sussex
PO18 0PX 01243 755055
www.goodwood.com

Great Dixter House
Northiam, Rye, East Sussex TN31 6PH
01797 252878
www.greatdixter.co.uk

Haddon Hall
Bakewell, Derbyshire DE45 1LA
01629 812855
www.haddonhall.co.uk

Hampton Court Palace
Surrey KT8 9AU 020 3166 6646
www.hrp.org.uk

Hardwick Hall
Doe Lea, Chesterfield, Derbyshire
S44 5QJ 01246 850430
www.nationaltrust.org.uk

Hardwick Old Hall
Doe Lea, Chesterfield, Derbyshire
S44 5QJ 0370 333 1181
www.english-heritage.org.uk

Harewood House
Harewood, Leeds,
West Yorkshire LS17 9LE
0113 2181010
www.harewood.org

Harlech Castle
Harlech LL46 2YH
www.harlech.com

Hatfield House
Hatfield, Hertfordshire AL9 5HX
01707 287010
http://www.hatfield-house.co.uk

Heaton Hall
Heaton Park, Manchester M25 5SW
0161 773 1231
www.manchestergalleries.org/html/heaton/heaton_home.jsp

Left: Edinburgh Castle.

Hellens
Much Marcle, Ledbury, Herefordshire
HR8 2LY
01531 660504
www.hellensmanor.com

Herstmonceux Castle
Hailsham, Sussex BN27 1RN
01323 833816
www.herstmonceux-castle.com

Hever Castle
Hever, Edenbridge Kent TN8 7NG
01732 865224
www.hever-castle.co.uk

Highclere Castle
Newbury, Berkshire RG20 9RN
01635 253210
www.highclerecastle.co.uk

Holkham Hall
Wells-next-the-Sea, Norfolk
NR23 1AB 01328 713111
www.holkham.co.uk

Holyroodhouse Palace
Canongate, The Royal Mile
EH8 8DX 0131 556 5100
www.royalcollection.org.uk

Houghton Hall
Houghton, King's Lynn, Norfolk
PE31 6TY 01485 528569
www.houghtonhall.com

Housesteads Roman Fort
near Haydon Bridge, Northumberland
NE47 6NN
0370 333 1181
www.english-heritage.org.uk

Hughenden Manor
High Wycombe HP14 4LA
01494 755573
www.nationaltrust.org.uk

Ightham Mote
Mote Road, Ivy Hatch, Sevenoaks, Kent
TN15 0NT
01732 810378
www.nationaltrust.org.uk

JEWEL TOWER
Abingdon Street, Westminster, London
SW1P 3JX
0370 333 1181
www.english-heritage.or.uk

KEDLESTON HALL
Derby DE22 5JH
01332 842191
www.nationaltrust.org.uk

KENILWORTH CASTLE
Kenilworth, Warwickshire CV8 1NG
0370 333 1181
www.english-heritage.org.uk

KENSINGTON PALACE
London W8 4PX
0870 751 5170
www.hrp.org.uk

KENWOOD HOUSE
Hampstead Lane, London NW3 7JR
0370 333 1181
www.english-heritage.org.uk

KEW PALACE
Kew Gardens, Kew, Richmond, Surrey
TW9 3AB
020 8332 5655
www.hrp.org.uk

KIDWELLY CASTLE
Kidwelly, West Glamorgan SA17 5BG
01554 890104
www.cadw.gov.wales

KILLYLEAGH CASTLE
Killyleagh, Downpatrick, Co Down
BT30 9QA
028 4482 8261
www.discovernorthernireland/
killyleaghcastle

KNEBWORTH HOUSE
Knebworth, Hertfordshire SG3 6PY
01438 812661
www.knebworthhouse.com

KNOLE
Knole, Seveoaks, Kent TN15 0RP
01732 462100 www.nationaltrust.org.uk

LAYER MARNEY TOWER
near Colchester, Essex CO5 9US
01206 330784
www.layermarneytower.co.uk

LEEDS CASTLE
Maidstone, Kent ME17 1PL
01622 765400
www.leeds-castle.com

LEWES CASTLE
169 High Street, Lewes, Sussex
BN7 1YE
01273 486290
www.sussexpast.co.uk

LINLITHGOW PALACE
Linlithgow, West Lothian EH49 7AL
01506 842896
www.historicenvironment.scot

LONGLEAT HOUSE
Longleat, Warminster, Wiltshire
BA12 7NW
01985 844400
www.longleat.co.uk

LOSELEY PARK
Guildford, Surrey GU3 1HS
01483 304440
www.loseleypark.com

LUDLOW CASTLE
Castle Square, Ludlow, Shropshire
SY8 1AY
01584 873355
www.ludlowcastle.com

LULLINGSTONE ROMAN VILLA
Lullingstone Lane, Eynsford, Kent DA4 0JA
0370 333 1181
www.english-heritage.org.uk

MANDERSTON
Duns, Berwickshire, Scotland TD11 3PP
01361 883450
www.manderston.co.uk

MAPLEDURHAM HOUSE
Mapledurham, Reading RG4 7TR
01189 723350
www.mapledurham.co.uk

Above: Windsor Castle.

MARBLE HILL HOUSE
Richmond Road, Twickenham
TW1 2NL 0370 333 1181
www.english-heritage.org.uk

MIDDLEHAM CASTLE
Castle Hill, Middleham, Leyburn,
North Yorkshire DL8 4QR
0370 333 1181
www.english-heritage.org.uk

MONTACUTE HOUSE
Montacute, Somserset TA15 6XP
01935 823289
www.nationaltrust.org.uk

MUNCASTER CASTLE
Ravenglass, Cumbria CA18 1RD
01229 717614
www.muncaster.co.uk

NORTON CONYERS
Near Ripon, North Yorkshire
HG4 5EQ 01765 640333
www.nortonconyers.org.uk

NOTTINGHAM CASTLE
Nottingham NG1 6EL 0115 9153700
www.nottinghamcastles.org.uk

ORFORD CASTLE
Orford, Woodbridge, Suffolk
IP12 2ND
0370 333 1181
www.english-heritage.org.uk

Above: Arundel Castle.

Osborne House
Osborne House, Royal Apartments,
East Cowes, Isle of Wight PO32 6JT
0370 333 1181
www.english-heritage.org.uk

Osterley Park
Jersey Road, Isleworth, Middlesex
TW7 4RB 020 8232 5050
www.nationaltrust.org.uk

Oxburgh Hall
Oxborough, King's Lynn, Norfolk
PE33 9PS 01366 328258
www.nationaltrust.org.uk

Palace of Westminster
London SW1A 0AA 020 7219 3000
www.parliament.uk

Pembroke Castle
Pembroke SA71 4LA 01646 681510
www.pembrokecastle.co.uk

Pendennis Castle
Falmouth, Cornwall TR11 4LP
0370 333 1181
www.english-heritage.org.uk

Penrhyn Castle
Bangor LL57 4HT 01248 353084
www.nationaltrust.org.uk

Penshurst Place
Penshurst, near Tonbridge, Kent
TN11 8DG
01892 870307
www.penshurstplace.co.uk

Petworth House
Petworth, West Sussex GU28 0AE
01798 342207
www.nationaltrust.org.uk

Pevensey Castle
Pevensey, Sussex BN24 5LE
0370 333 1181
www.english-heritage.org.uk

Peveril Castle
Market Place, Castleton, Hope Valley
Derbyshire S33 8WQ
0370 333 1181
www.english-heritage.org.uk

Polesden Lacey
Great Bookham, near Dorking, Surrey
RH5 6BD
01372 452048
www.nationaltrust.org.uk

Portchester Castle
Portsmouth, Hampshire PO16 9QW
0370 333 1181
www.english-heritage.org.uk

Portland Castle
Castletown, Portland, Weymouth, Dorset
DT5 1AZ
0370 333 1181
www.english-heritage.org.uk

Powis Castle
near Welshpool SY21 8RF
01938 551944
www.nationaltrust.org.uk

Prior Park Landscape Garden
Ralph Allen Drive, Bath BA2 5AH
01225 833977
www.nationaltrust.org.uk

Queen's House, Greenwich
Park Row, Greenwich, London SE10 9NF
020 8312 6608
www.rmg.co.uk

Raby Castle
Staindrop, Darlington, Co Durham
DL2 3AH 01833 660202
www.raby.co.uk

Raglan Castle
Raglan NP15 2BT
01291 690228
www.cadw.gov.wales

Rhuddlan Castle
Castle Gate, Castle Street, Rhuddlan
LL18 5AD 01745 590777
www.cadw.gov.wales

Richmond Castle
Tower Street, Richmond, North Yorskhire
DL10 4QW
0370 333 1181
www.english-heritage.org.uk

Rochester Castle
The Lodge, Rochester-upon-Medway,
Medway ME1 1SW
0370 333 1181
www.english-heritage.org.uk

Rousham House
near Steeple Aston, Bicester, Oxfordshire
OX25 4QX
01869 347110
www.rousham.org

Royal Pavilion, The
Brighton, East Sussex BN1 1EE
03000 290900
www.brightonmuseums.org.uk

St Mawes Castle
St Mawes, Cornwall TR2 5DE
0370 333 1181
www.english-heritage.org.uk

St Michael's Mount
Marazion, near Penzance, Cornwall
TR17 0HS
01736 710265
www.stmichaelsmount.co.uk

Sandringham House
Sandringham, Norfolk PE35 6EN
01485 545400
www.sandringhamestate.co.uk

Scone Palace
Perth PH2 6BD 01738 552300
www.scone-palace.co.uk

Seaton Delaval Hall
Seaton Sluice, Whitley Bay,
Northumberland NE26 4QR
0191 237 1493
www.nationaltrust.org.uk

Stirling Castle
Castle Wynd, Stirling FK8 1EJ
01786 450000
www.stirlingcastle.scot

Stoke Park Pavilions
Stoke Bruerne, Towcester,
Northamptonshire
NN12 7RZ 01604 862329
www.stokeparkpavilions.co.uk

Stokesay Castle
near Craven Arms, Shropshire
SY7 9AH 0370 333 1181
www.english-heritage.org.uk

Stourhead
near Warminster BA12 6QF
01747 841152
www.nationaltrust.org.uk

Stowe House
Contact Visitor Services Manager,
Stowe School, Buckingham
MK18 5EQ 01280 818000
www.stowe.co.uk

Stowe Landscape Gardens and Park
near Buckingham MK18 5EQ
01280 817156
www.nationaltrust.org.uk

Strawberry Hill
St Mary's, Strawberry Hill,
Waldegrave Road, Twickenham
TW1 4ST
020 8744 1241
www.strawberryhillhouse.org.uk

Sudeley Castle
Winchcombe, Gloucestershire
GL54 5JD
01242 604244
www.sudeleycastle.co.uk

Sulgrave Manor
Manor Road, Sulgrave, Banbury,
Oxfordshire OX17 2SD
01295 760205
www.sulgravemanor.org.uk

Syon House
Syon Park, Brentford TW8 8JF
020 8560 0882
www.syonpark.co.uk

Tattershall Castle
Tattershall, Lincoln LN4 4LR
01526 342543
www.nationaltrust.org.uk

Tintagel Castle
Tintagel, Cornwall PL34 0HE
0370 333 1181
www.english-heritage.org.uk

Tower of London
London EC3N 4AB
www.hrp.org.uk

Uppark
South Harting, Petersfield GU31 5QR
01730 825415
www.nationaltrust.org.uk

Upton House
Banbury, Warwickshire OX15 6HT
01295 670266
www.nationaltrust.org.uk

Vyne, The
Sherborne St John, Basingstoke RG24 9HL
01256 883858
www.nationaltrust.org.uk

Waddesdon Manor
Waddeson, near Aylesbury,
Buckinghamshire HP18 0JH
01296 820414
www.waddesdon.org.uk

Walmer Castle
Walmer, Deal, Kent CT14 7LJ
0370 333 1181
www.english-heritage.org.uk

Warwick Castle
Warwick CV34 4QU
01926 830820
www.warwick-castle.co.uk

Weston Park
Weston-under-Lizard, near Shifnal,
Shropshire TF11 8LE
01952 852100
www.weston-park.com

Wilton House
Wilton, Salisbury SP2 0BJ
01722 746700
www.wiltonhouse.co.uk

Winchester Castle Great Hall
Winchester SO23 8PU
01962 846476
www.hants.gov.uk/thingstodo/greathall

Windsor Castle
Windsor, Berkshire
SL4 1NJ
030 3123 7304
www.windsor.gov.uk

Woburn Abbey
Woburn, Bedfordshire
MK17 9WA
01525 290333
www.woburnabbey.co.uk

Wollaton Hall
Wollaton, Nottingham
NG8 2AE
0115 915 3900
www.wollaton.org.uk

Right: Stourhead.

INDEX

Page numbers in *italics* refer to captions.

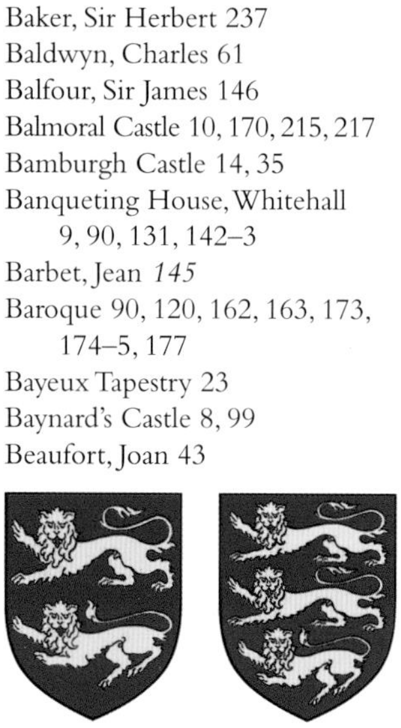

ACKNOWLEDGEMENTS

ABOUT THE AUTHOR

Charles Phillips is an established writer of popular history and the author of *The Illustrated History of Knights and the Golden Age of Chivalry* and *The Illustrated History of the Kings and Queens of Britain*, both published by Lorenz Books. He was a key writer on Time Life's *Myth and Mankind* series, which blends mythology with the art and history of ancient cultures. His other books include *How to Think*, *The Medieval Castle Manual*, *The Ancient World in Minutes* and *50 Leaders who Changed History*. Charles is a graduate of Oxford University and holds an MA from the University of Westminster.

This edition is published by Lorenz Books
an imprint of Anness Publishing Ltd
info@anness.com
www.lorenzbooks.com
www.annesspublishing.com

Publisher: Joanna Lorenz
Editor: Joy Wotton
Designer: Nigel Partridge
Illustrators: Anthony Duke, Rob Highton and Vanessa Card
Production Controller: Ben Worley

A CIP catalogue record for this book is available from the British Library.

Page 1: Rochester Castle
Page 2: Castle Howard
Page 3: Windsor Castle
Above right: Bodiam Castle

PICTURE ACKNOWLEDGEMENTS

Alamy: AA World Travel Library: 73t, 210b; Keith Allan: 166-7; Arcaid: 141br; Jon Arnold Images: 106br; Tim Ayers: 4; 18-19; Sandra Baker: 6b; Alastair Balderstone: 180b; Roger Bamber: 165tr; Quentin Bargate: 138t; Peter Barritt: 60b, 225br; Pat Behnk: 220bl; Bildarchiv Monheim GmbH: 5, 7t, 11b, 21t, 109b, 110, 187t, 190-1, 192t, 192bl, 193t, 193b; BL Images Ltd: 11t, 55b, 206t; Michael Booth: 4, 31t, 58-9, 70b, 130-1, 216b, 236bl; G P Bowater: 119b; Brinkstock: 221bl; David Cattanach: 81t; Adrian Chinery: 85t, 140; Gary Cook: 57b; David Copeman: 143b; CW Images: 93tr, 126t; Detail Nottingham: 129tc; Ros Drinkwater: 225t; EDIFICE: 121b; Rod Edwards: 184bl; Guy Edwardes Photography: 6t, 69t; Elmtree Images: 88–9; Bernie Epstein: 29b; Robert Estall photo agency: 40b; Europhotos: 133t; Mary Evans Picture Library: 96b, 102, 118cr, 207b; eye35.com: 9t, 106bl, 152b, 206b; B E Eyley: 68bl; Paul Felix Photography: 53t, 124br; Joe Fox: 93c, 147t; Alan Gallery: 146t; Chris Gloag: 60t, 61b, 61t; Tim Graham: 161br, 212t, 212b; Greenshoots Communications: 223b; Duncan Hale-Sutton: 78t; Robert Harding Picture Library Ltd: 4, 94-5; Andrew Harris: 7b; Mike Haywood: 159tr; John Henshall: 218t; Jeremy Hoare: 38b, 141t; The Hoberman Collection: 161bl; Holmes Garden Photos: 184t; Doug Houghton: 20b; Michael Jenner: 34t, 70t, 107t, 145b; Hywel Jones: 69b; Iconotec: 16, 71b; Imagebroker: 172-3; ISP Photography: 237tr; iX Images: 31b; Justin Kase: 4, 90tc, 112-13, 121t; David Kilpatrick: 211b; Mike Kipling Photography: 42b, 43b, 66t; Ian Leonard: 168tr, 211t, 235tc; Nick Lewis Photography: 210tr; Pawel Libera: 99t; Liquid Light: 47t, 55t; Pedro Luz Cunha: 40t; David Lyons: 10b, 29t, 127b; Manor Photography: 39tr; The Marsden Archive: 226tr; Neil McAllister: 124t, 177b; David Millichope: 54b; Jeff Morgan: 127t, 222t; nagelstock.com: 107b, 120b, 123b; Eric Nathan: 209tr; Frank Naylor: 136; David Newham: 80b, 77t, 227bl; North Wind Pictures Archives: 157t; David Norton Photography: 3, 153b; one-image photography: 50t; Peter Packer: 115b, 115t; Derek Payne: 65t; PCL: 224b; John Peter Photography: 239bl; Photofrenetic: 103tl; The Photolibrary Wales: 52b; Pictorial Press Ltd: 165br; David Poole: 12-13; Popperfoto: 105bl, 163b, 230b; Powered by Light/Alan Spencer: 111c; Purestock: 137b; Ben Ramos: 186b; Rob Rayworth: 4, 36-7, 245; David Reed: 84t; Nigel Reed: 109t; Matthew Richardson: 76t; Rolf Richardson: 45, 117b, 204tr; David Rowland: 73br, 73bl; Ruleofthirds: 240t; Stephen Saks Photography: 79b; David Sanger Photography: 137t; Scottish Viewpoint: 239t; Brian Seed: 99c, 139t; Ian Shaw: 213t; ShelbyImages.com: 44t; Shenval: 170; Simmons Aerofilms Ltd: 20t, 135t, 235b; Skyscan Photolibrary: 21bl, 25t, 34b, 46b, 54t, 108b, 116, 123t, 144t, 171t, 180t, 219t, 223tl; Nigel Stollery: 154t; Homer Sykes: 242bl; Howard Taylor: 26b; John Taylor: 220t; Travel Ink: 50b; Travelshots.com: 225bl; V&A Images: 183b; Darryl Webb: 17b, 41bl; www.white-windmill.co.uk: 72b; David Wootton: 227t; Worldwide Picture Library: 32t, 71t, 118bl
The Art Archive: 27t, 27b, 49t, 86t, 144b, 178bl; Dagli Orti: 209tl; Jarrold Publishing: 2, 8b, 22t, 26t, 38t, 39tl, 67t, 99b, 139br, 147bl, 171c, 171b, 187b, 201t, 224t, 240b; Musée de la Tapisserie/Dagli Orti: 23b; Musée du Chateau de Versailles/Dagli Orti: 78b; Palazzo Barberini Rome/Dagli Orti: 108t; Private Collection MD: 232b, 233t, 227br; Private Collection/Eileen Tweedy: 183tr; Neil Setchfield: 92; Victoria & Albert Museum London/Eileen Tweedy: 98b; John Webb: 142t
Courtesy of Berkeley Castle Charitable Trust: 68br
The Bridgeman Archive: © Ashmolean Museum, University of Oxford: 21br, 200t; John Bethell/Audley End, Essex: 138b; Cardiff Castle, Cardiff, Wales: 223b; Chiswick House, London: 179c, 181t; Compton Wynyates, Warwickshire: 96t; Hardwick Hall, Derbyshire: 122t; Hatfield House, Hertfordshire: 134b; Hedingham Castle, Essex: 32b; Kedleston Hall, Derbyshire: 198t, 198b, 199b; Kenwood House, London: 199t; Knole House, Sevenoaks, Kent: 133b, 132b; Osterley Park, Middlesex: 10t; Plas Newydd, Anglesey: 237bl; Stourhead, Wiltshire: 178t; Syon House, Middlesex: 196bl; Blenheim Palace, Oxfordshire: 176t; © Bonhams, London/Private Collection: 192br; © Bronte Parsonage Museum, Haworth, Yorkshire: 83bl; © Burghley House Collection: 189bl; © Chetham's Library, Manchester: 24t; © Christie's Images/Private Collection: 218br; © City of Westminster Archive Centre, London: 176b; © Collection of the Earl of Pembroke, Wilton House, Wilts: 145t; © Collection of the New-York Historical Society, USA: 104t; J. Collins & Son Fine Paintings, Devon: 30b; Corning Museum of Glass, New York, USA: 105t; Crathes Castle, Kincardineshire, Scotland: 119t; Eastnor Castle, Herefordshire: 207t; Mark Fiennes, Hatfield House, Hertfordshire: 134t; Giraudon, Bibliotheque Nationale, Paris, France: 226tl; © Guildhall Art Gallery, City of London: 208; Heveningham Hall, Suffolk: 200bl; Hever Castle Ltd, Kent: 100tr; Kew Gardens, London: 194t; Knebworth House, Hertfordshire: 226b; © Leeds Museums and Art Galleries (Temple Newsam House): 183tl; Longleat House, Wiltshire: 62t; © Mallett Gallery, London: 33b/ Private Collection: 129b; Marlborough House, London: 141bl; John Martin Robinson: 243b, 243t; Roy Miles Fine Paintings: 67b; Montacute House, Somerset: 129tl; © Philip Mould, Historical Portraits Ltd, London/Private Collection: 184br; National Portrait Gallery, London: 114t; National Trust Photographic Library/John Hammond, Hardwick Hall, Derbyshire: 122b/Patrick Prendergast, Castle Coole, County Fermanagh, Northern Ireland: 201bl; © Newport Museum and Art Gallery, South Wales: 35b, 48t; Petworth House, Sussex: 150b/National Trust Photographic Library/Rupert Truman: 189br; Philadelphia Museum of Art, Pennsylvania, PA, USA: 179br; Polesden Lacey, Great Bookham, Surrey: 231b; Private Collection: 132t, 143t, 181b, 205t, 205b; Rousham House, Oxfordshire: 186t; © The Royal Cornwall Museum, Truro, Cornwall: 117t; Scottish National Portrait Gallery, Edinburgh, Scotland: 197br; Society of Antiquaries, London: 42t; Syon House, Middlesex: 152t; The Stapleton Collection, Private Collection: 46t, 103tr, 142b, 161t, 150t, 182t, 185tr, 195t, 196br, 196t, 208t, 213b; Topham Picturepoint, Compton Wynyates, Warwickshire: 97t/Penshurst Place, Kent: 62t/Petworth House, West Sussex: 151b; © Walters Art Museum, Baltimore, USA: 44b; Ken Welsh/Private Collection: 159b; © Christopher Wood Gallery, London, Private Collection: 175; © Yale Center for British Art, Paul Mellon Collection, USA: 194b, 200br
Jonathan Buckley: 87b
Cadw. Crown Copyright: 48b, 49b, 51t, 52t, 56t
Carew Castle: 126bl, 126br
Corbis: Peter Aprahamian: 165bl; Bettmann: 209b, 235bm; Chris Bland/Eye Ubiquitous: 128b; Mike Finn-Kelcey/Reuters: 163t; Angelo Hornak: 185tl; Hulton-Deutsch Collection: 124bl; Massimo Listri: 205b; Clay Perry: 156b; Adam Woolfitt: 65b, 242br
Ynys Crowston-Boaler: 157b
Darryl Curcher, Pennington PR: 5, 214-215, 221br
© **EHS Built Heritage**: 39t, 41br, 41t
Mary Evans Picture Library: 77b, 162t, 182b, 210tc
Tim Graham Picture Library: 82b, 202t, 202b, 203t, 232t, 238bl, 238t, 238br
Haddon Hall: 86bl, 86br, 87tr, 87tl
Leeds Castle: 64t, 101t, 101b
Karita Lightfoot: 17t, 56b, 57tl
Loseley Park: 125b, 125tc, 125tr
Norton Conyers: 83t, 83br
© **Penshurst Place**: 63b
Pictures of Britain: Jeffrey Beazley: 154b; John D Beldom: 158b; John Blake: 9b, 97b; Norman Browne: 179t; Dorothy Burrows: 23t, 28c, 53b; Mike Cowen: 159t; Keith Ellis: 195br; Norman Feakins: 231t; Brian Gadsby: 106t; Brian Gibbs: 4, 74-75, 103b; Ron Gregory: 82t, 111b, 156t; Antony Hebdon: 151t; John Husband: 22b; Vera Hunter: 33t, 51b, 72t; John Larkin: 84b; Deryck Lister Hallam: 14m, 43t, 197t, 218b; Paul I Makepeace: 104b, 105br; John Mole: 111t; Chris Parker: 100t; Tom Parker: 35t; Adam Swaine: 5, 228-229; Adina Tovy: 1, 24b, 30t, 47b, 222bl; John Tremaine: 139bl; Jeffery Whitelaw: 76b, 128t; Julian Worker: 114b, 174b
Rex Features: 202bl; BNP/NAP: 120t; Alexander Caminada: 189t; Chris Capstick: 100bl; Mauro Carraro: 239br; James Fraser: 240t; Patrick Frilet: 234t, 234b; Richard Gardner: 188tr; David Hartley: 177t; JD/Keystone USA: 202b; LXO: 230t; Peter Macdiarmid: 174t; Mykel Nicolaou: 85b; Simon Roberts: 164b; Dan Sparham: 236t, 236br; The Travel Library: 5, 148-149, 155, 217b, 217t; Jaime Turner: 64b; Joan Williams: 233b; John Winders: 135b
© **David Sellman**/Penshurst Place: 62b
Shutterstock 221t. **Stowe House Preservation Trust**/Jerry Hardman-Jones: 188tc, 188b
Joy Wotton: 8t, 14tl, 90tl, 90tr, 98tc, 98tr, 160b, 160tc, 160tr, 162b, 164t, 168tc, 195bl, 246, 247, 249
Peter Wotton: 14tr, 28b, 68t, 80t, 81b, 168tl, 178br, 241br, 251, 256